MW01634520

# Photographs by Norman Parkinson

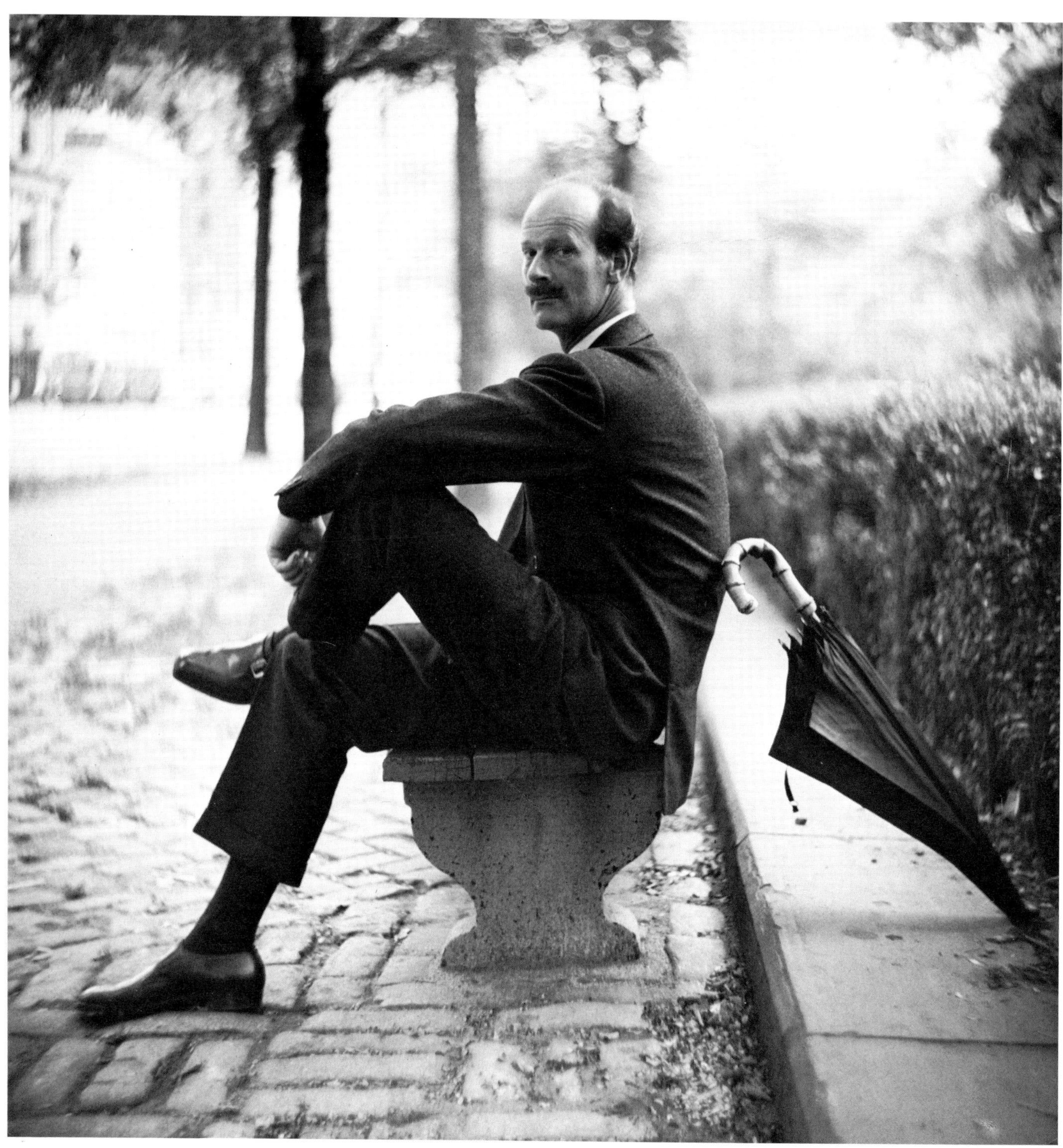

**Norman Parkinson, by Frances McLaughlin, New York, 1949**

Photographs by

# Norman Parkinson

Fifty years of portraits and fashion

Terence Pepper

Gordon Fraser

## Contents



## Acknowledgements

This exhibition would not have been possible without the active cooperation of the Condé Nast organisation, and the National Portrait Gallery is particularly grateful to Beatrix Miller, editor of British *Vogue*, for making the comprehensive magazine archives available to us and enlisting *Vogue*'s art director, Susan Mann, to design the catalogue. In New York we are grateful to Diana Edkins, curator of American *Vogue*'s archive, for lending us other material relating to the 1950s and 1960s, while for the more recent work included in the exhibition we owe thanks to *Town and Country* magazine and to the French and Italian editions of *Vogue*. I would also like to thank Mrs Parkinson for her written contribution to this book, and Norman Parkinson himself who has given up so much of his time to help with all aspects of the exhibition. His assistant Robert Pascall has similarly provided much invaluable and patient help throughout the last six months. Georgina Howell's book *In Vogue: Six Decades of Fashion* provided the original inspiration, and her advice and suggestions have proved most helpful. Finally I would like to thank my many colleagues on the National Portrait Gallery staff for their support and encouragement.

T.P.

Published in connection with
the exhibition held at the
National Portrait Gallery from
7 August to 25 October 1981

Exhibition organisers Colin Ford and Terence Pepper
Exhibition designer Michael Jones

© National Portrait Gallery, London 1981
Published by The Gordon Fraser Gallery Ltd,
London and Bedford

British Library Cataloguing in
Publication Data
Norman Parkinson.
1. Photography, Artistic
I. Title
779'.092'4 TR653
ISBN 0-86092-061-5

Designed by Susan Mann

Printed in England by Jolly & Barber Ltd, Rugby
Colour separations by Klaus-Peter Beckmann, Hamburg

*Front cover* **Portrait after Kees Van Dongen 1959**

*Back cover* **Norman Parkinson New York 1960**

## Foreword

Twelve years ago, the National Portrait Gallery mounted its first exhibition of photography. A retrospective of almost fifty years of photographs by Cecil Beaton, it enjoyed an unprecedented critical and public success and helped to establish portrait photography as a major area of concern for the Gallery. It also heralded a series of eighteen more photographic exhibitions between 1972 and 1980, divided almost equally between historical and contemporary subjects. For our twentieth photographic exhibition, we have again chosen a photographer whose career has spanned half a century, and who specialises in elegant, glamorous portraiture and fashion: Norman Parkinson.

During his five decades as a professional, 'Parks' has always managed to keep a step in front of other photographers, through his command of colour, his use of outdoor locations and his skill at suggesting movement in a still photograph. Above all, he has always been totally dedicated and professional, though never over-earnest. He has shown a remarkable ability to capture accurately the spirit of the period in which he is working. One can date a Parkinson photograph without much difficulty from its look and feel, as well as from the changes – and growth – in his style. It is rare to be able to arrange an exhibition in decades as Michael Jones has so elegantly done, and be confident that the characters of the pictures in each room will be so clearly differentiated.

Norman Parkinson is an extremely busy photographer, his talents more in demand than ever. We are doubly grateful to him, not only for wholeheartedly accepting our suggestion for an exhibition and making his work freely available for it, but for turning his back on a number of assignments over the last few months, so that he could be on hand at every stage of preparation. The result is, I believe, one of the most colourful, amusing, and altogether pleasurable exhibitions the Gallery has put on in recent years.

**John Hayes**
Director
National Portrait Gallery, June 1981

## Chronology

| | |
|---|---|
| **1913** | 21 April. Born Ronald William Parkinson Smith |
| **1927–31** | Educated at Westminster School |
| **1931–3** | Apprenticed to court photographers Speaight & Sons of Bond Street |
| **1934** | Opens own studio with Norman Kibblewhite at 1 Dover Street, Mayfair |
| **1935** | 15–23 October. One-man studio exhibition |
| **1935–40** | Works for British edition of *Harpers Bazaar* and *The Bystander* |
| **1937** | Collaborates with Francis Brugière on photo-mural for the British Pavilion at the Exposition Universelle in Paris |
| **1937–9** | Extended series of photographic essays on the British Armed Services for recruiting purposes |
| **1937–70** | Farming in Gloucestershire, Worcestershire and Oxfordshire |
| **1938** | Takes colour photographs for *Harpers Bazaar* |
| **1939** | Travels to New York to photograph the World Fair |
| **1940–5** | Combines farming and reconnaissance photography over France for the RAF with occasional work for *Vogue* |
| **1945** | Marries Wenda Rogerson |
| **1945–60** | Works for *Vogue*, taking fashion and portrait photographs |
| **1949** | First annual trip to New York to work for American *Vogue* |
| **1952** | First advertising work |
| **1957** | Included in 1st Biennale International Photographic Exhibition, Venice |
| **1960** | Exhibition at Jaeger showrooms |
| **1960–4** | Becomes associate contributing editor of *Queen* |
| **1963** | Moves to Tobago, West Indies |
| **1965** | Assignments for French and Italian editions of *Vogue*, and for *Life* |
| **1967** | BBC Television documentary, *One Pair of Eyes* |
| **1968** | Elected Honorary FRPS |
| **1969** | Takes official photographs for the Investiture of Prince Charles and for Princess Anne's nineteenth birthday |
| **1973** | Takes official photographs for Princess Anne's engagement and wedding |
| **1975** | Assignments for *Town and Country* |
| | Takes official photographs for the Queen Mother's seventy-fifth birthday |
| | Elected FIIP |
| **1978** | Exhibition at The Photographers' Gallery, and publication of *Sisters Under the Skin* |
| **1979** | BBC Television documentary in collaboration with Fyfe Robertson, *A Ripe Old Age* |
| **1980** | Takes official photographs for the Queen Mother's eightieth birthday |
| **1981** | Awarded CBE |

## Introduction by Terence Pepper

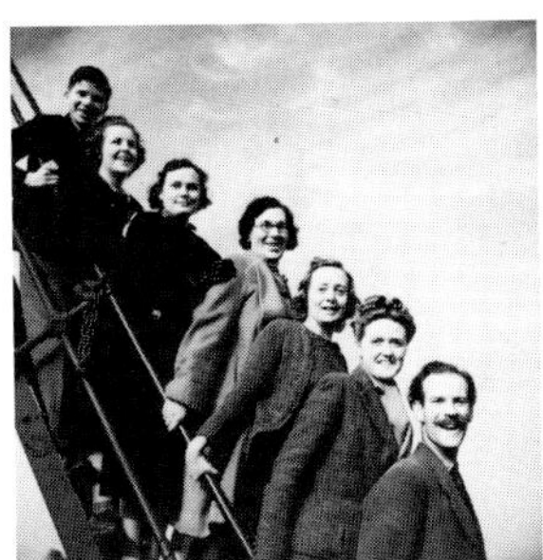

*Fig. 1* **Dover Street staff**

Norman Parkinson was born in 1913 in Roehampton, one of three children. His father was a barrister-at-law and through his mother, who was half Italian, he was descended from Luigi Lablache, the famous *basso profundo* who created the title-role in *Don Pasquale* and was music teacher to Queen Victoria. Parkinson was educated at Westminster School, where his strongest subject was art, and he claims that much of his innate ability to see and see quickly was brought out by the art master there, the painter and poster designer, Henry S. Williamson.

When he left school at eighteen in 1931, Parkinson was apprenticed to Speaight & Sons of Bond Street, an established and respected firm of court photographers. Here, in return for a premium of £300, he was to be paid £1 a week and taught the fundamental principles of portrait photography. In the studio he focused the cumbersome and immovable studio camera, preparing it for Richard Speaight to press the cable release, and in the darkroom he learned to print by assisting Mr Smart. His enthusiasm for trying out new ideas was not entirely appreciated in this very conservative studio, and after only two years of his three-year apprenticeship, he was given a reference that read, in part: 'I am sure that one day he will take a good photograph', and asked to leave.

Aged twenty-one, Parkinson now opened his own studio, where he was assisted for a time by Norman Kibblewhite, another ex-pupil of Speaight's. The studio was at 1 Dover Street, Piccadilly, the heart of fashionable photographers' London. Paul Tanqueray had portrait studios at No. 6, opposite Bertram Park, Yvonne Gregory and Marcus Adams at No. 43, while Hugh Cecil and Dorothy Wilding were established nearby.

Although Parkinson kept his portrait studio open until the outbreak of war, his main creative work was the fashion and portrait photography which he did, mostly on location, for the British edition of *Harpers Bazaar*, and the portraits, reportage and pictorial work he contributed to *The Bystander*, a society magazine with good general news coverage, edited by Reginald Hooper. His pictorial work is now strongly evocative of the period. For example, a picture called 'Dawn' shows an aeroplane about to take off in the early morning light, capturing the excitement and novelty of air travel, and his 'London Cameo, 1936' is a wry comment on the abdication crisis. Reportage work for *The Bystander* took Parkinson to theatrical garden-parties, race-track meetings, Wimbledon, and to Switzerland to photograph life at fashionable ski resorts. In 1937, following Edward VIII, he went to Merthyr Tydfil to take a compassionate series of pictures of miners and their families in the depth of the depression (Fig. 3). 'With the Services' was another contribution. This was a series of extended photo-essays documenting Britain's re-arming forces, a basically serious propaganda exercise to which he brought characteristic touches of humour. In 1939 he travelled by sea to New York for a weekend to photograph the World Fair, and in 1937 he covered the Paris Exposition Universelle. In the preparations leading up to this exhibition he not only photographed the contributing British artists in their studios, eg Bawden, Sheringham and Skeaping, but also collaborated with Francis Brugière (plate 3), the *avant-garde* photographer who designed a giant photo-mural for the British Pavilion. This showed typical British trades and traditional customs which Parkinson had travelled round the country to photograph.

*Fig. 2* **Studio brochure, 1935**

NORMAN PARKINSON IS SOCIETY'S NEWEST PHOTOGRAPHER—IN A FEW MONTHS HIS STRIKING WORK HAS BECOME KNOWN THROUGHOUT THE WEST END

BEFORE FINALLY DECIDING WHO SHALL TAKE YOUR COURT PHOTOGRAPHS NORMAN PARKINSON INVITES YOU TO VISIT HIS STUDIO AT NUMBER ONE DOVER STREET PICCADILLY AND SEE HIS OUTSTANDING PORTRAITS

ON COURT NIGHTS THE STUDIO IS OPEN UNTIL ONE A.M.

TELEPHONE REGENT 4388

During the war years, Parkinson combined farming in Gloucestershire with reconnaissance photography over France for the RAF. In the 1940s he joined the Condé Nast organisation and was to work principally for the British and American editions of *Vogue* until 1960, when for four years he became a contributing associate editor of *Queen* magazine. In 1964 he moved to Tobago, where he turned his attention to his first love, farming. Since then, he has worked freelance for many of the major international magazines, including the various editions of *Vogue*, *Life*, *Elle* and, most recently, since 1975, the American periodical *Town and Country*. He has also established an international reputation for his portraits of the royal family.

Parkinson's career as a fashion photographer has grown almost in tandem with the development of this particular branch of photography. At the outset, fashion photography was a studio-bound activity practised by only a very few British photographers, of whom the best was probably Shaw Wildman. In the 1930s Wildman gradually moved his models out-of-doors, but despite settings such as Brooklands race-track, the pictures remained essentially static. Parkinson was really the first British photographer to get his models to move and look natural in outdoor locations. The European photographers Martin Munkacsi and Jean Moral had pioneered this kind of work, but Parkinson found the style instinctive and translated it to a British context. In 1935, when he was recruited to the staff of *Harpers Bazaar* by the art editor, Alan McPeake, he used a £17 hand-held Graflex he had bought especially for the occasion to photograph models strolling in Hyde Park. This was the genesis of the 'running-jumping' picture that was to remain one of the hallmarks of his style. 'My aim', he said, 'was to take moving pictures with a still camera', and McPeake's creative layouts, in which pictures were overlapped and tilted on the page, emphasised the movement captured in the photographs. With the passage of time the movement became more pronounced, as can be seen in his 1939 photographs of Pamela Minchin on a beach leaping high in the air in a Fortnum swimsuit (plate 10), or two girls energetically golfing at Le Touquet (plate 9). These pictures were important milestones, demonstrating that the fashion photograph could be convincingly and enjoyably spontaneous.

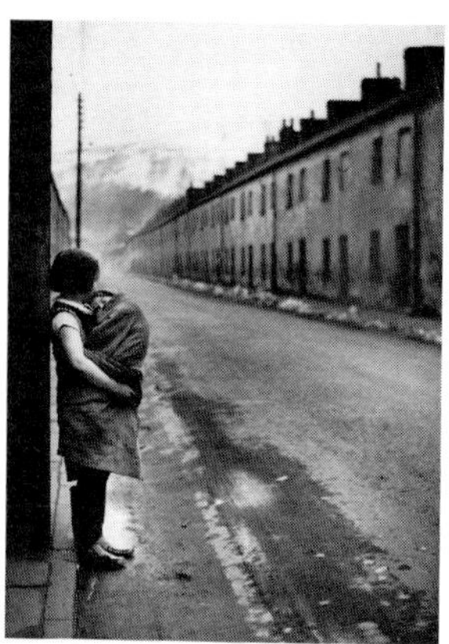

*Fig. 3* **Miner's family, 1937**

Photographed in the studio, the model had usually been a rarefied and exquisite creature, remote from the realities of everyday life. Parkinson's women were different. 'I wanted my women to live, and live with me, to be my friends. I wanted them to be out there in the fields jumping over the haycocks.' His women have liveliness and warmth as well as elegance. They have a certain breezy independence. They were the kind of women with whom the readers of *Harpers* and *Vogue* wished to identify themselves. Parkinson's 1940s pictures of his wife, Wenda Rogerson, typify all that is most characteristic of this new style. Wenda Rogerson, originally an actress, had first been photographed as a fashion model by his admired rival, the American photographer Clifford Coffin, and his pictures of her show her as delicate and idealised. In one photograph she stands at the foot of a staircase in a bombed house in Grosvenor Square; she is as pale and remote as a porcelain figure, her dreamlike fragility emphasised by the heavy gleaming draperies of her long skirt. Parkinson's pictures of her show her in quite a different light. She stands in front of a Peabody Trust Building, smiling and capable in her Simpsons' suit and sensible shoes, a pram visible in the background (plate 55). She sits demurely among ferns in a hedgerow to show off her 'Country Classic' tweeds (plate 60), or enjoys the fun of a family picnic on the grass. Back in London, she poses with Barbara Goalen on the steps of the National Gallery (plate 31), and, silhouetted in their New Look outfits, they present the quintessential image of the well-groomed post-war woman about town.

The fashions themselves were made to look eminently more credible and accessible for being seen worn in real life situations. John Parsons, art editor of *Vogue* (1940–65), particularly liked this approach and encouraged Parkinson to take pictures that would suggest a mood and a story, such as the lyrical and romantic melancholy conjured up by his picture the 'Iron Road', taken at a country railway station in 1947 (plate 57). Parkinson was similarly successful when he created unworldly settings for more sumptuous clothes. In 1947, for example, he photographed evening dresses in ruined abbeys, and in a 1951 picture, a magnificent Hartnell ballgown is worn by a model who stands in front of Clytha Park, the wind-blown branches above her and her blurred skirt suggesting a ghostly and mysterious atmosphere (plate 56).

More typically, it is Parkinson's anarchic sense of humour that sets the mood of his work, as when his wife, for an article on taste in the 'More Dash than Cash' series, grapples messily with the pleasure of eating spaghetti while wearing a smart little cocktail hat and pearls (plate 61). Parkinson's humour has helped to push back the boundaries of what constitutes a successful fashion shot, and has shown that fashion can be equally appealing if it is funny or even anarchic. A model tows along a small toy horse which is then sat upon by an extremely overweight passer-by, or, for a 1960 feature on Lancashire fashion, three laughing and black-grimed miners hold aloft a startled model in her best new dress (plates 85 and 86).

Parkinson's ideas for fashion pictures have frequently involved outrageous stunts. As early as 1938, when he photographed two girls at the top of a 'big wheel' overlooking Brighton pier, the caption writer described him as Norman 'Daredevil' Parkinson. On location in Africa Mrs Parkinson was posed on the back of an ostrich which turned out to move at an incredible speed. As she disappeared into the distance clinging on for dear life, her husband, intent on his view-finder, was heard to cry after her, 'More profile, Wenda! More profile!'. In the 1960s a huge crane was hired to hoist models to the top of London monuments for a feature in *Queen*, while recently in Sri Lanka, photographing the bikini-clad Pilar Crespi, he posed her, not like Dovima in Avedon's photograph, between two fettered elephants, but among untethered elephants, lying on their backs or scrubbing them with a huge brush.

One of Parkinson's particular skills is his ability to portray children in a natural and spontaneous way – Stella McCartney jumping joyously on a Jamaican beach, or the Duke of Devonshire's children in sailor-suits posing on a bridge in front of Chatsworth. He was one of the first photographers to introduce children successfully into fashion pictures. In the 1940s and 50s he shows them at picnics, being bridesmaids and pages at weddings or being pushed in prams. In the early 1950s one particularly successful Aquascutum advertisement for a dinner-jacket showed a small pyjama-clad child clambering up to adjust her grandfather's bow tie (plate 62). With pictures such as these, Parkinson brought fashion into the rough and tumble of family life.

In the post-war period the image of the ideal fashion model has changed remarkably, and Parkinson's use of models has reflected and anticipated many of these changing tastes and possibilities. In the late 1940s and early 1950s Mrs Parkinson appears as the ideal of the well-groomed, approachable and companionable model of the time, equally at home in the town and country, living in London or travelling smartly abroad.

Another of Parkinson's successful collaborations was with the South African-born Enid Boulting (née Munnik), wife of the film producer Roy Boulting. In 1950, in one of Parkinson's now classic fashion photographs, she appears full-face and threequarter-length wearing a Helena Geffers suit, a box jacket over a narrow skirt. The suit was called 'Impertinence', and Parkinson shows her as a mid-century image of the new brutalism in fashion (plate 29). In her lips she holds an unlit cigarette and with her short hair and gamin looks she strikes a forthright and liberated pose. The picture appeared in the same year as Irving Penn's Dior-suited idealised model who smokes a cigarette in the only acceptable *Vogue* way, using a long cigarette-holder. Parkinson's photograph caused a furore in America; *Vogue*'s editor-in-chief, Edna Woolman Chase, cabled from New York: 'Smoking in *Vogue* so tough so "unfeminine".' Nevertheless, Parkinson had created a fiery independent new breed of women. In 1951 he photographed his wife posing in a classic twinset and pearls in the public bar of a country pub, sitting next to a cowman (plate 58). This caused another ripple with the less progressively minded members of the magazine's staff, who complained that no reader would ever be seen in such a situation, but was stoutly defended by the socialistically inclined editor, Audrey Withers, who was prepared to print his pictures.

In 1955 Enid Boulting, now with a three-year-old son and two-year-old twins, portrayed another image of woman in an imaginary series portraying the events in her busy day. In different outfits she was shown to be looking after children and husband, and then entertaining guests in the evening after a hard working day combining high fashion modelling with painting her husband's portrait. In 'A cheerful crowd go out in dirty weather' (plate 63), one of the pictures in the series, she is seen wearing her herringbone suit, walking out in the rain with her three small raincoated charges. Here in *Vogue* was the image of the woman who had time both for children and a career. In the same year, in the 'Young Idea' section, created to appeal to the newly-found clothes purchasing power of the seventeen to twenty-five age group, Parkinson photographed Joan Cox, a primary school teacher in an East End school (plate 64). She wears Jaeger separates as she leads her charges in a merry snake-like procession around the playground. At the time it was a remarkable idea for a fashion photograph.

In the 1960s, when working for *Queen*, it was the face of Celia Hammond, one of many models whose career Parkinson launched, that appeared most frequently, representing the younger age group at which fashion in the period was aimed. At the time, Parkinson, describing her dedication to work and her professionalism, summed up her qualities: 'Celia has tremendous imperfections, yet I think these add to her attraction because other women feel that if they tried really hard they could look as good as she does'.

In the 1970s, the spirit and style of Parkinson's work can best be summed up by the carefree energetic professionalism of the model Jerry Hall. She it is who is glimpsed in a riot of red striding through Russia from Red Square to a fire temple in the remote outback (plate 45), or, hair streaming back, leaning over a gilded rail in Marie Antoinette's bedroom at Versailles (plate 44). The accent today is usually predominantly on youth, and it has been particularly interesting to see in some of Parkinson's most recent work the reappearance at fifty of the model Carmen, at work again after a gap of twenty years, still looking strikingly elegant.

*Fig. 4* **London fashion, 1949**

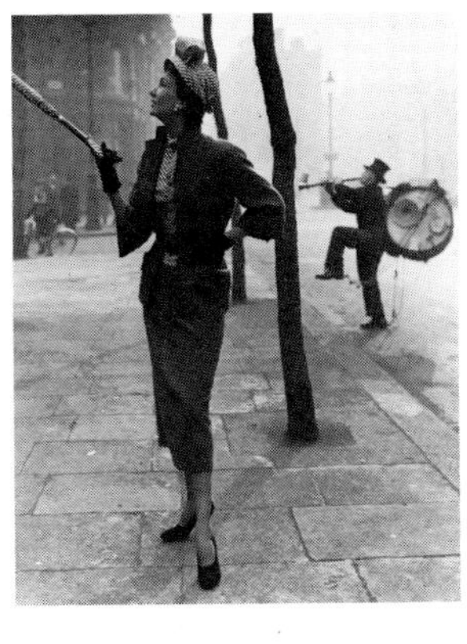

Although fashion photography has perhaps taken up the main part of Parkinson's photographic career, throughout his life he has consistently worked in the field of portraiture, producing here some of his strongest and most compelling images. At the beginning of his career, newly established in his Dover Street studios, he found that he was spending most of his time turning out the kind of standard studio portrait that his clients expected. Only occasionally could he enliven the monotony by experimenting with a movable lighting system to produce such pictures as his romantically baroque portrait of Vivien Leigh (plate 5), and his study of Diana Napier against a background of dramatically-lit folds of material radiating out from behind her (plate 6). It was portrait commissions from *Harpers*, ranging from the family of Joseph Kennedy, the American Ambassador, to the dress designer, Charles James, that first gave him the opportunity to do location work. He found that this was the kind of portraiture he infinitely preferred, partly because the sitter is more at ease, more truly himself in his own surroundings, but mainly because the different settings stimulate a fresh eye and a variety of approach. 'I like to think that I'm a photographer who has not got stuck. Any photographer who surrounds himself with a studio is doomed. What you have to do is to ignite the enthusiasm to get out of the studio.'

*Fig. 5* **London fashion, 1949**

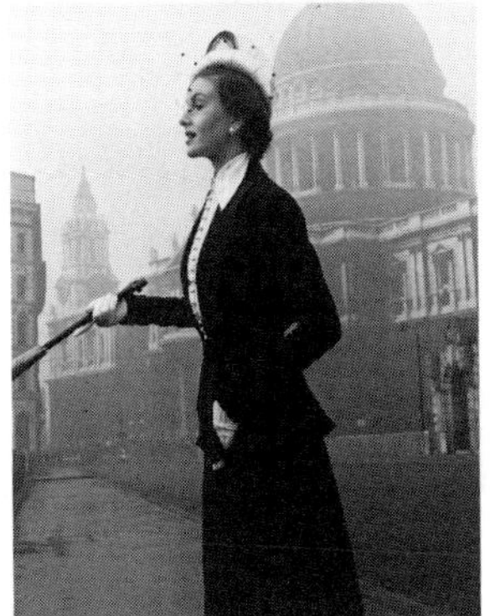

There are occasional Parkinson portraits – Lord David Cecil, Charles Morgan and Walter de la Mare (plates 19, 23 and 14) – in which the subject's head is allowed to fill the frame, but more often Parkinson likes to show his sitter in apposite and telling surroundings. The Sitwells, artists and patrons of the arts, stand solemnly before an elaborate *trompe-l'oeil* wall-painting in Osbert's Chelsea garden (plate 1). Sir Arthur Bliss is shown striking a theatrical pose, a dramatic and flamboyant figure standing alone in a deserted and wintry street (plate 79). The ghost story writer Algernon Blackwood sits by a window that overlooks traffic-filled Park Lane, an aged timeless creature weaving a tale of ancient horrors while the modern world thunders by (plate 22). In a 'society' portrait of the Wyndham-Quin sisters (plate 76), the girls stand smiling in pale and exquisite ballgowns on either side of a table under which (a typical Parkinson touch) their poodle dozes. On the walls behind them and on the table itself is a collection of old master portraits, a sombre and formal contrast to the girls' bright elegance. Another very different painterly reference appears in his 1939 portrait of Edward James (plate 2). Here, in a surrealist fantasy, James's disembodied head lies beside Magritte's plaster cast of Napoleon's death-mask painted with clouds.

Parkinson plans his portraits carefully, occasionally, as with a royal portrait, finding it helpful to reconnoitre the surroundings beforehand. Normally, when the pressure is on and time is limited, he will use the few moments of arrival and exchange of pleasantries at a location to observe the surroundings, deciding where best to position his sitter. He will occasionally rearrange objects to achieve the best effect, as, for example, in the portrait of Tyrone Guthrie (plate 21), where the scattered pit stools were reorganised into a satisfying and effective 'L' shape. In his 1953 series of musicians with their instruments, the instruments themselves become the environment: Jimmy Blades smiling over a long expanse of xylophone (plate 26), George Eskdale peeping under his glasses through the coils of his trumpet (plate 25).

Parkinson uses natural light whenever possible, either taking his sitter outside or, as with his portraits of Algernon Blackwood or of Clifford and Arnold Bax (plates 22 and 78), by using light from a window. He likes to capture the textures of skin and material: the network of lizard-like wrinkles on Charles Morgan's face, the rough weave of Katherine Hepburn's linen jacket or the stitches of Ralph Vaughan Williams's knitted pullover, the crumbling outside wall of Maria Korchinska's Maida Vale flat (plates 23, 71 and 12). Often the arrangement of the sitter's hands gives a tension and unity to the composition. Montgomery Clift raises a hand to the furrowed lines of his forehead; Tyrone Guthrie, in a suitably theatrical gesture, reaches into his breast-pocket for a handkerchief; Father D'Arcy grasps the lapels of his jacket, and his hands lead the eye upwards towards his face and to the Madonna and Child statue behind him (plates 70, 21 and 13).

Parkinson's eye for an effective composition gives his photographs of groups a particular unity and cohesion. In his picture of the Sitwells, for example (plate 1), Edith, hair newly crimped, stands between her brothers, their heads on the same level. Parkinson then photographed them from above so that the three faces look up, alike and united before the camera. Similarly, in his 1963 photograph of the Beatles (plate 82), he emphasised their group identity by lining them up with their heads close together, four famous haircuts in a row. When he was invited to take the official photographs for the Queen Mother's eightieth birthday, the three blue satin cloaks he devised and had made especially for the pictures that show her with the Queen and Princess Margaret simplify the composition and unify the family group.

One of Parkinson's most elaborately arranged group photographs is his 'Ten young actresses of 1953' (plate 65), taken to illustrate an article on the young look in the theatre. The picture recalls Irving Penn's relentlessly elegant 1947 group of '*Vogue*'s ten most famous models'. The arrangement of the actresses has been carefully organised so that the evening-dressed ones are at the base of the picture with those in trousers above them. But instead of the timeless and unspecific background used by Penn, Parkinson has arranged his sitters on a climbing-frame in a gym, and included himself upside-down at the very top, sending up the whole carefully composed tableau. Combining stylishness with humour, the picture is very typical of his self-deprecating attempts to defuse the pretensions of photography. Most of Parkinson's other theatrical work is more formalised, and shows his ability to frame tightly the leading characters of a play in a powerful or interesting construction. Richard Burton grasping Claire Bloom in a tense moment in a rehearsal of *Hamlet* at the Old Vic is presided over by Michael Benthall, the director, in the background, showing a tightly constructed group (plate 69); Jeremy Spencer and Carol Wolveridge appearing in *The Innocents* stare knowingly and menacingly out of their composition (plate 68); Margaret Rutherford's expansive and characteristic gesture with her arms diagonally thrown across the composition tightly frames a scene from *Time Remembered*, in which Paul Scofield and Mary Ure are seen in embrace in the background. Perhaps Parkinson's most famous theatrical group is the assemblage of the creators of the play *The Dark is Light Enough*, a pyramidical composition in which Edith Evans is the central pivot, surrounded by Oliver Messel, James Donald, Christopher Fry and Peter Brook. As well as the theatre, Parkinson has also photographed a number of film stars on sets, and of these his photograph of John Huston playing cards on the set of the film of *Moby Dick* is a stunning *tour de force*; Hustons's huge looming figure caught in concentration towers over the scene (plate 73). Taken with a Rollieflex placed on the flat deck, the bulk of Huston's massive figure dominates the composition, from his shining black leather shoes to his corduroy cap.

On the other hand, Parkinson is equally successful with his photograph of Audrey Hepburn off the set of *War and Peace*, sitting by a stable door, her long legs protruding and seemingly inextricably mixed up with those of a pet donkey with whom she is posed (plate 72). The total effect emphasises the gentleness and humour of the picture.

Parkinson's name has perhaps become most familiar to the public through his photographs of the royal family. His first official commission came in 1969, when he was asked to take the pictures for Prince Charles's Investiture and for Princess Anne's nineteenth birthday. His photographs of Princess Anne, particularly one of her riding her horse High Jinks in Windsor Great Park, brought a new freshness and informality into royal portraiture, and his subsequent elegiac engagement and wedding pictures of her and Captain Mark Phillips are among the most romantic royal pictures ever taken (plate 50). He had similar success when he took the official photographs for the Queen Mother's eightieth birthday, portraying her in sparkling gown and jewels through a rain-spotted window, thereby combining subject and setting in perfect harmony (plate 49).

Parkinson's preferred technique is to photograph against the light, using to a greater or lesser extent fill-in foreground flash. His London street fashion photographs of 1949 and his recent 'royal blue trinity' photographs are two examples. 'I'm Mr Contre-jour', he says. He hasn't used an exposure metre since the invention of polaroid film, as he finds that the preliminary polaroid shots he now always takes can tell him with greater accuracy exactly where the light is coming from, and can also be used to give the sitter confidence, to show them that they are going to look good. Parkinson likes to show people at their best. 'If you have the responsibility of using your lens to record people for history, do it well. Everybody can look a little handsome, a touch beautiful – record them that way. Don't destroy them and make them look hideous for the sole purpose of inflating your own photographic ego.' To keep his sitter at ease, Parkinson brings to his portrait sittings a barrage of chat and off-beat jokes. Though working with manic energy his manner is relaxed and amiable, his eyes amused but observing everything. He is a distinguished 6 feet 5 inches tall and his clothes are stylishly eccentric. He always wears a Kashmiri wedding hat while he is working to bring him luck, and he will occasionally adopt the air of a faded colonel who has just taken up photography as a pleasant hobby to relax the tensions, but each session is planned with a military precision. Seizing the moment is part of the skill, and in the end, there is no substitute for it. He once spent the best part of a day photographing the composer Georges Enesco on a tuition visit to Bryanston School. It was only at Salisbury station, just as he was leaving, that he captured the picture that satisfied him, a stolen snapshot in which Enesco's stooped figure seems to be performing a crablike and secret dance among the station pillars (plate 16).

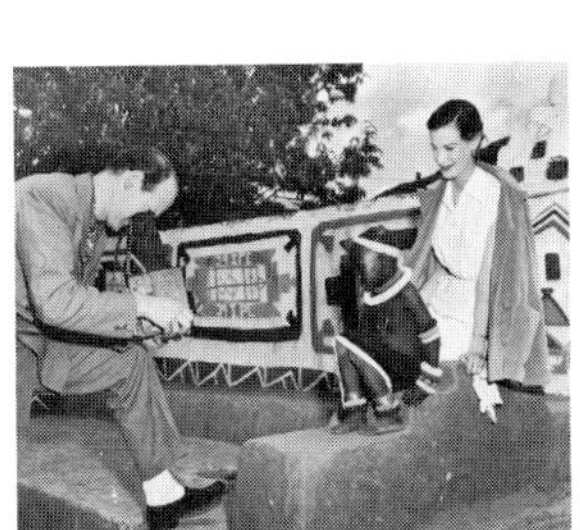

*Fig. 6* **South Africa, 1951**

Parkinson has always preferred to work in colour whenever he can, and in the late 1930s his 35mm Kodachrome pictures were among the first colour work to appear in the British edition of *Harpers Bazaar*. After the war opportunities for colour photography greatly increased, and through his work for *Vogue*, Parkinson has become one of the world's best-known colour photographers. He is one of the very few photographers who are able to handle both black and white and colour with equal skill. His feeling for colour is bold and instinctive, yet he nearly always uses it with a telling restraint and subtlety.

In his 1971 Seychelles fashion photograph of a girl in black calling to a black dog along the white deserted sandy beach (plate 43), the colours are all the more dramatic for being so few. It is a typical trademark that Parkinson uses only a limited range of colour to stunning effect, whether he is posing Wenda Rogerson in a caramel coloured Molyneux satin gown leaning on a Silver Ghost Rolls-Royce in 1950 (plate 35), or Anne Gunning in a pink mohair coat by a ceremonial elephant outside the City Palace in Jaipur, India, to create a dazzling location photograph of a cacophony of reds, pinks and magentas (plate 39). Sometimes one contrasting single splash of colour will be added to an otherwise narrow range. In his first distant location pictures in South Africa he photographed his wife in a blue and black striped dress against the almost monochromatic blues and greens of jungle shrubbery and cascading water of the Victoria Falls, but brought off the final Rousseauesque effect by the addition of a pink belt, shoes and collar. In his more recent 1970s portrait of the artist John Piper (plate 53), the sitter's striped shirt is seen as the only dash of colour in a predominantly pale composition of grey flint wall and withered sunflowers.

Working in colour, Parkinson sometimes makes reference to the work of those painters he most admires. For a 1959 fashion picture of a woman wearing an Otto Lucas scarlet velvet toque, he pays homage to Van Dongen's work (front cover). He focused on a richly embroidered decaying hanging behind the model, so throwing her out of focus and accentuating her khol-rimmed eyes and the bright red of her lips and hat in a typical Van Dongen manner. Other pictures, such as his portrait of Princess Alexandra seated on a carved stone bench wearing her mother's eighteenth-century embroidered dress, are reminiscent of a grand Zoffany or Gainsborough pose, validly translated into photographic terms. Since the early 1930s Parkinson has experimented with the effects of double exposure, usually to combine a photograph of a girl and a painted image, and he regards these as some of his best work. The effect he aims for is a photographic equivalent to the layers of a painter's oil paint on canvas.

Despite this interest in painterly effects Parkinson is always adamant in his debunking of the pretensions of photographers and the claims of art-form status. He sees photography as primarily a means of communication, and to him professionalism, coupled with imagination and ability to portray one's own individual vision of the world, are the goals for which he has aimed. An article contributed to a 1962 photographic annual perhaps sums up better than anything else the approach he has adopted throughout a long career and his formula for success.

'Don't listen to what they are saying – photography is not an art!
A photographer is an engine-driver – get there on time!
A poet maybe,
A do-it-yourself chemist – mostly in the dark,
A diplomatist with the client who has been given a wonderful picture and can't see it,
A patient husband and father who rarely sees his family,
A cricket captain who always has one eye on the weather,
A journalist who uses his nut, and quickly.
If a photographer is all of these, then he is moving on – success is with him, or just around the corner!'

Terence Pepper

**May 1981**

## Norman Parkinson by Wenda Parkinson

Fifty years of photography and none of it easy, perhaps because with intentional purpose Parkinson never makes anything easy for himself. I speak with certainty and privileged knowledge since for more than thirty-five of those fifty years, both as his wife and the reason for some of his best-known pictures, I have shared his existence, and as photography is three-quarters of his life it has been necessary, though often baffling, to go along with the dedicated zeal with which he approaches his work.

Parkinson says firmly – and I am sure that he believes in what he says – that photography is not an art but a craft. I don't know whether I agree with him or not; it is certainly not a fashionable dictum. Surely there are a handful of photographers in the world whose vision strays over the edge of craftsmanship into the area of intangible communication which we recognise as art.

During fifty years of work I don't believe that Parkinson has ever been bored or grown tired of photography. He possesses an eye of innocence. What he sees through the lenses of his rather worn out cameras, his familiar friends, never ceases, even after so long, to surprise and delight him. There can be no one who is less blasé. Every sitting – however seemingly mundane – is capable of holding within it the magic he is always striving to find. Brought up in an age when fairy-tales were still read aloud to children by the warmth of the nursery gas fire, he has never lost his belief in magic. Indeed he talks about the existence of gremlins in his camera. The princes and princesses, the good and the bad fairy, appear, a little disguised, from the filed recesses of his imagination again and again.

He admits to being incurably romantic and sees no reason for being ashamed of this. His work is the antithesis of what he refers to as the 'rough realism' school of photography, but at the same time he is beware of the pretty-pretty. If it is undeniably pretty it also has to be witty.

Parkinson has been a farmer almost as long as he has been a photographer. A rather curious combination, or is it? Steichen bred delphiniums, Penn has a farm in Vermont. Parkinson comes on one side of his family from farming stock, the other side were opera singers. Both sides contribute, he admits, and laughs at his own theatricality. At the same time he never loses the sense, the bluntness and practicality of the countryman, which makes him shy away from affectation or whimsicality.

Parkinson believes that he suffers fools gladly, but as far as his work is concerned he does not, and he is incapable of dissembling. He is painstaking to the point of being irritating to those less patient; there is only one way to do a thing and that is the right way. Parkinson believes it to be his way. He has been described by those who work with him as ruthless. Fatigue, cold, heat, danger, the law, nothing is going to come between him and the picture he anticipates. Fortunately he is generally able to draw on a velvet glove of gaiety and wit to disguise his single-minded intentions.

There is an undeniable amount of painter reference in his work. He is not a frustrated artist but he has never been able to abandon his mental book of art reference. His lens looks through the eyes of many artists. Klimt, Gainsborough, Van Dongen, Zoffany, but it ends up Parkinson. This vision may be oblique but it is never forgotten and filters down into the instant image which is photography.

He is probably best known to the public, through his pictures of the royal family, as a portraitist of women. It is important that he loves women; he is for that reason protective towards them. He has never believed in retouching these objects of his affection – his retouching is achieved by lighting. He says 'I set out to get on film the look my sitter gives as a temptress to the privacy of her own looking glass'. He never betrays his sitters, and condemns those who feel that to show a man or woman at their worst gives their pictures strength. Parkinson believes that the best of a person is as truthful as the worst.

He always photographs his sitters in their own homes, believing that a studio is sterile, and he spends his time whilst the cameras are being set up absorbing the paintings and objects with which the sitter has surrounded himself. To be a good portraitist, he believes you also have to be a good detective.

He stands as a very simple photographer, without pretension. He never imposes himself upon a picture. He picks up his camera and then lets his eye speak: if it also speaks to others then he is content.

## List of plates

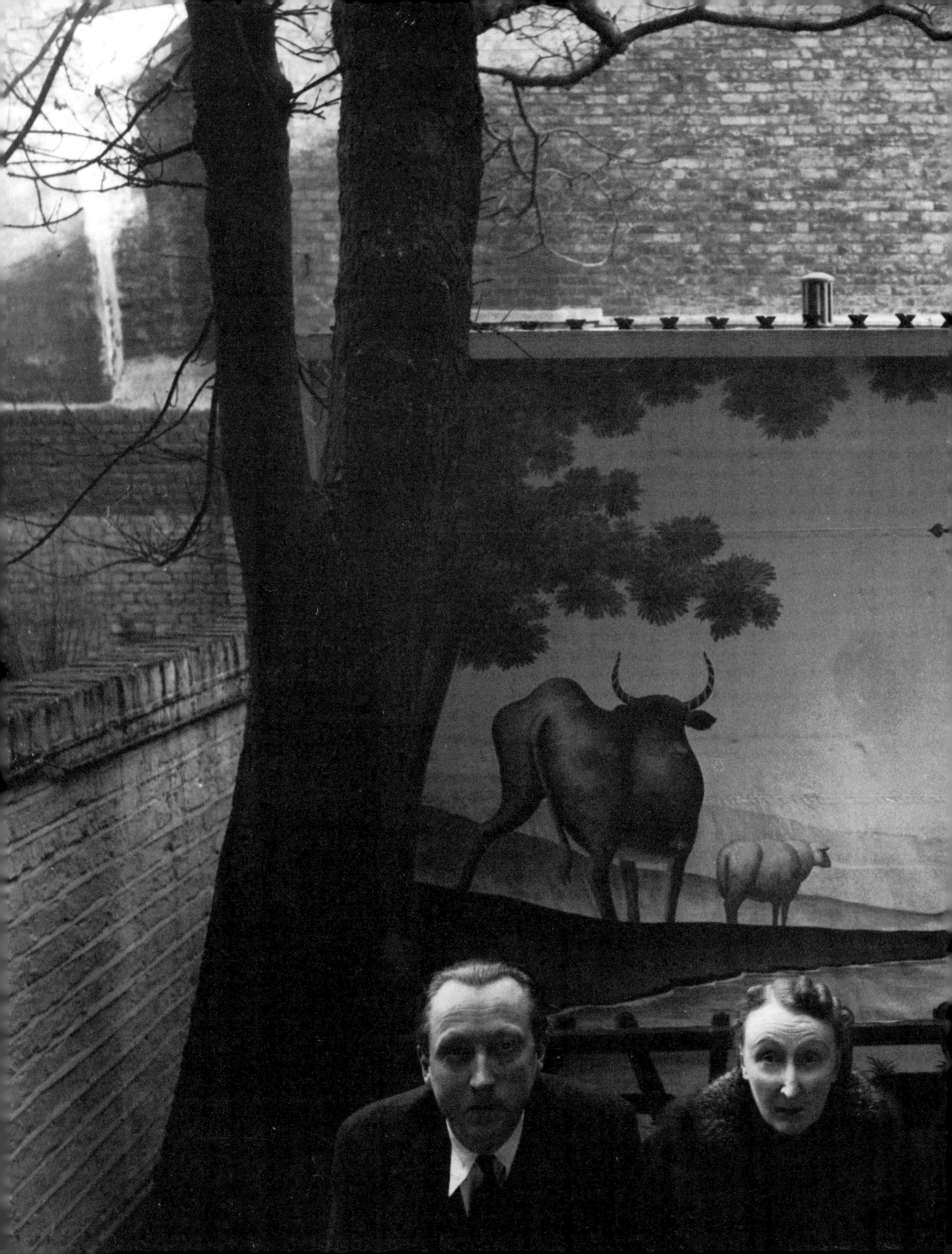

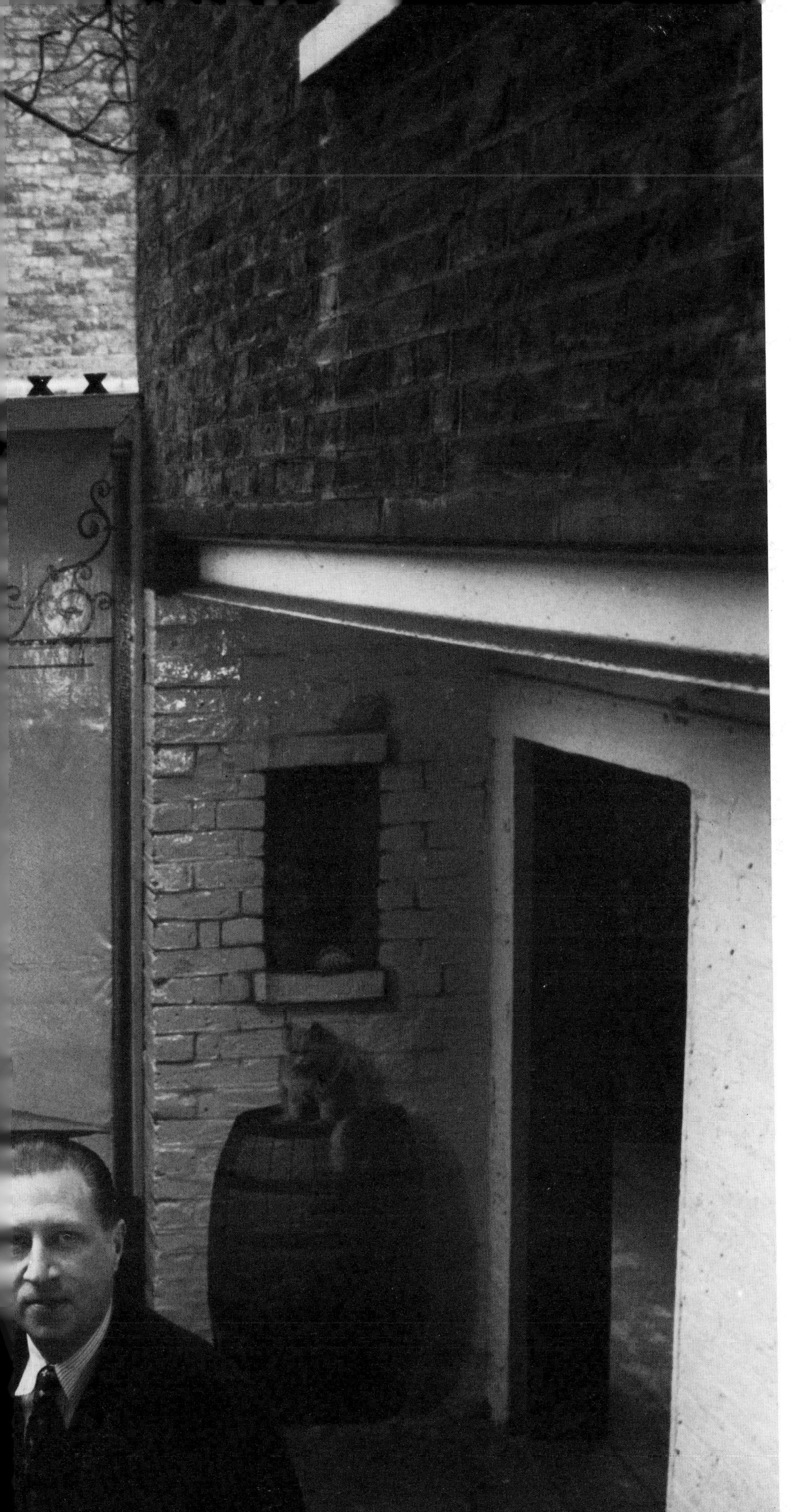

*1* **Sacheverell**
**Edith and Osbert Sitwell**
**Chelsea 1938**

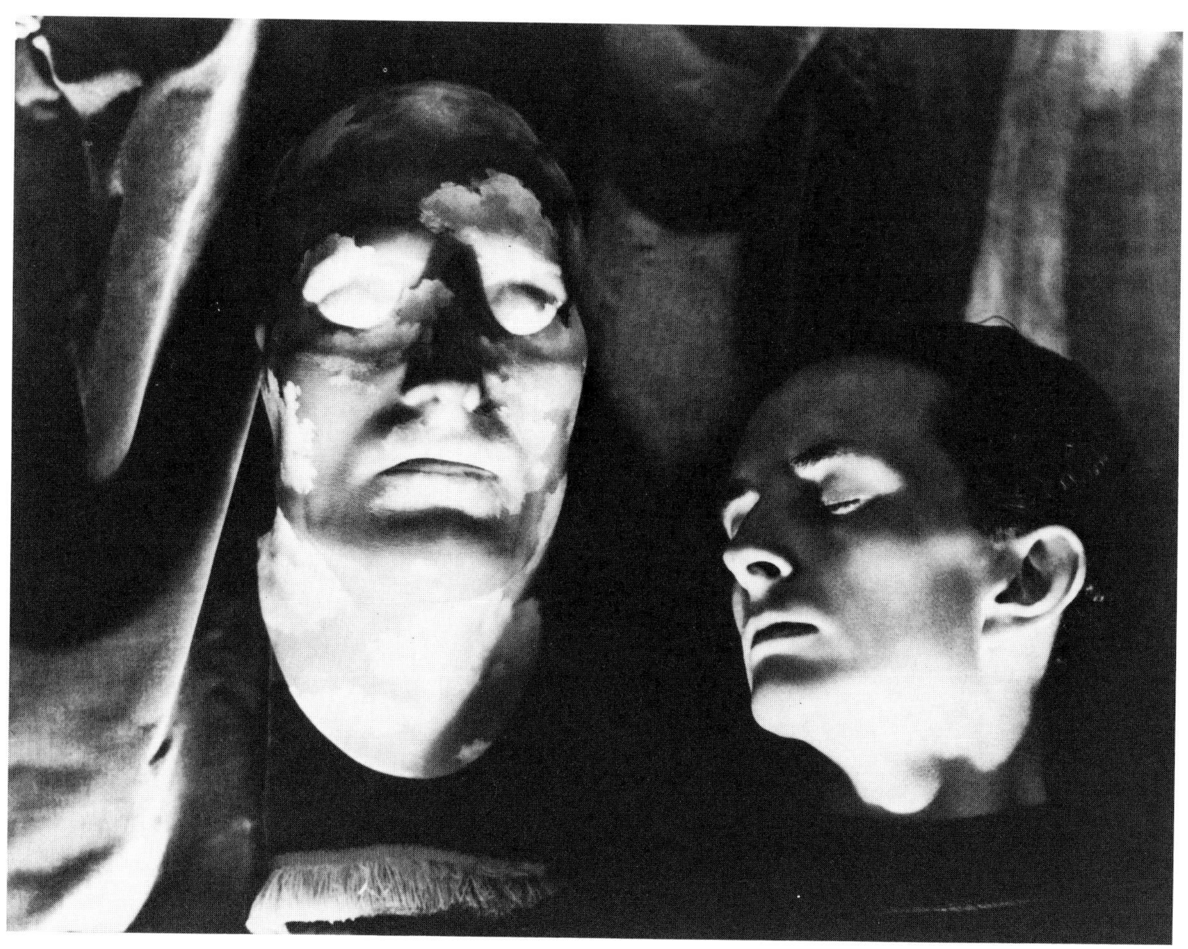

*2* **Edward James** **1939**

*3* **Francis Brugière** **1937**

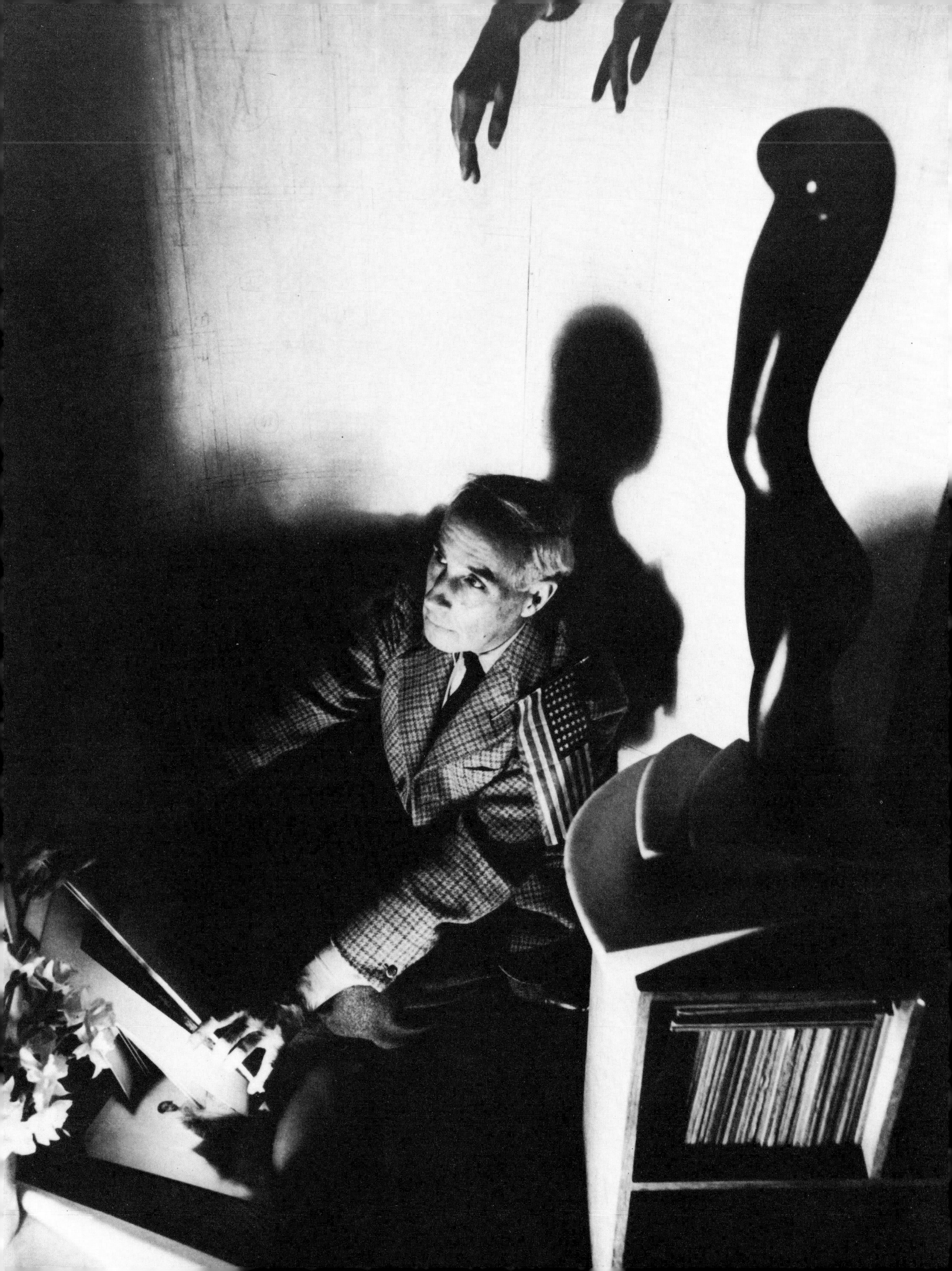

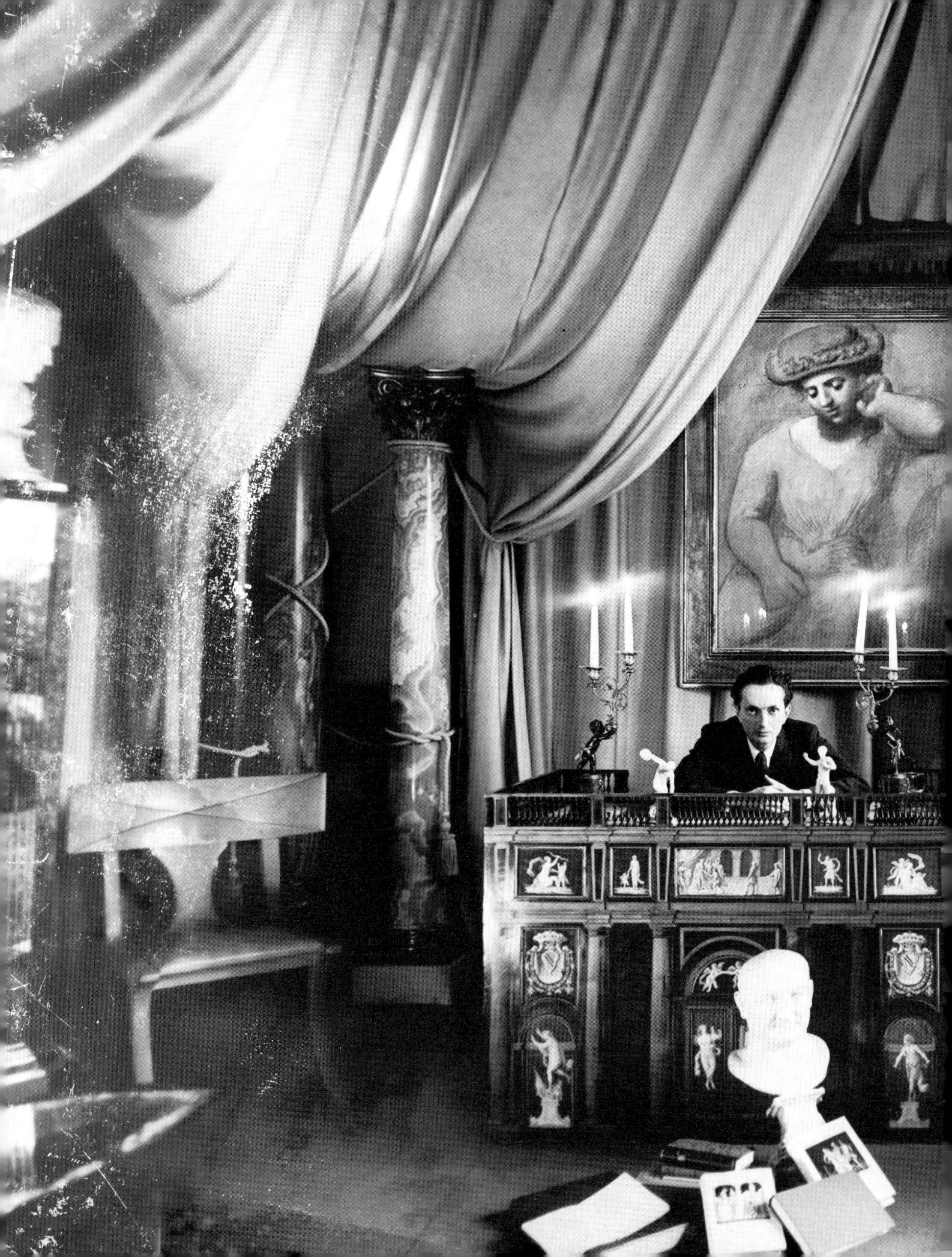

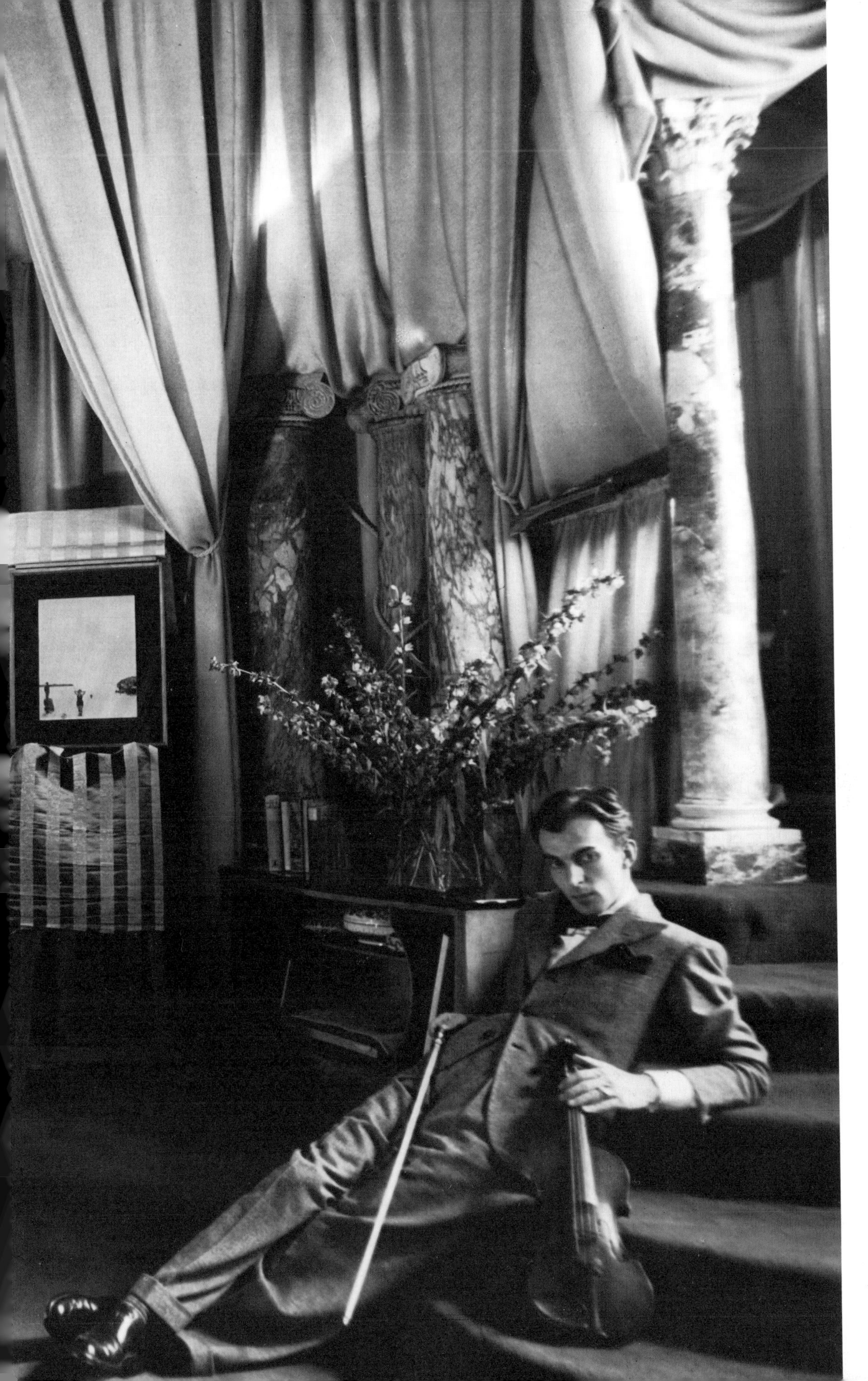

*4* **Edward James in his tent room 1939**

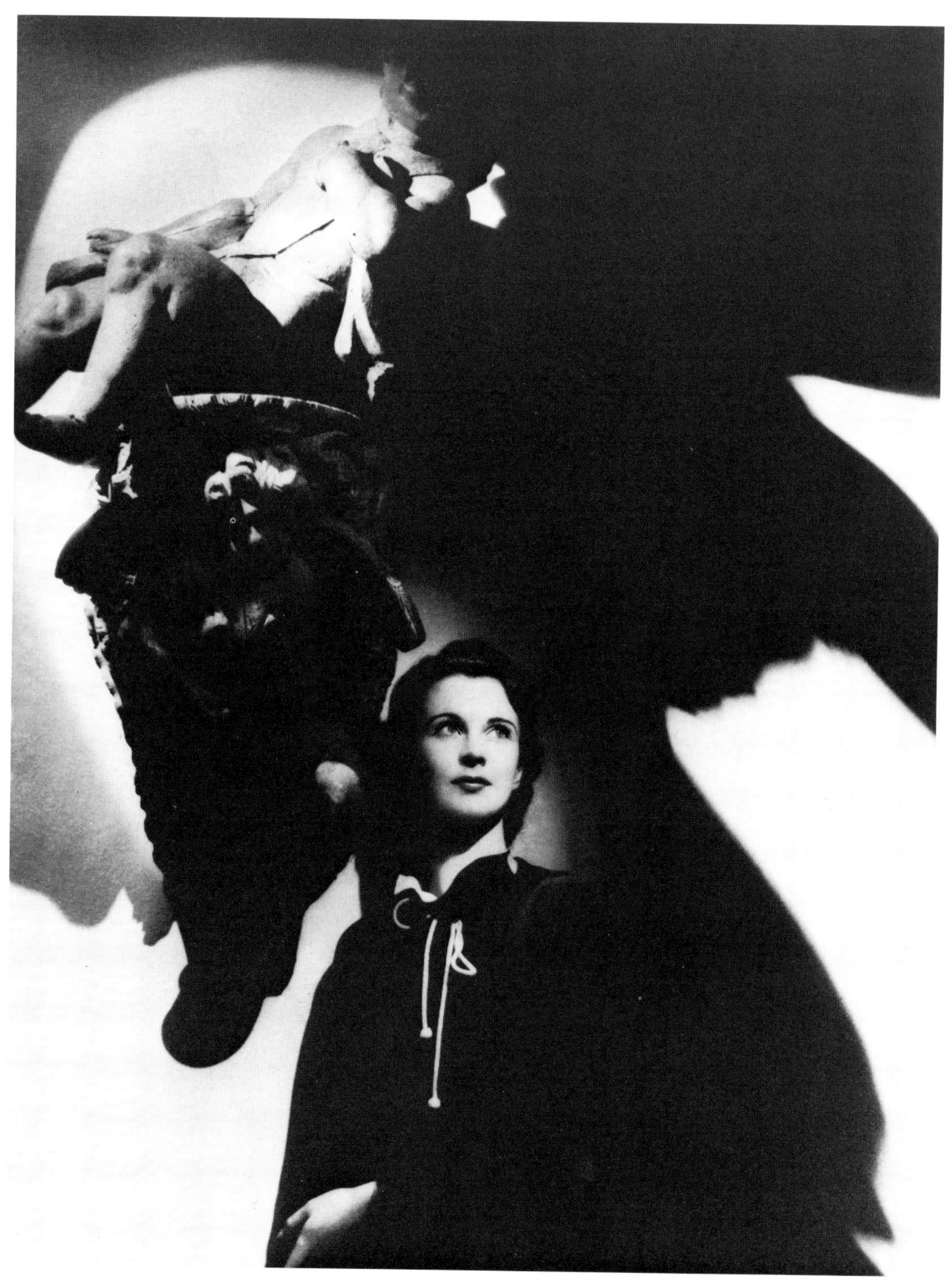

5 **Vivien Leigh** 1935

6 **Diana Napier (Mrs Richard Tauber)** 1935

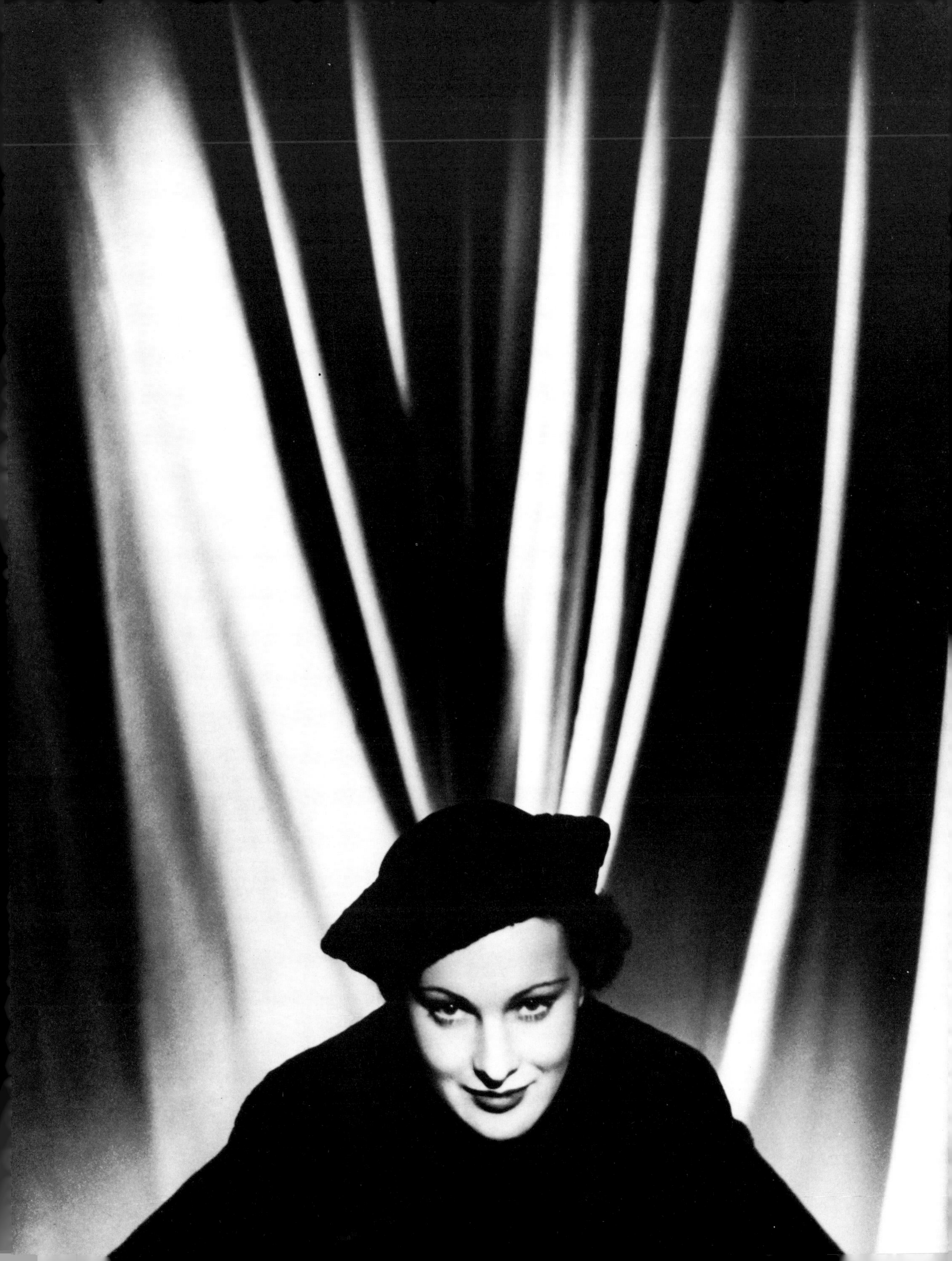

The Bystander, December 16, 1936

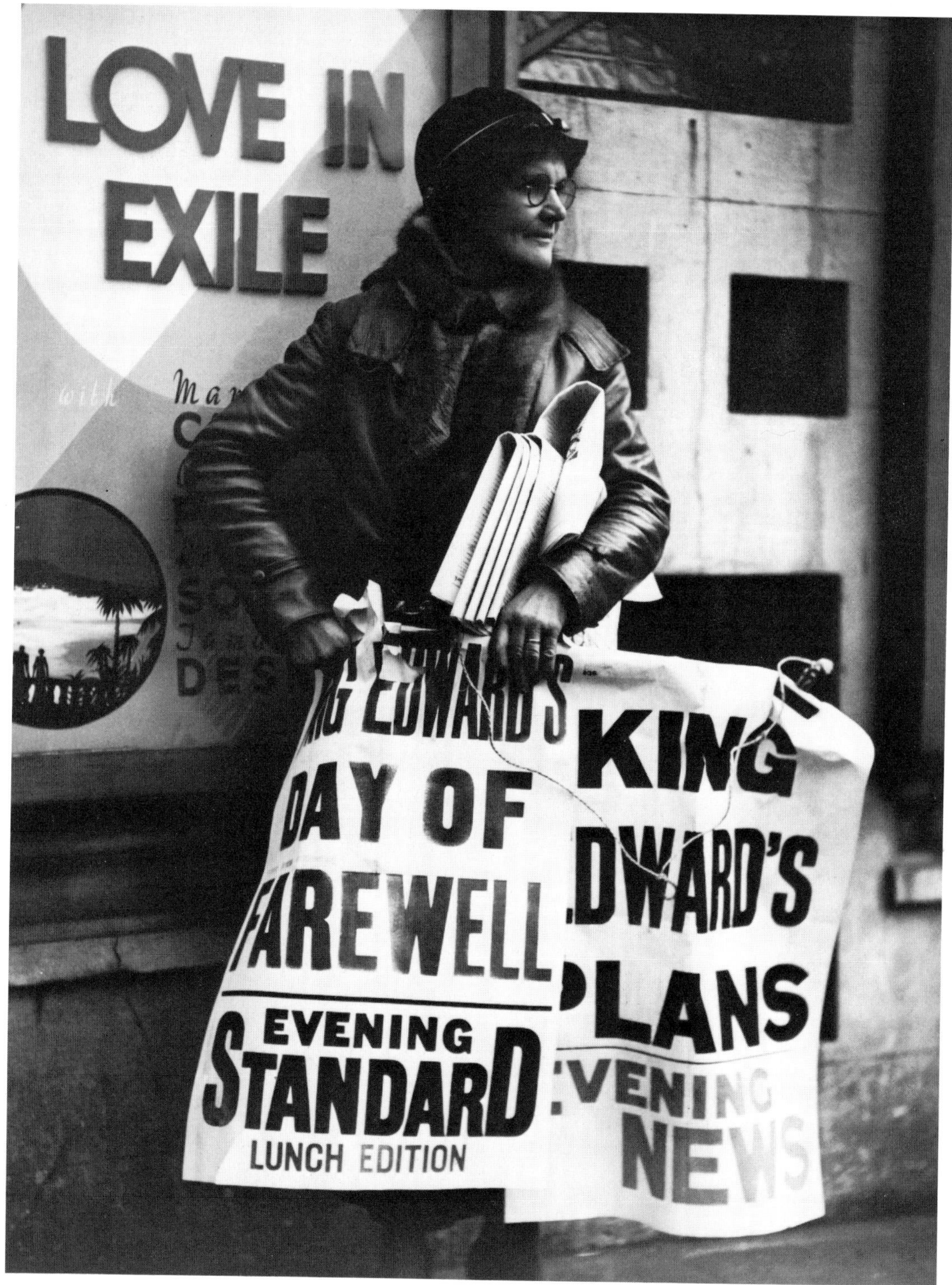


7 London Cameo, December 11th, 1936

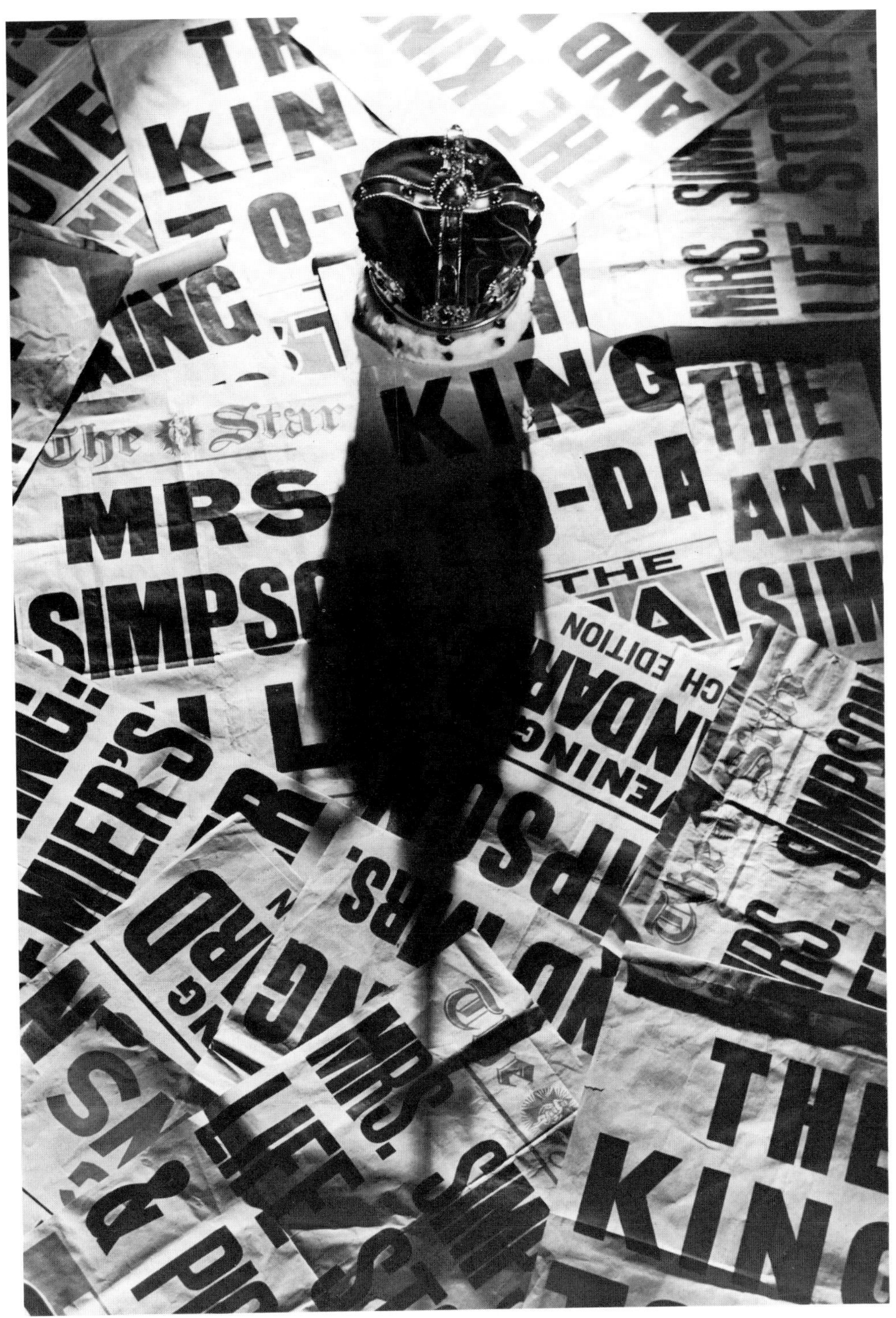


*8* December 3rd, 1936 : an Epitome

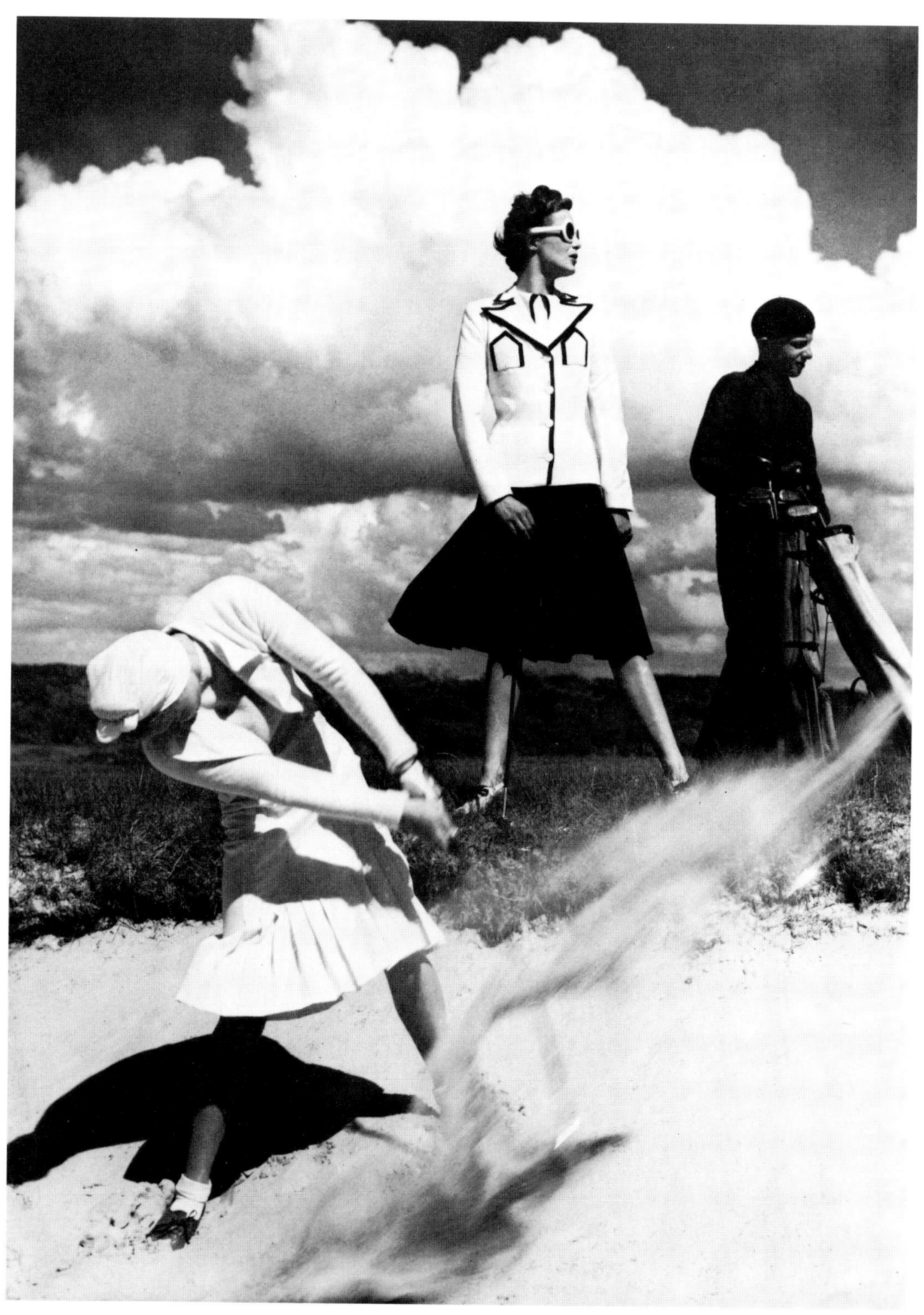

*9* **Golfing at Le Touquet** 1939

*10* **Swimsuit fashion Pamela Minchin** 1939

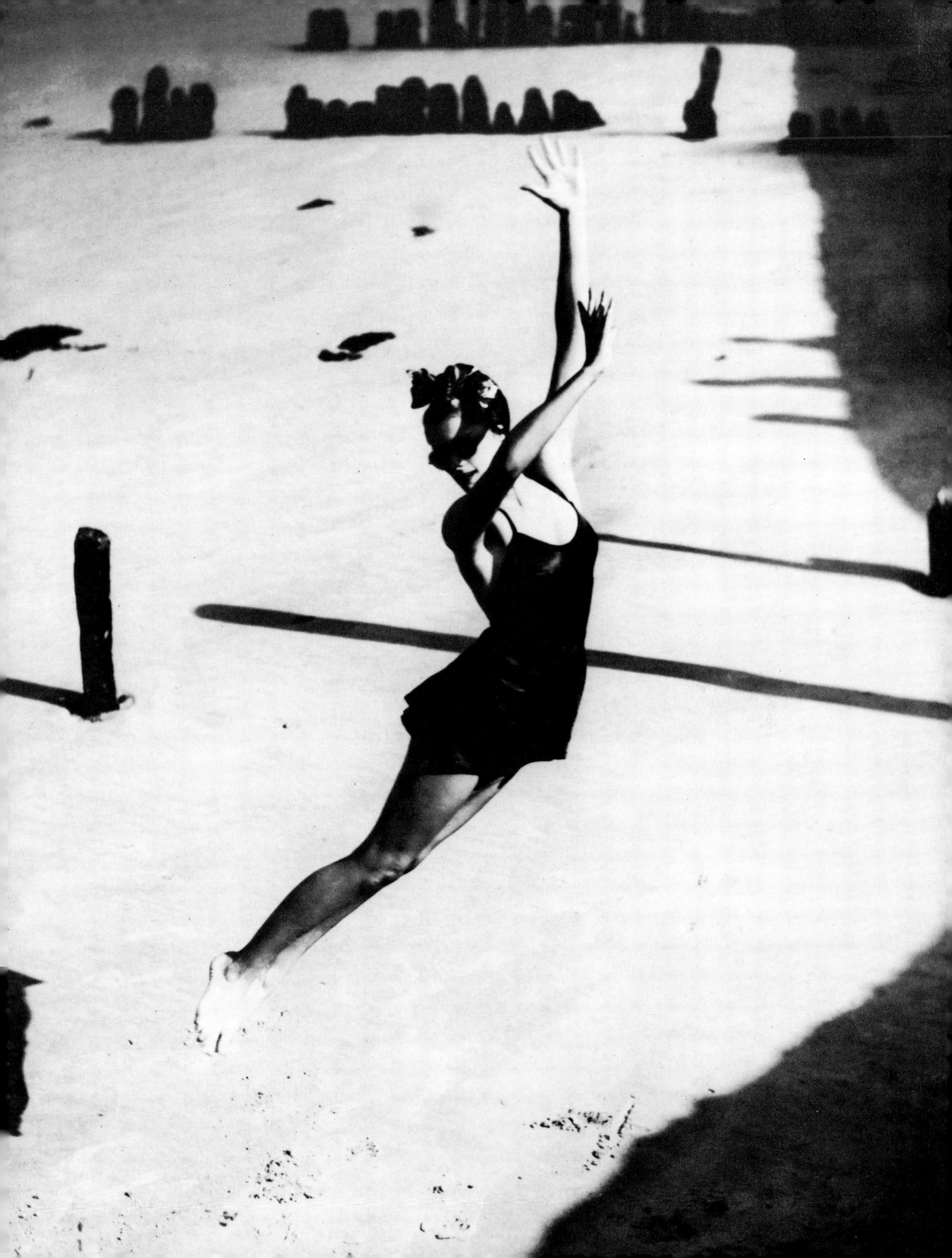

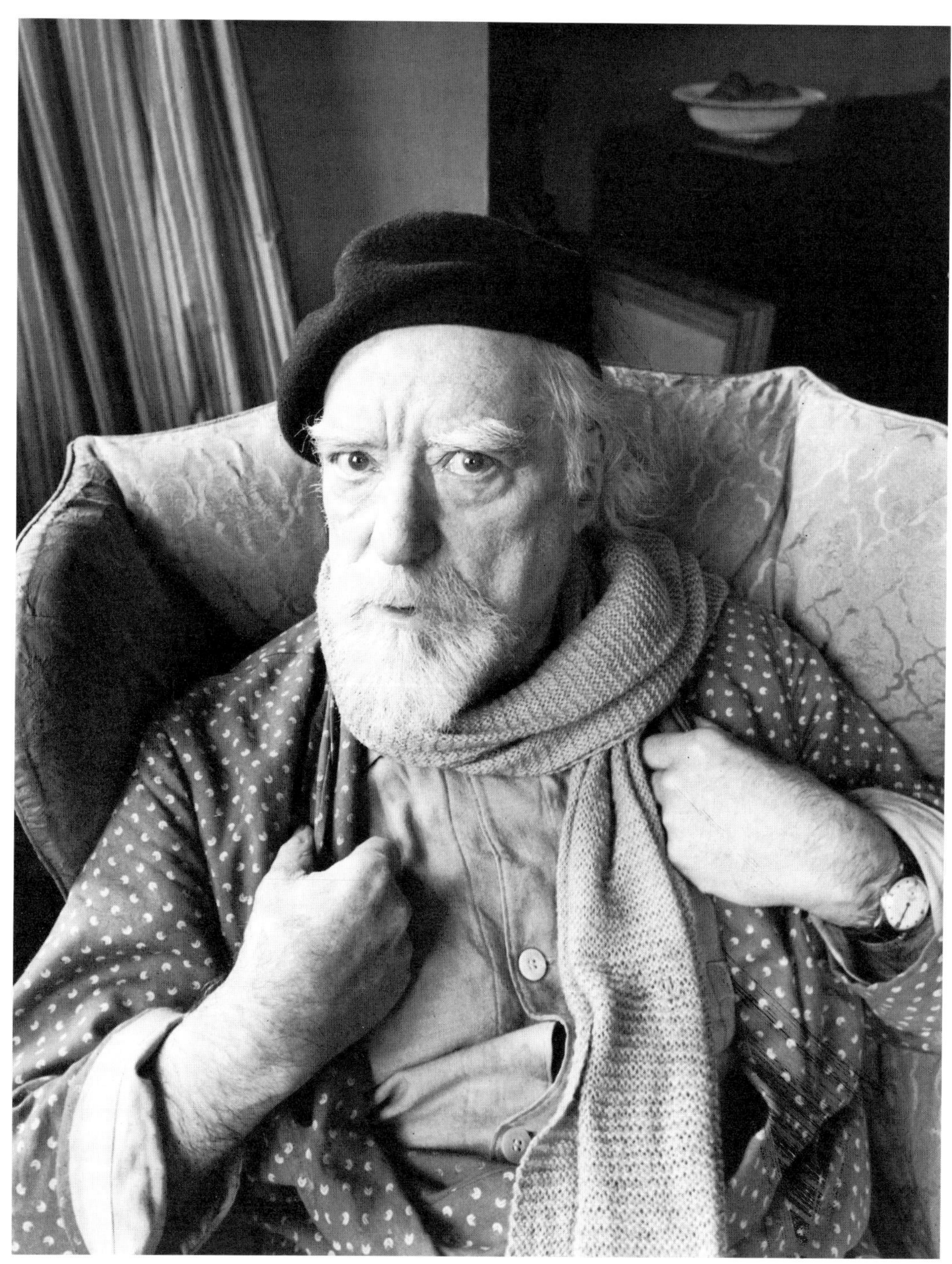

*11* **Augustus John 1951**

*12* **Ralph Vaughan Williams 1951**

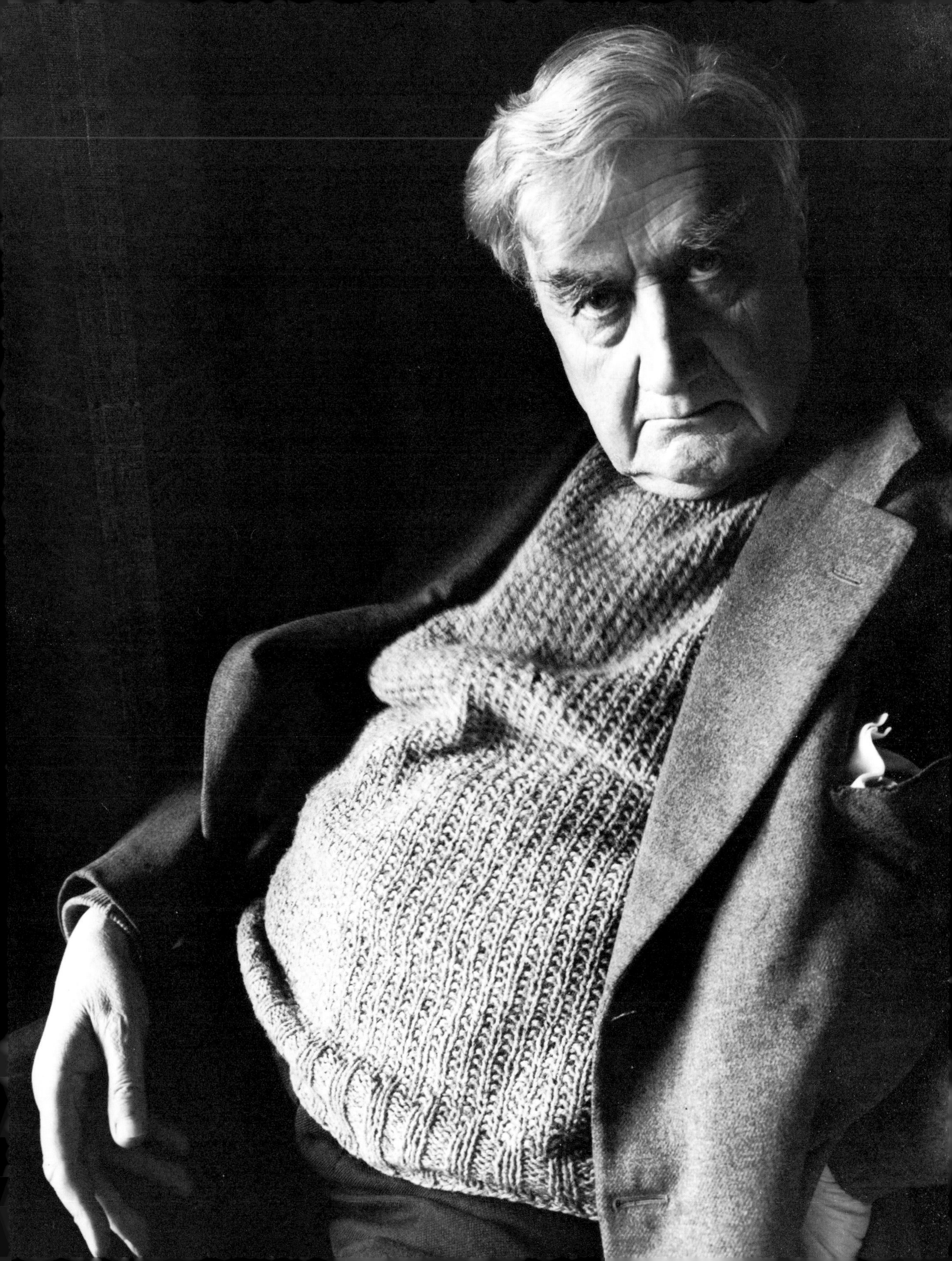

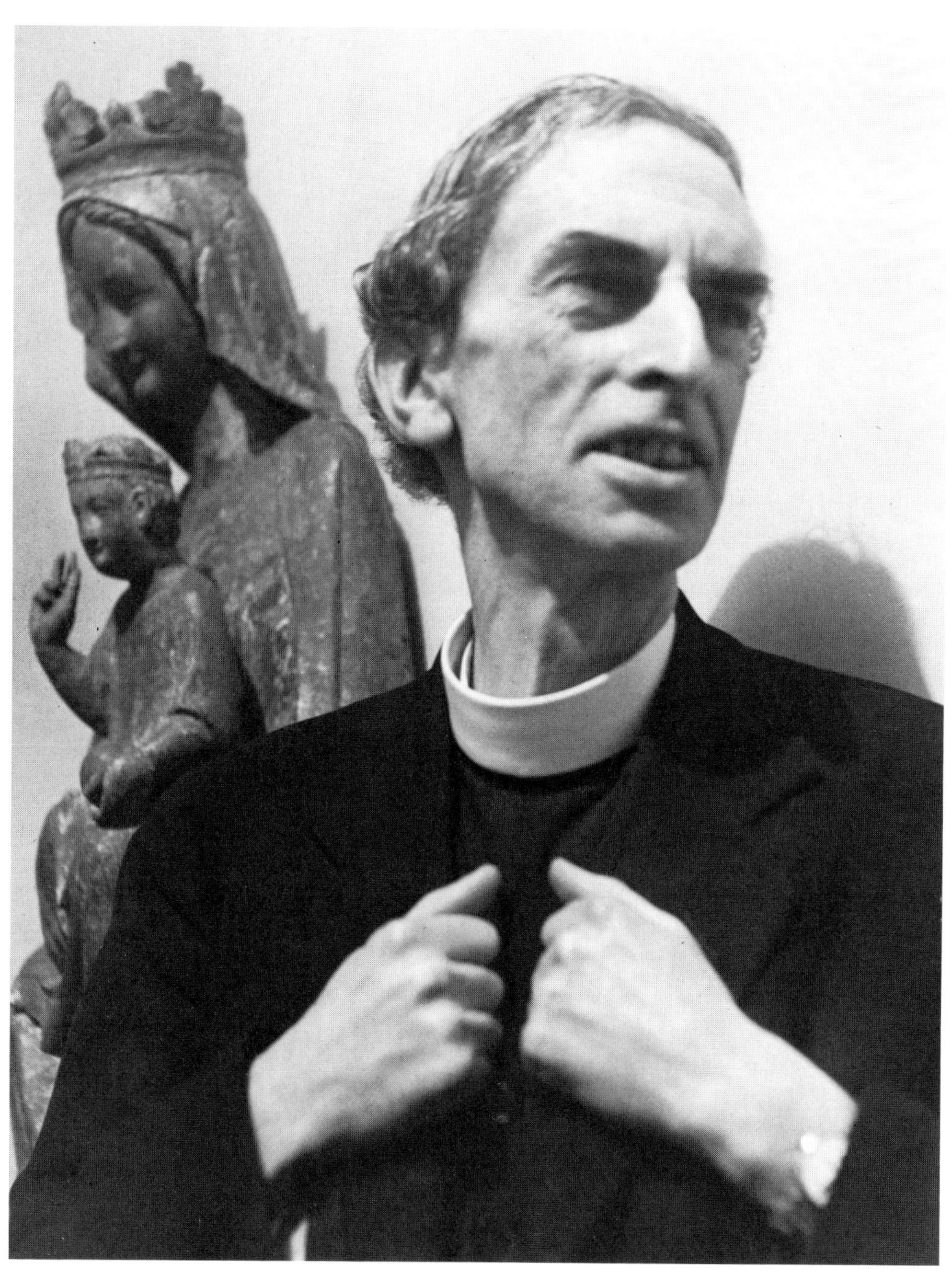

*13* **Father D'Arcy Oxford 1951**

*14* **Walter de la Mare 1951**

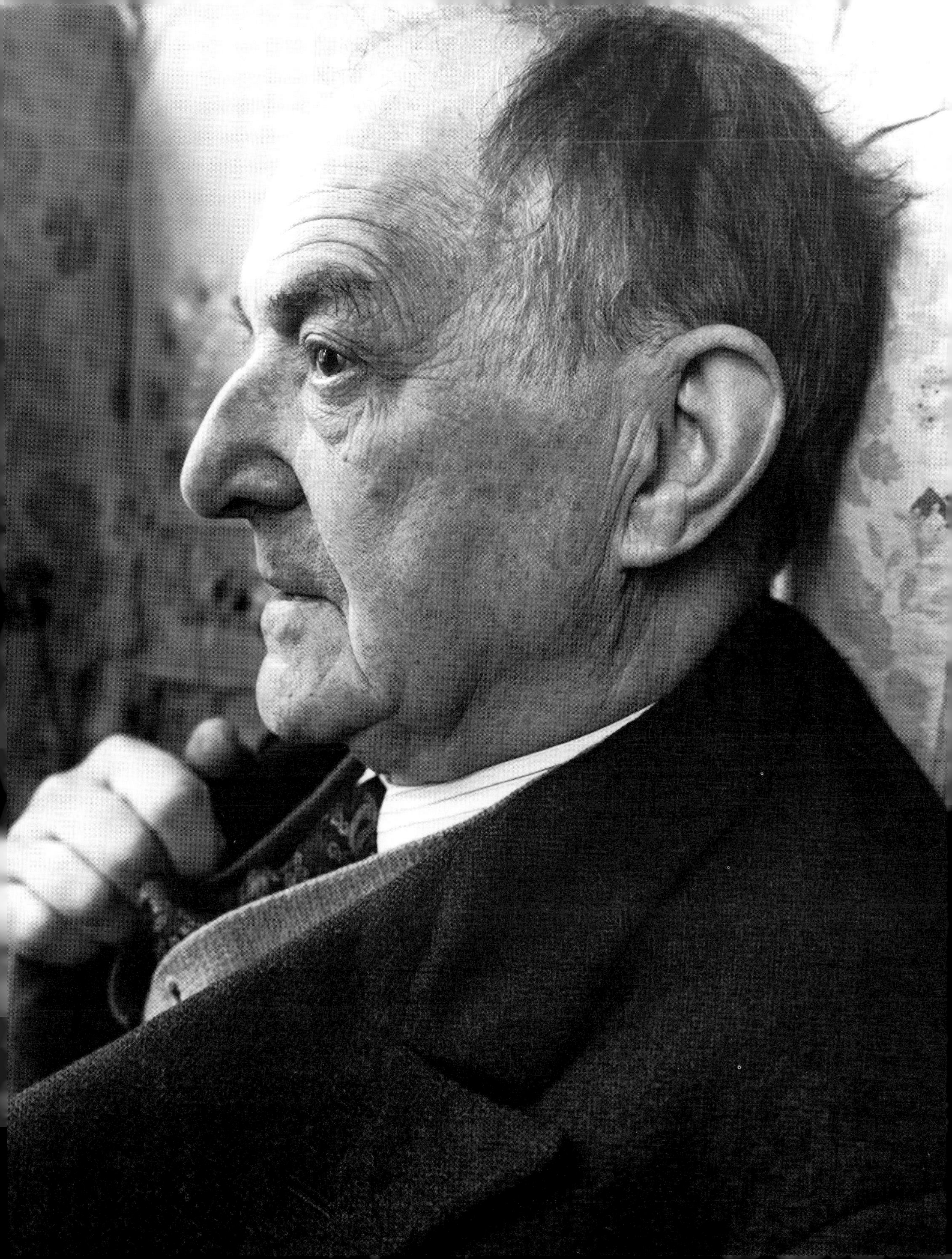

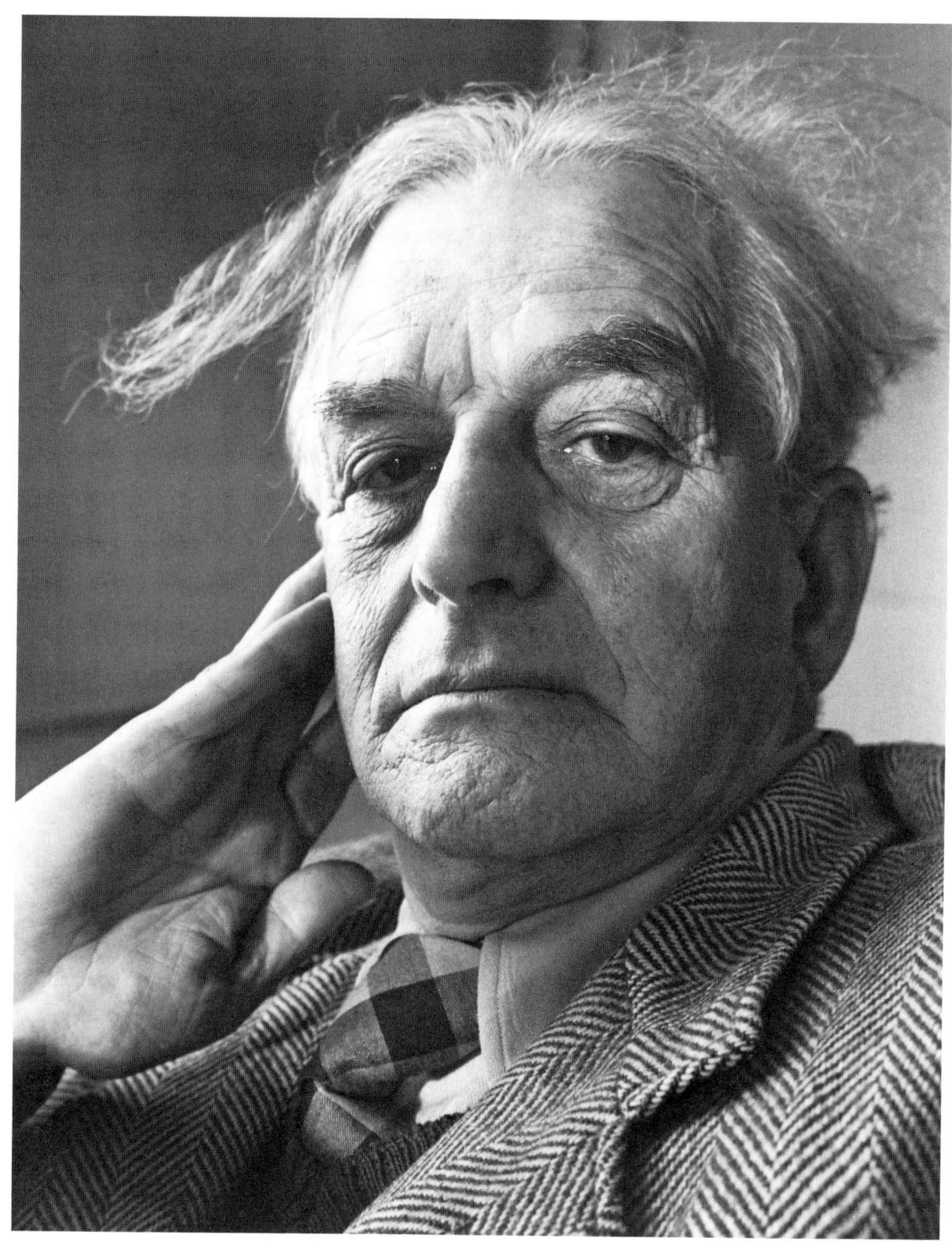

*15* **A. E. Coppard 1951**

*16* **Georges Enesco Salisbury Station 1953**

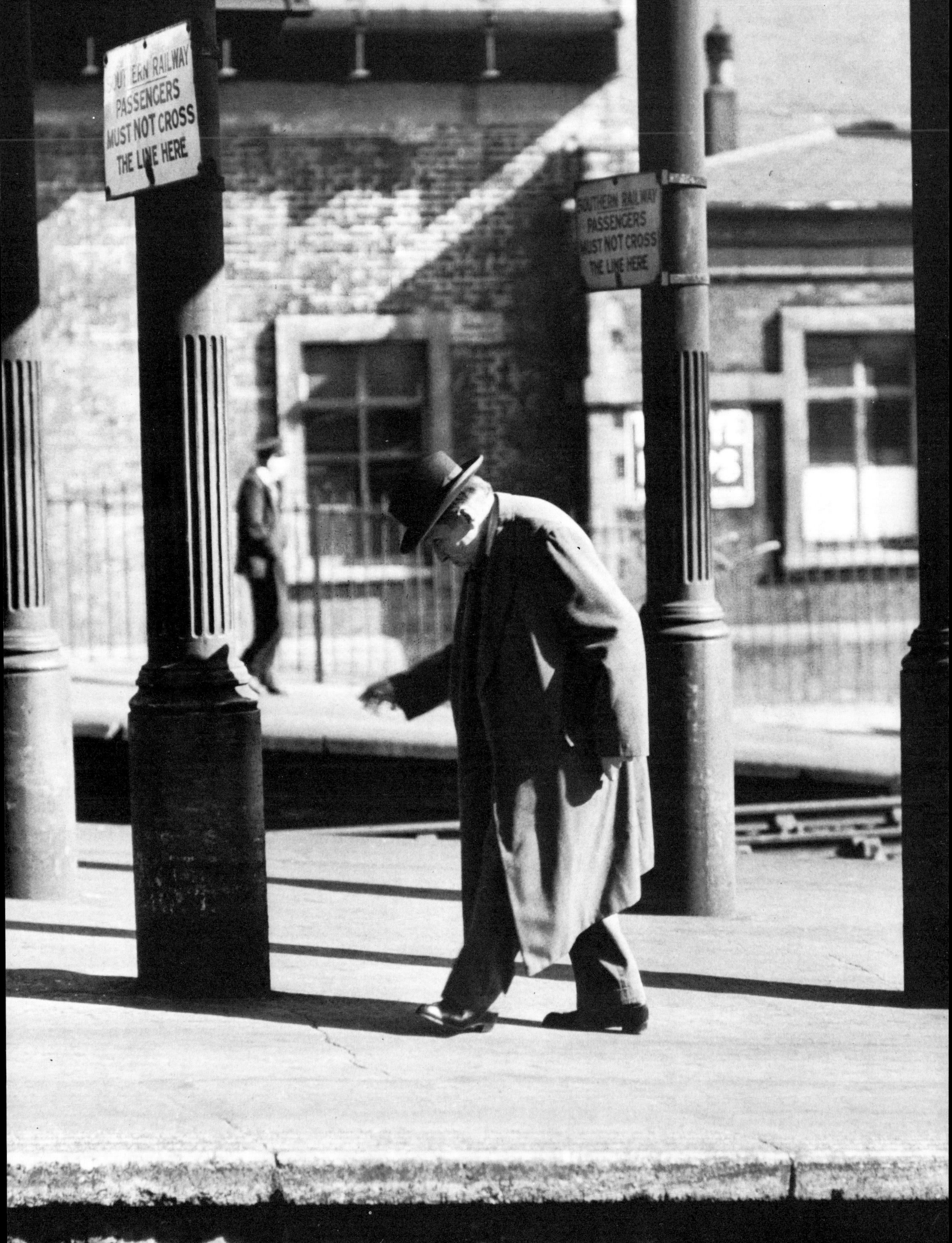
SOUTHERN RAILWAY
PASSENGERS
MUST NOT CROSS
THE LINE HERE
SOUTHERN RAILWAY
PASSENGERS
MUST NOT CROSS
THE LINE HERE

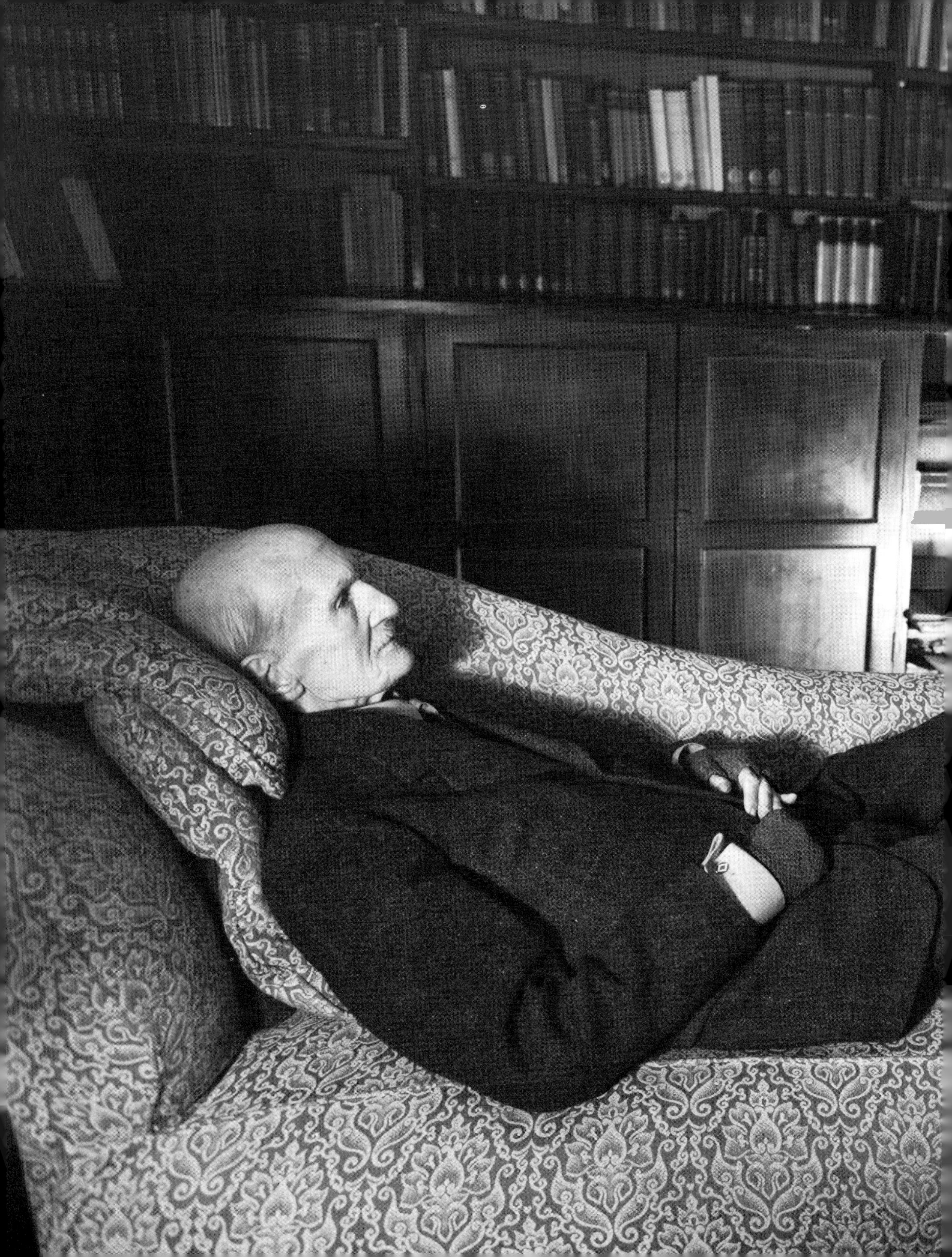

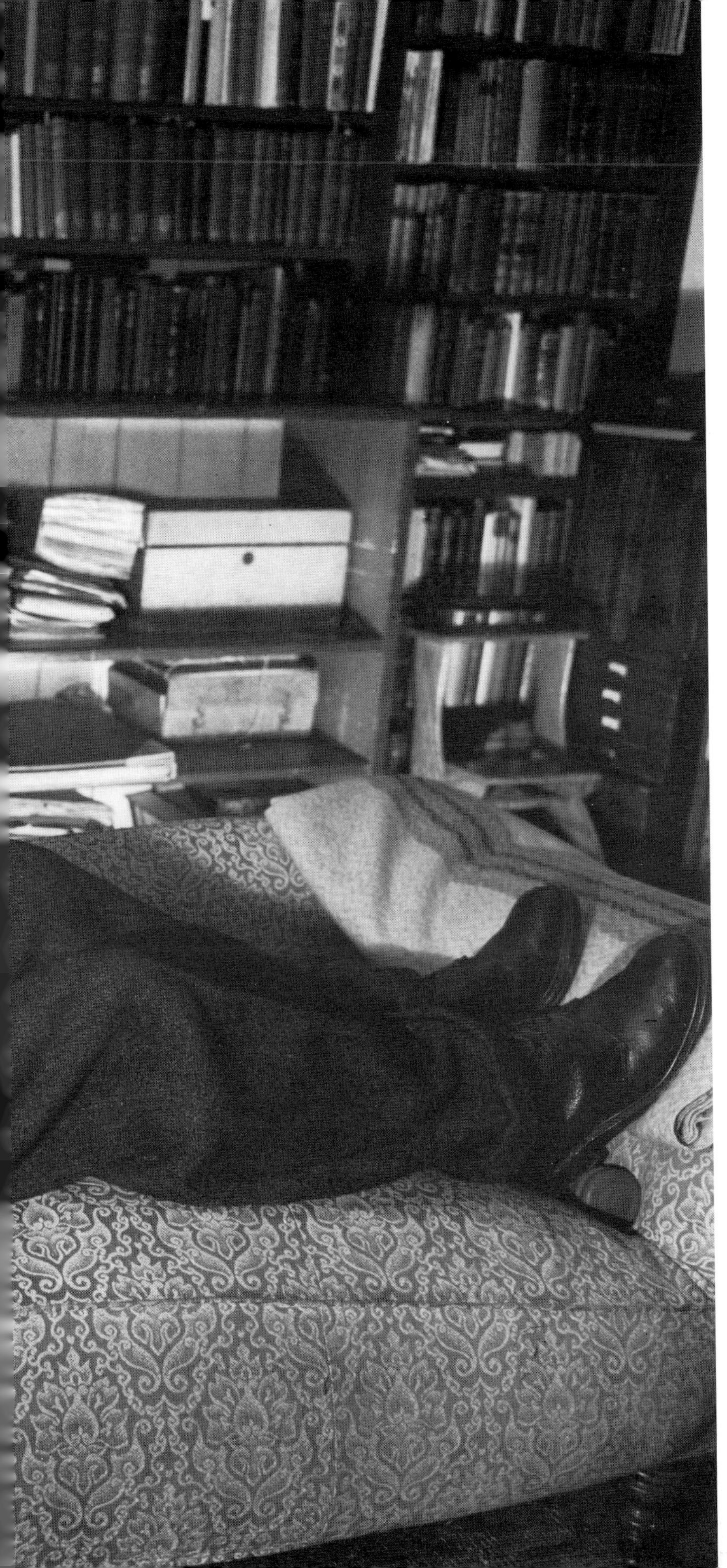

*17* **Professor Gilbert Murray** **1957**

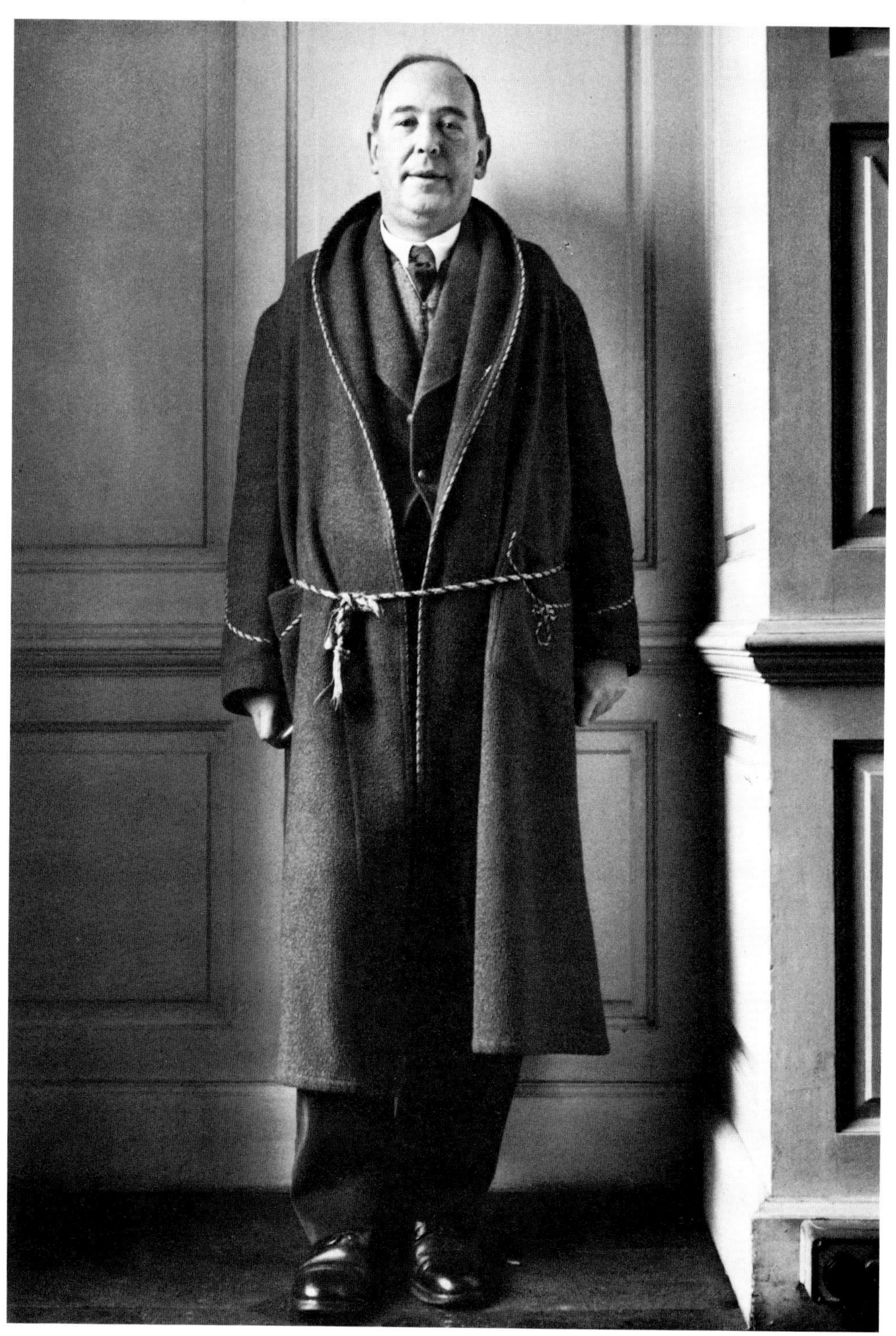

*18* **C. S. Lewis 1951**

*19* **Lord David Cecil 1951**

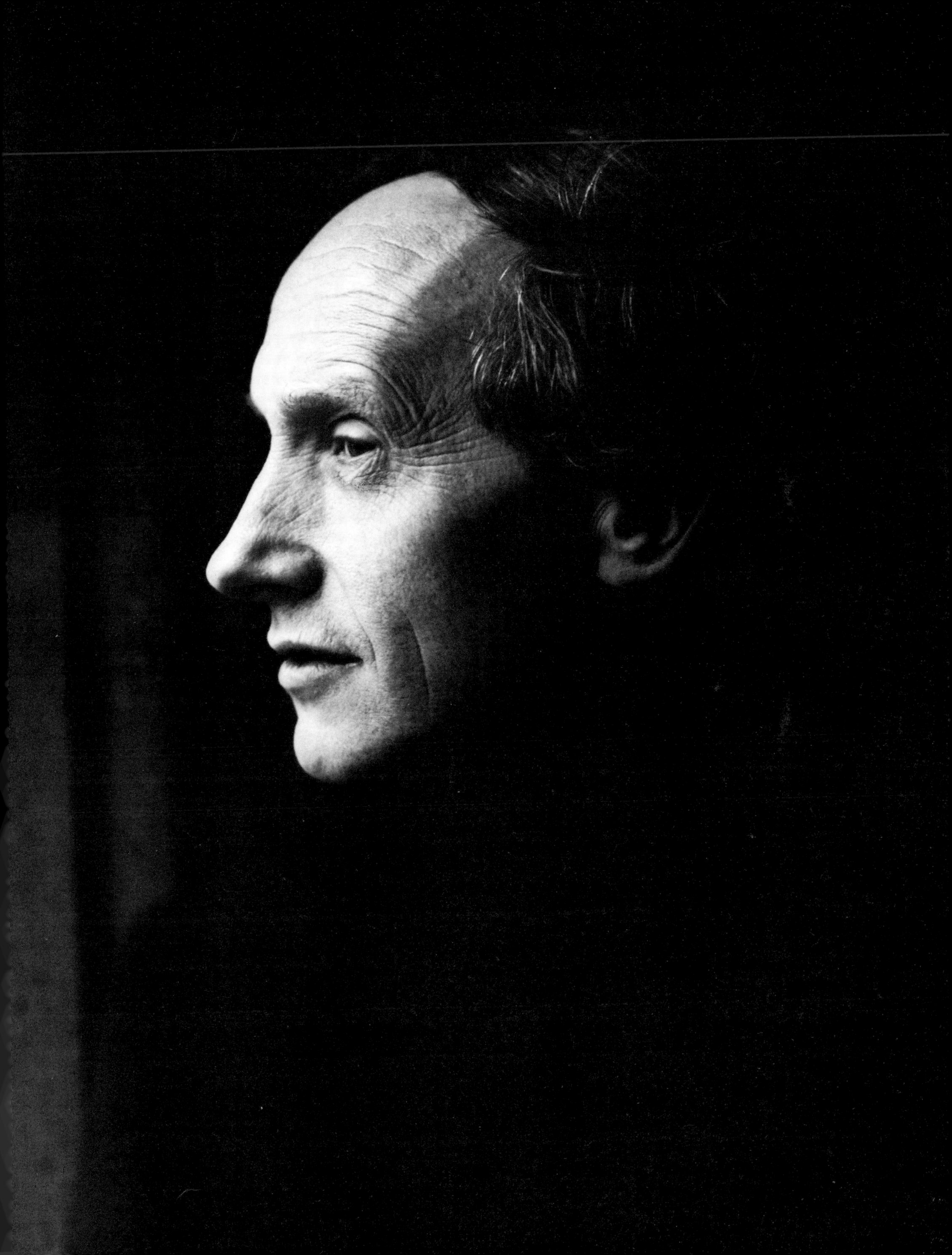

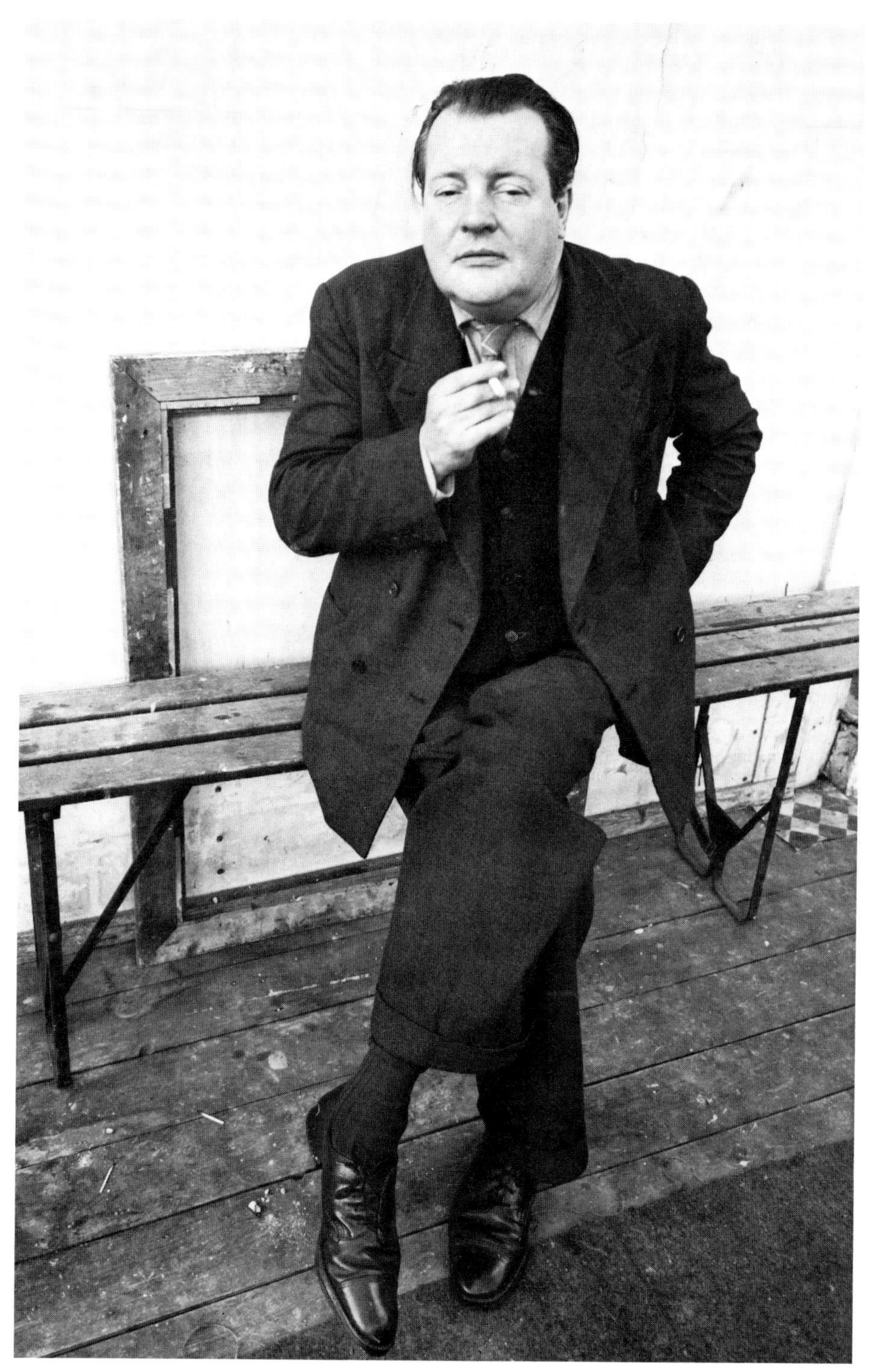

*20* **Constant Lambert 1950**

*21* **Tyrone Guthrie 1951**

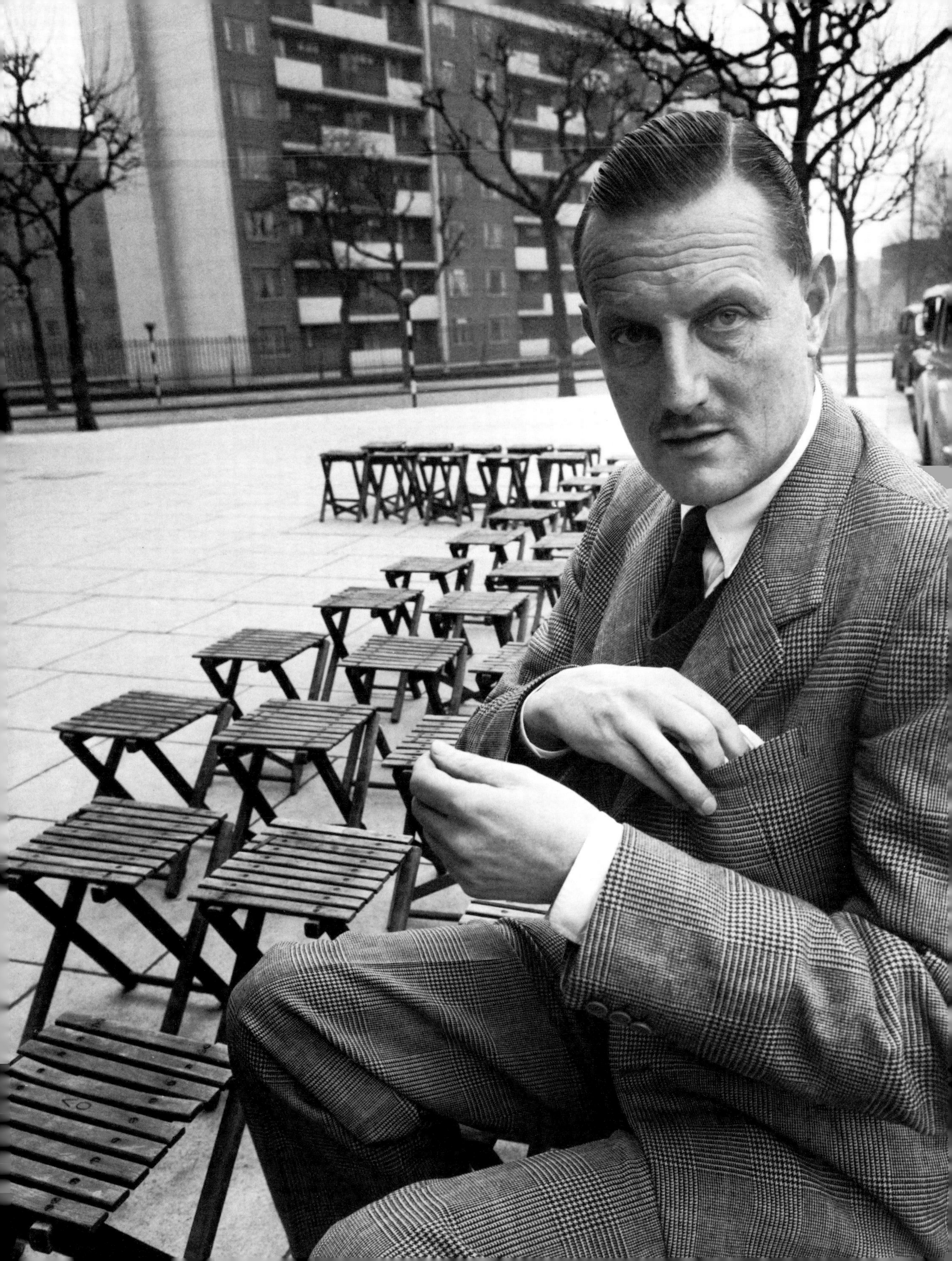

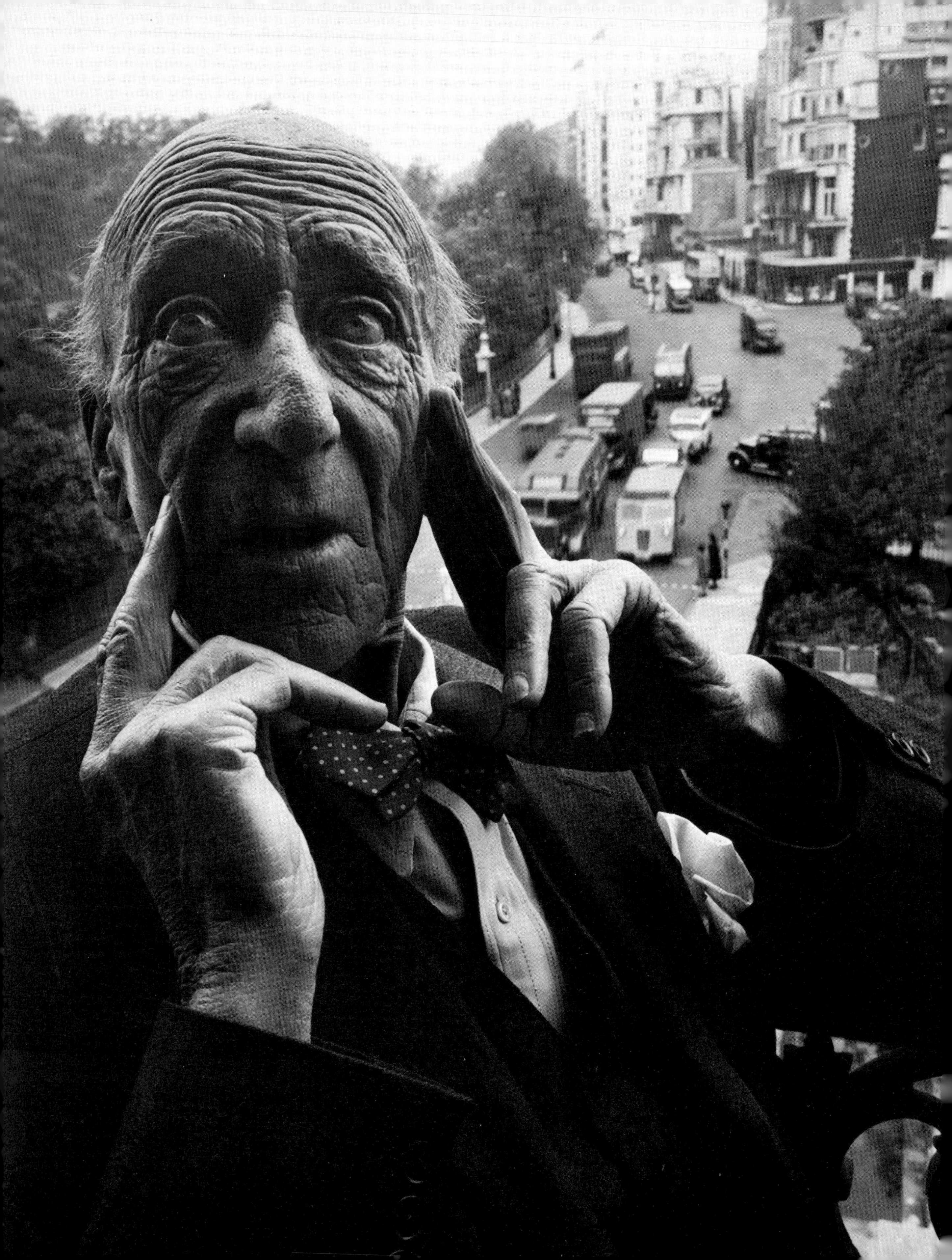

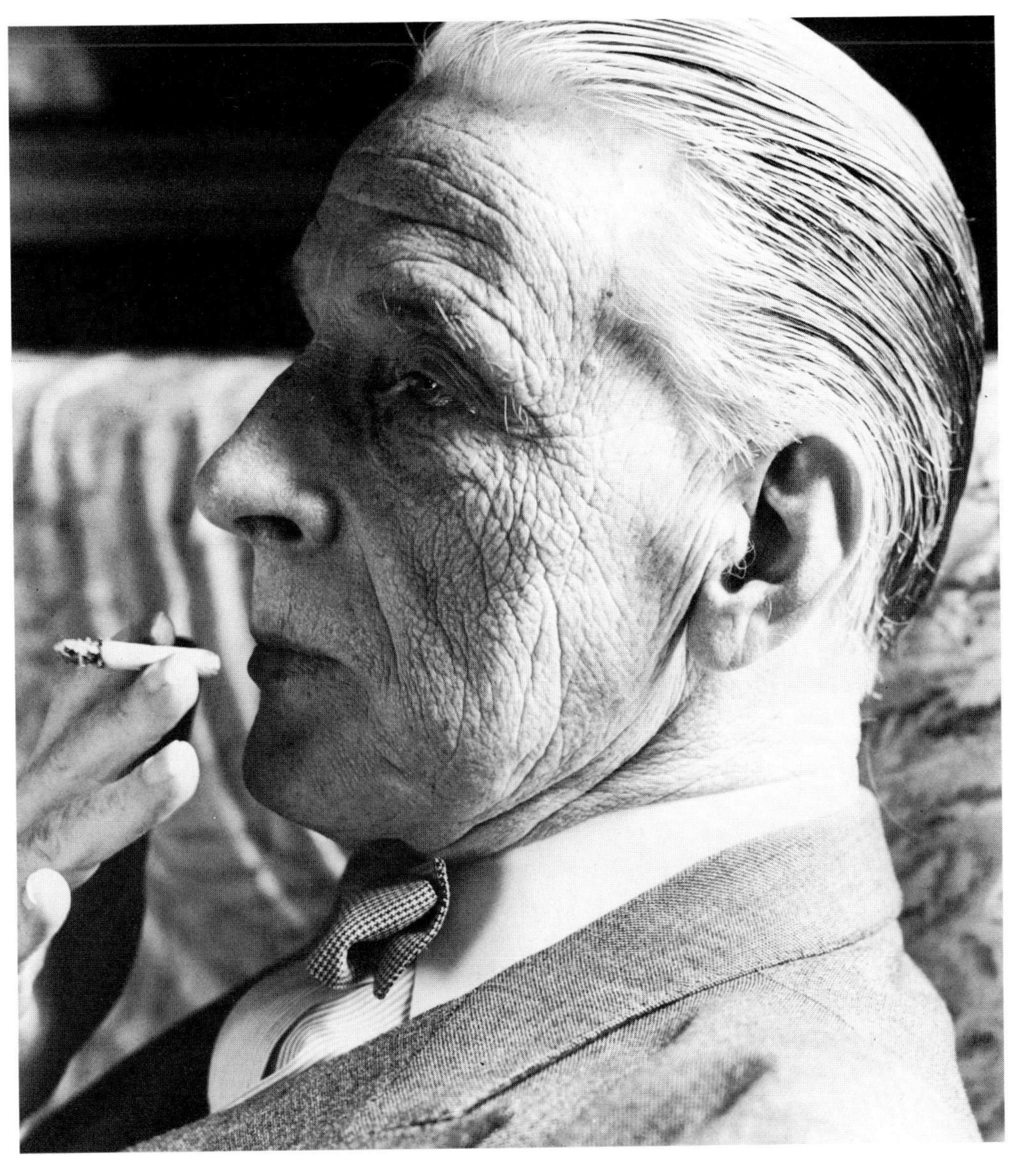

*23* **Charles Morgan 1952**

*22* **Algernon Blackwood 1951**

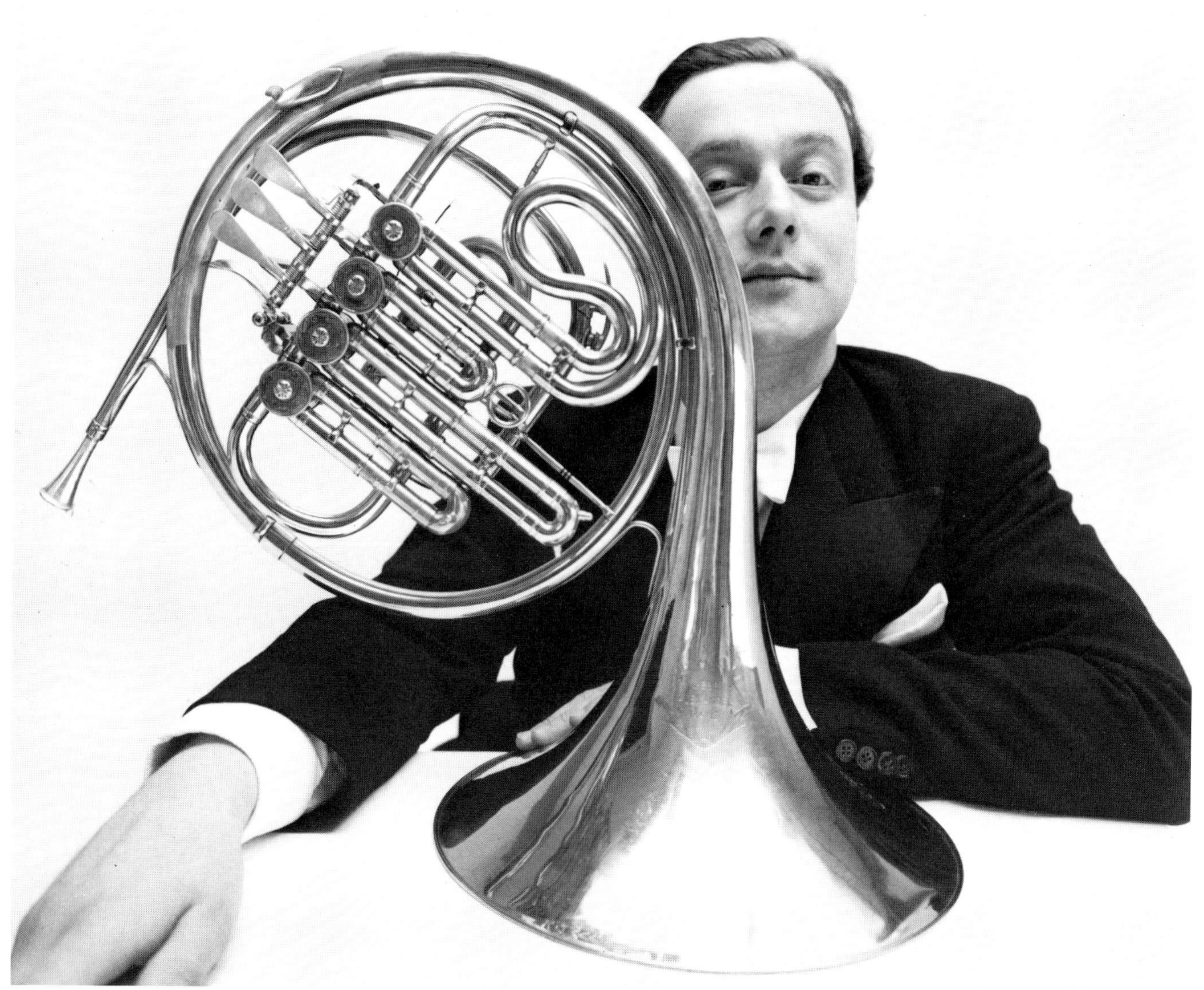

*24* **Dennis Brain** **1953**

*25* **George Eskdale** **1953**

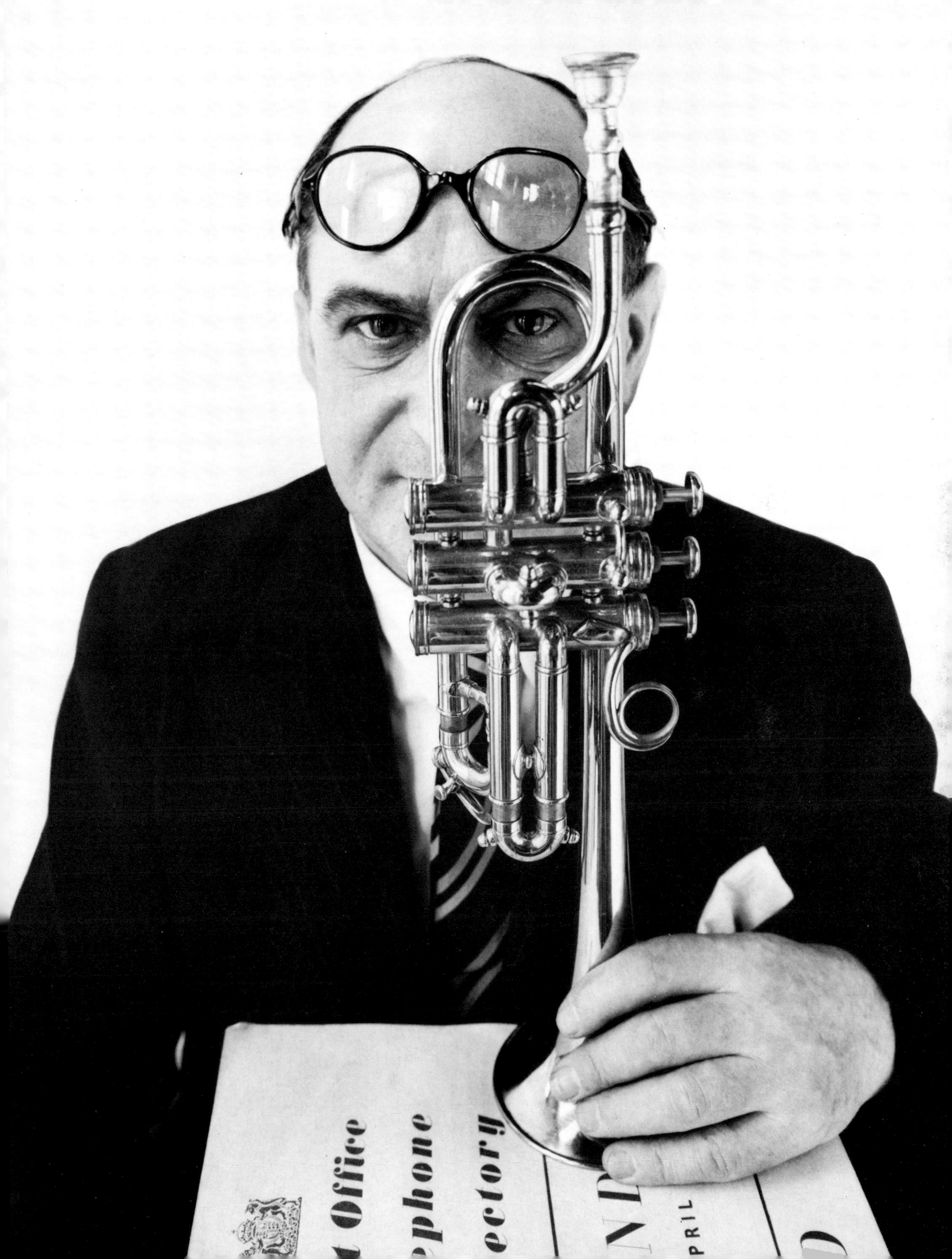
t Office
ephone
ectory
PRIL

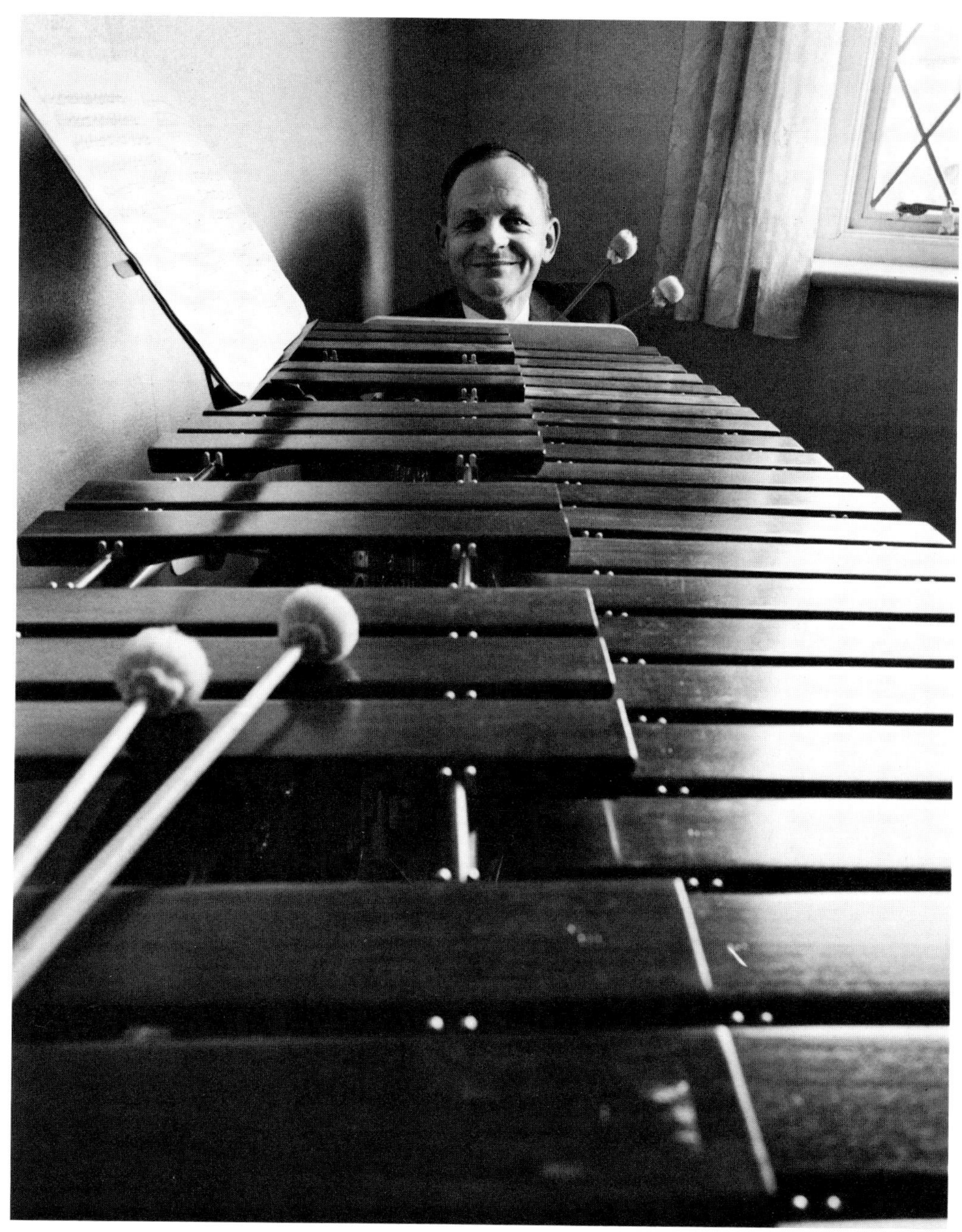

*26* **Jimmy Blades** 1953

*27* **Frederick Thurston** 1953

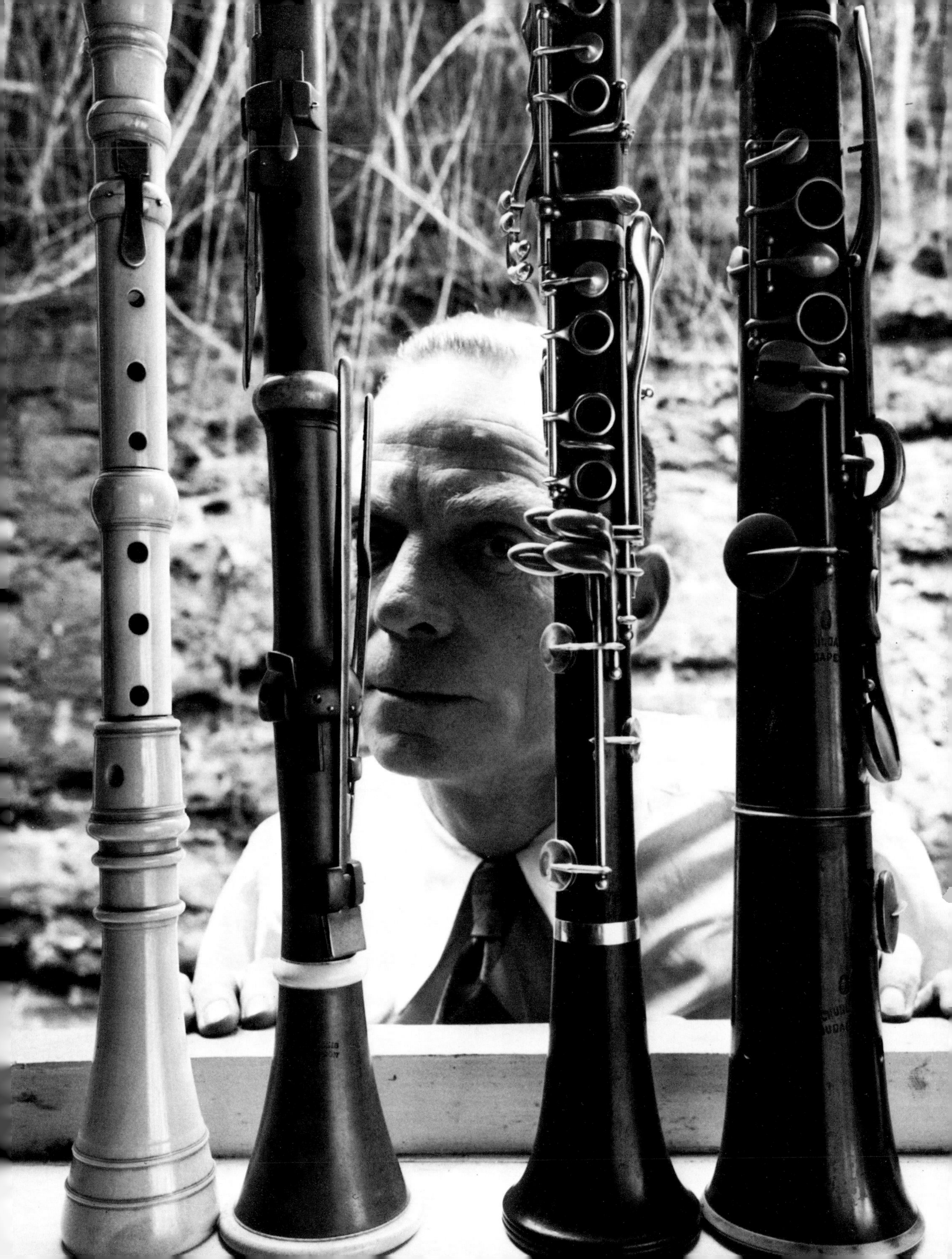

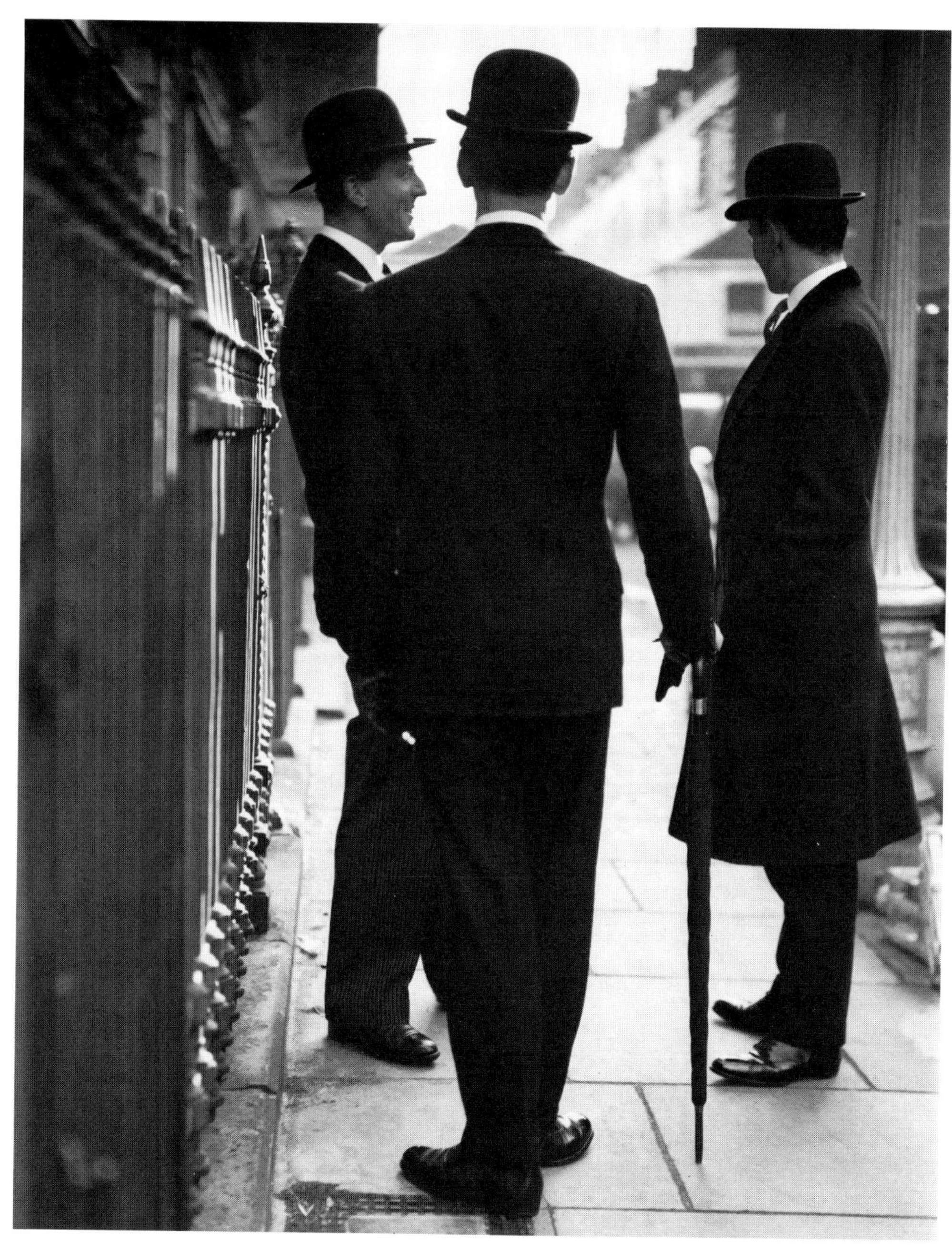

28 **Back to formality   Savile Row**
**Peter Coats   William Ackroyd   Mark Gilbey   1950**

29 **"Impertinence"   Helena Geffers suit**
**Enid "Scutty" Boulting   1950**

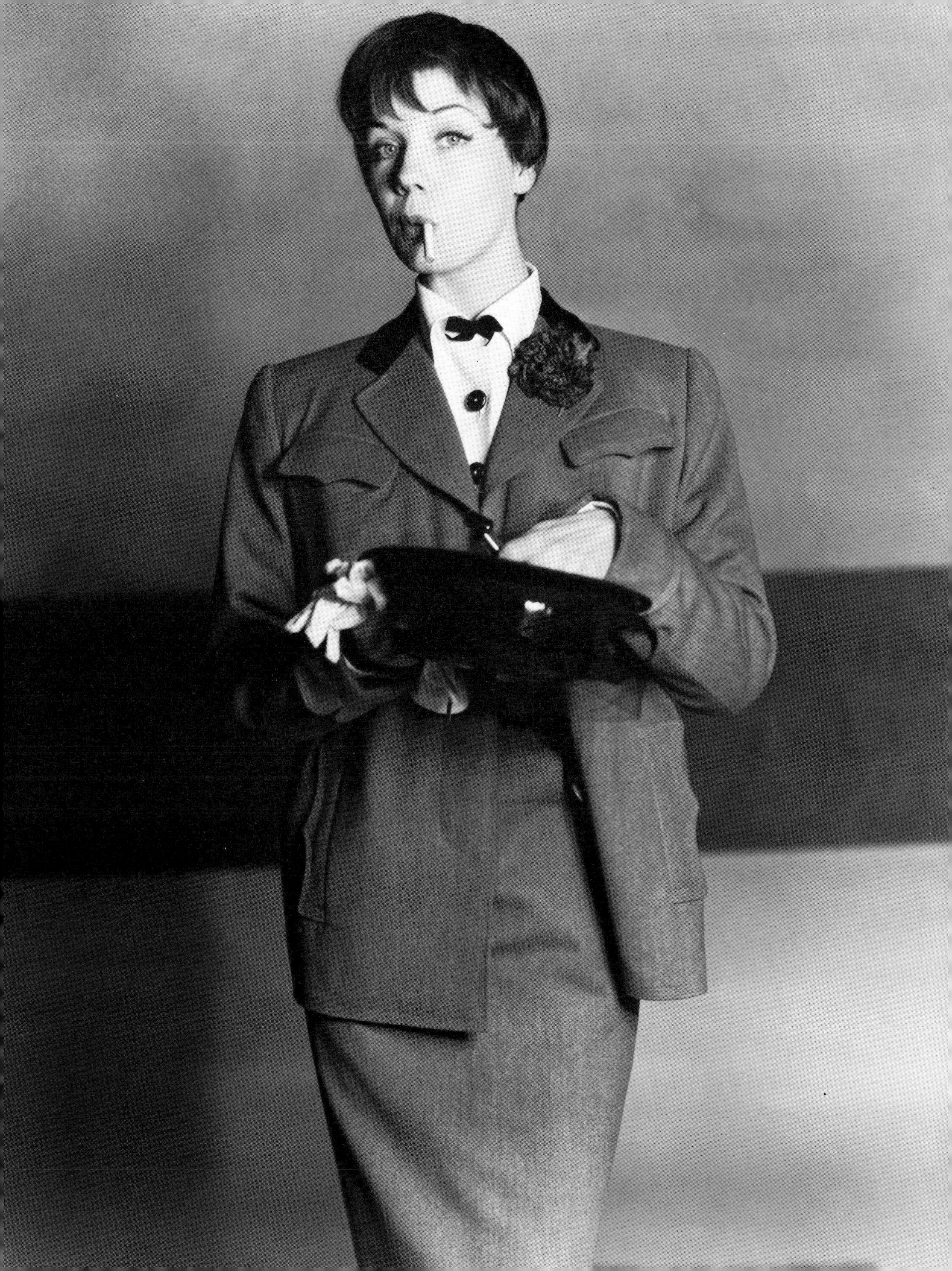

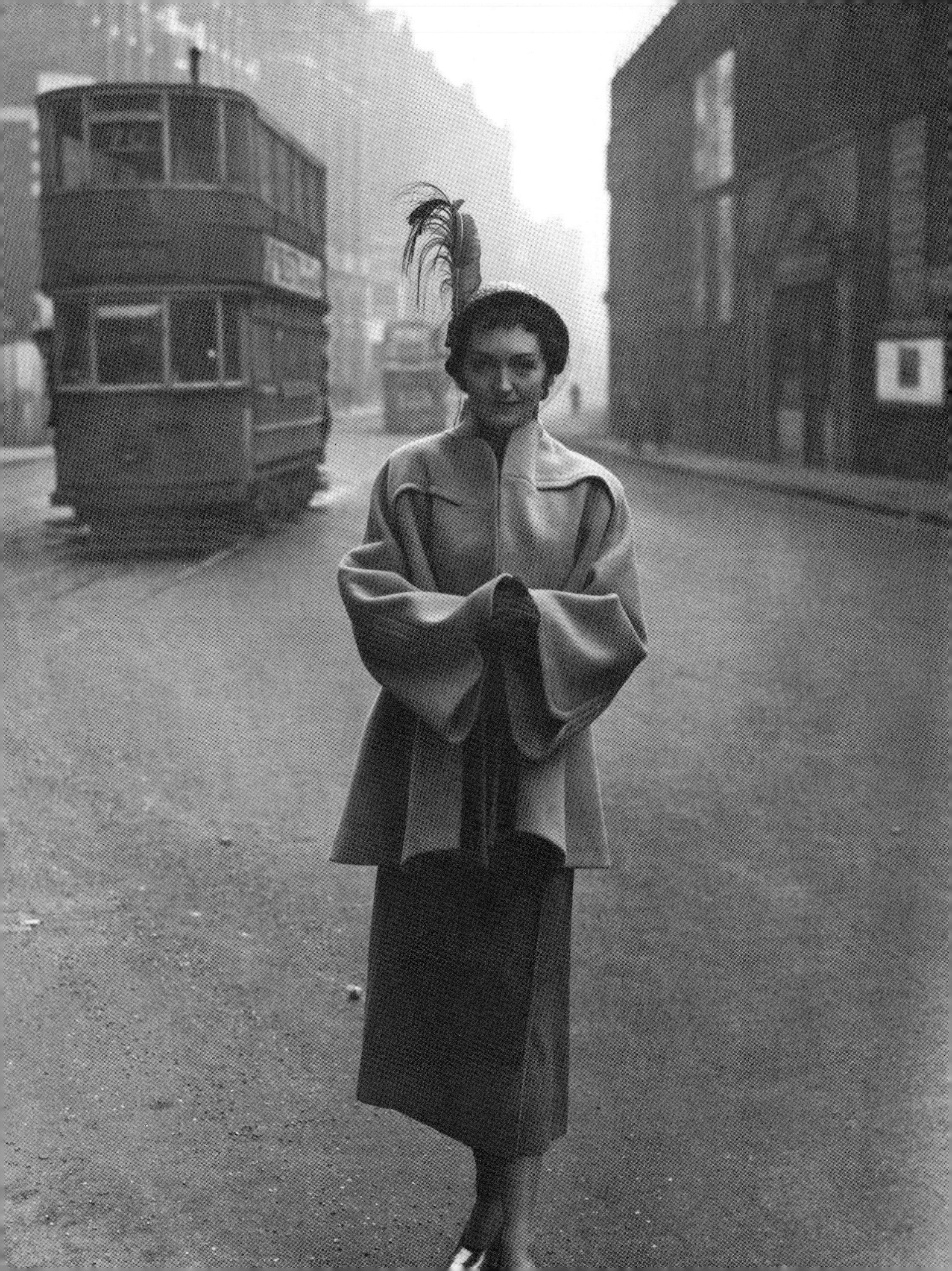

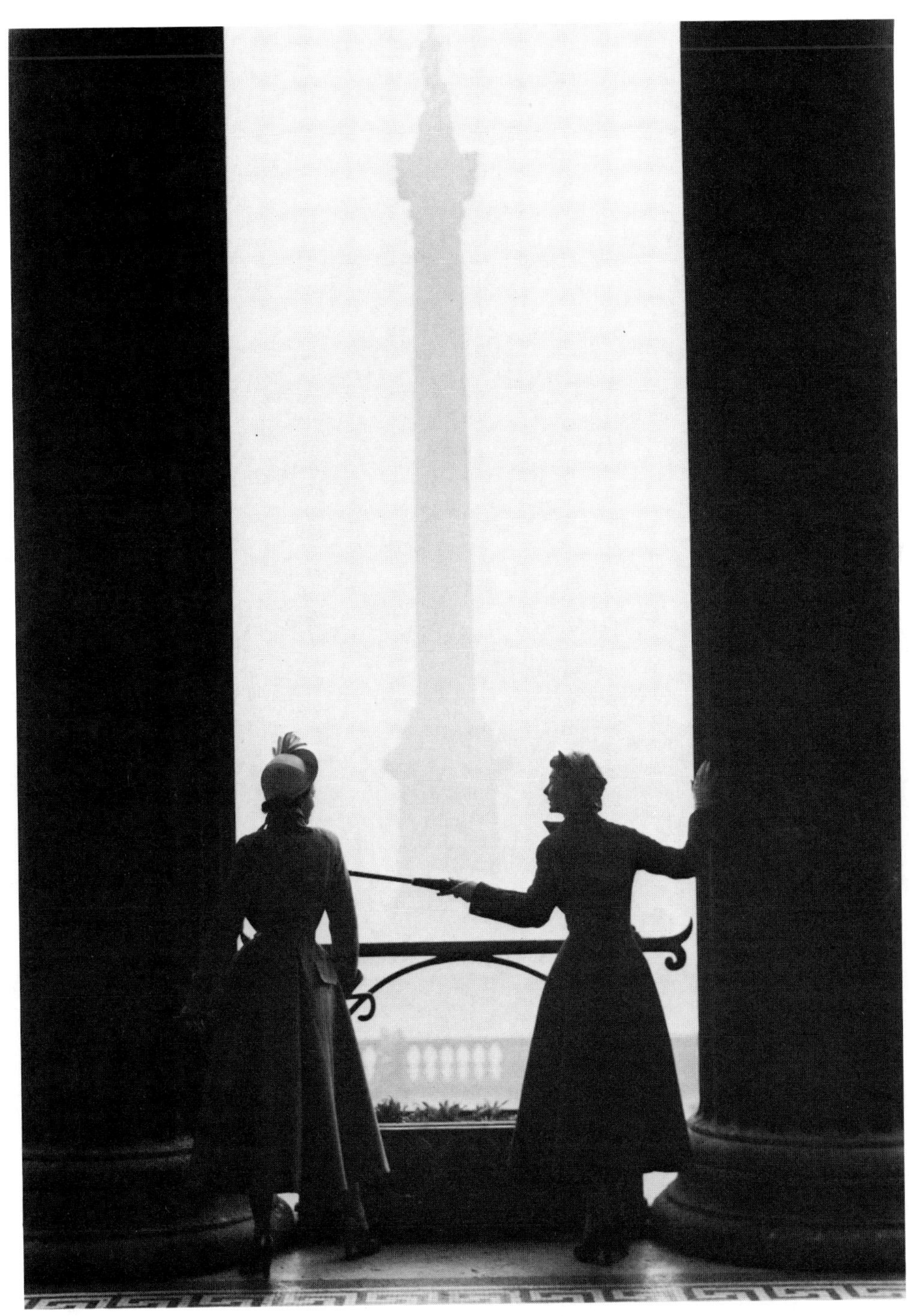

*31* **London Spring Collections New Look (Amies and Molyneux coats)**
**Barbara Goalen and Wenda Rogerson 1949**

*30* **Michael Sherard's bell-sleeved duffle jacket**
**Anne Chambers 1949**

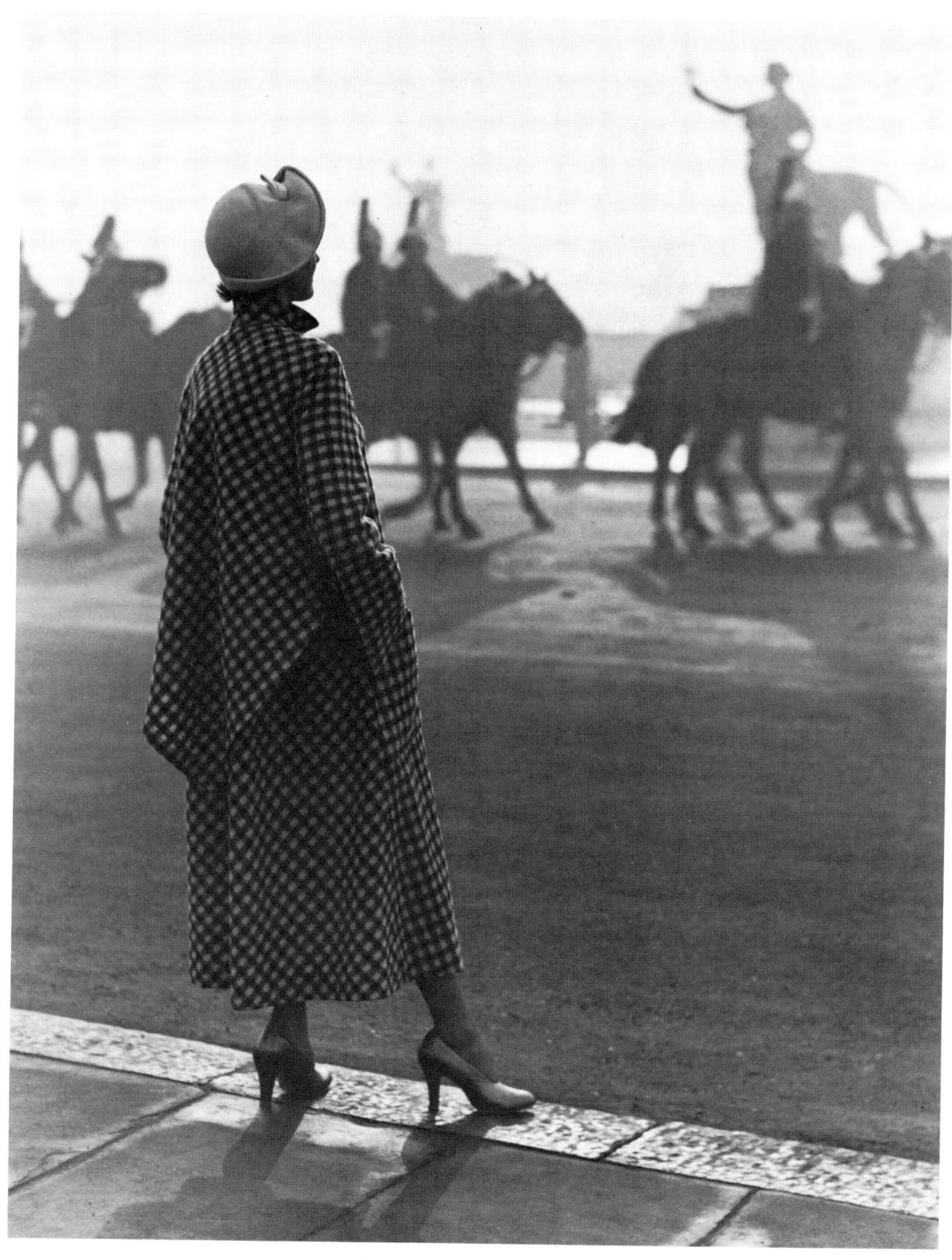

*32* **Bianca Mosca check coat Anne Chambers 1949**

*33* **Hardy Amies tweed coat**
***Vogue* March 1949 Cover**
**Wenda Rogerson**

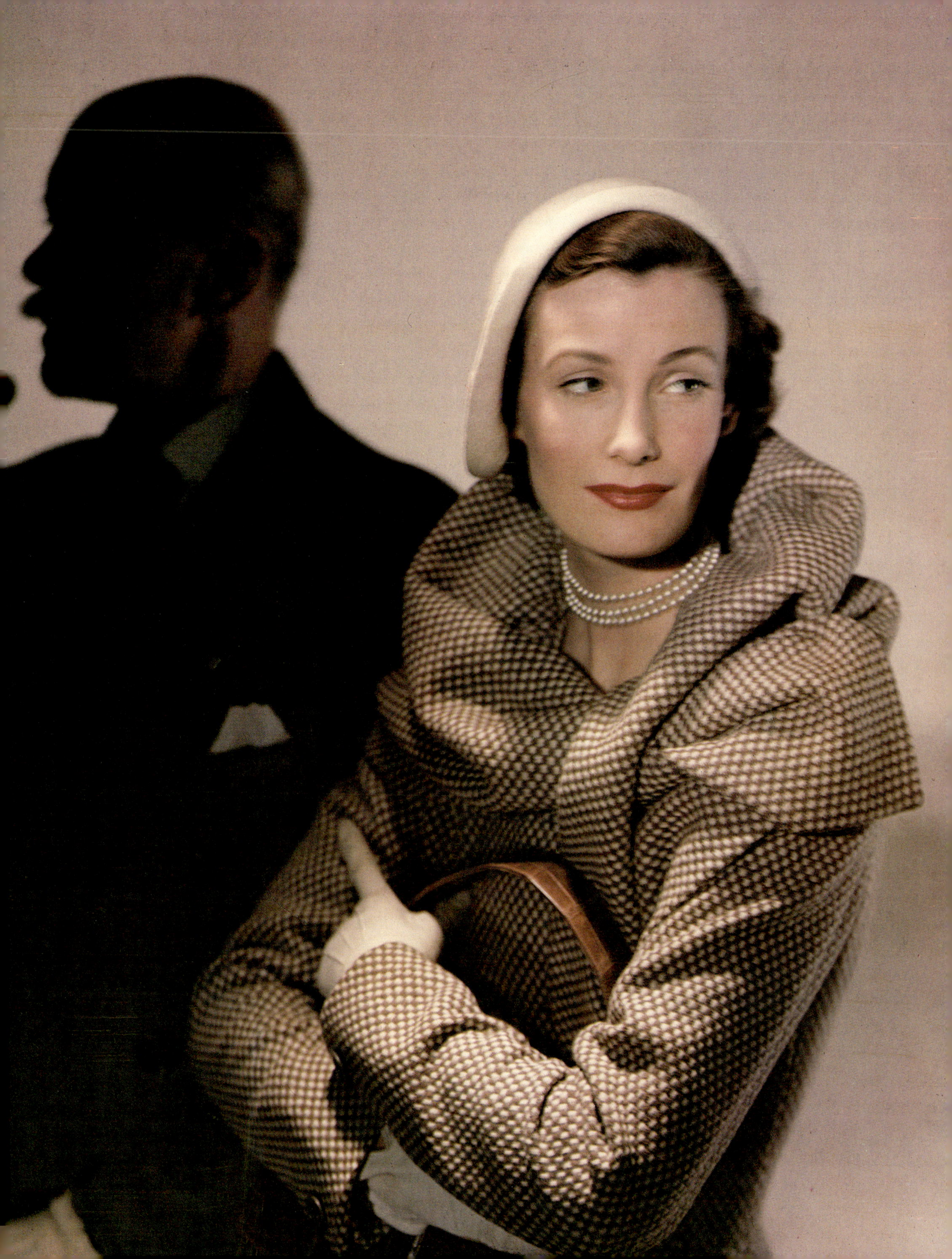

34 **Hon James Drummond Master Duncan Davidson**
**page-boys to the Duke of Norfolk**
**Arundel Castle 1953**

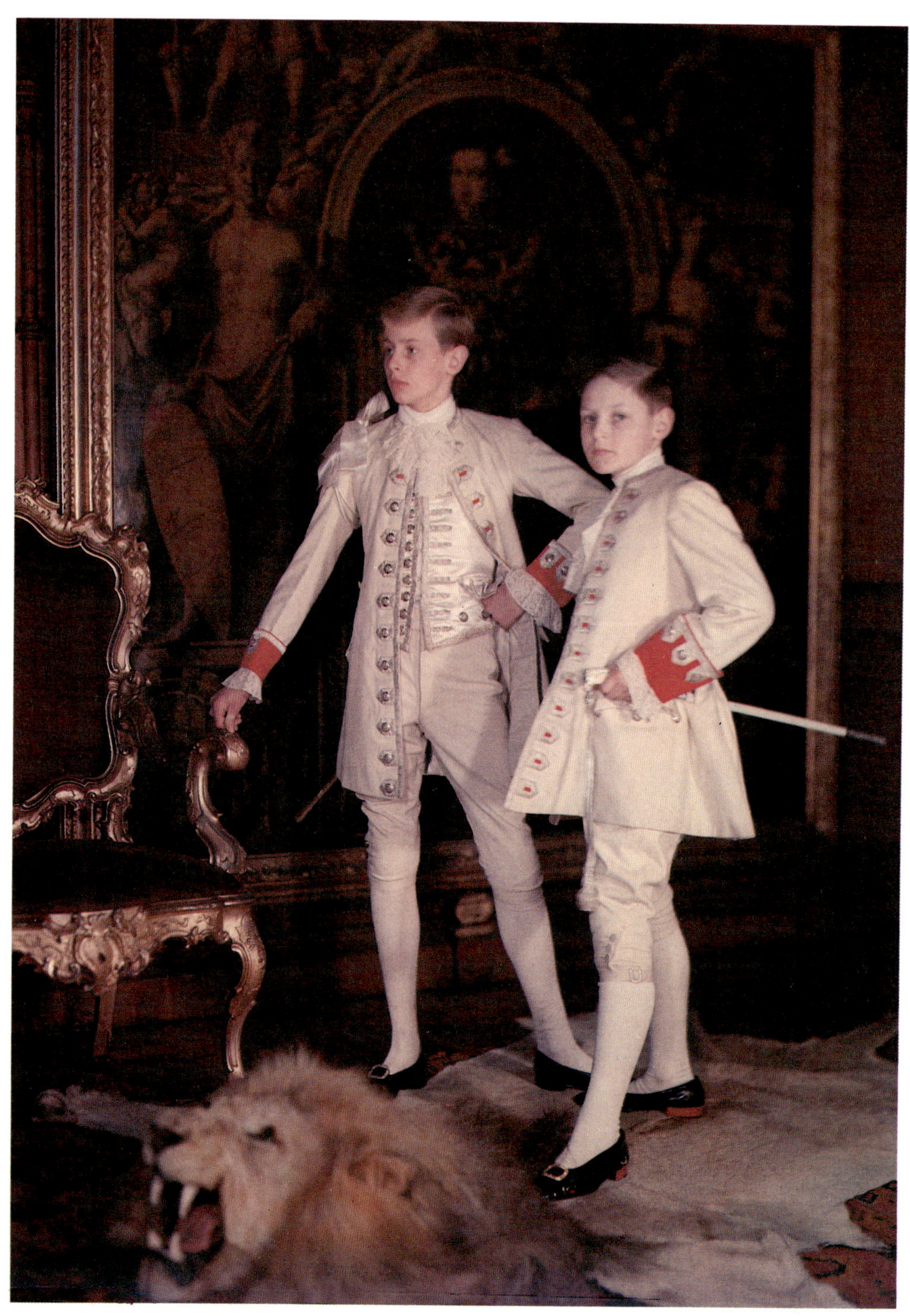

35 **Molyneux caramel satin evening dres**
**1907 Silver Ghost Rolls-Roy**
**Wenda Rogerson 19**

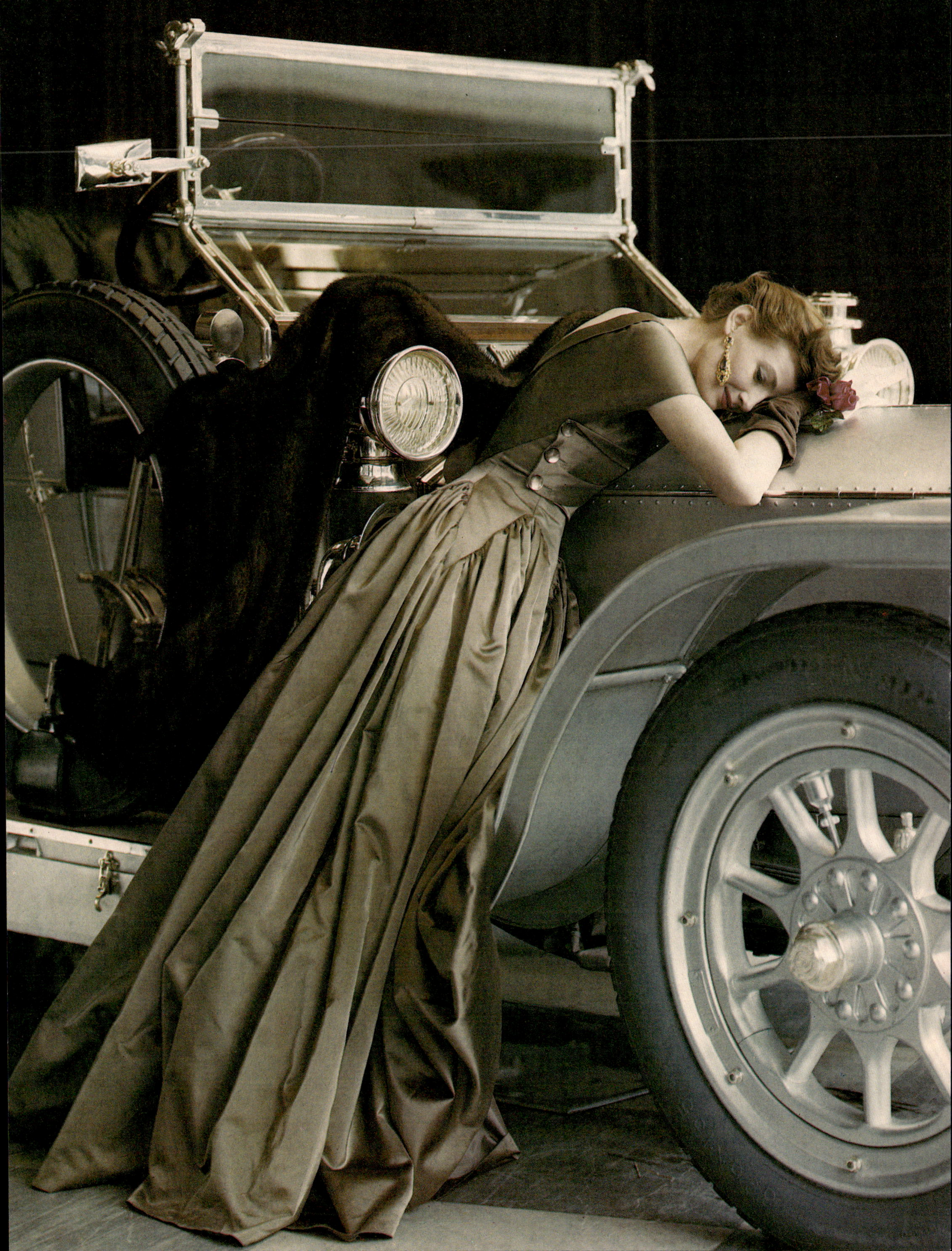

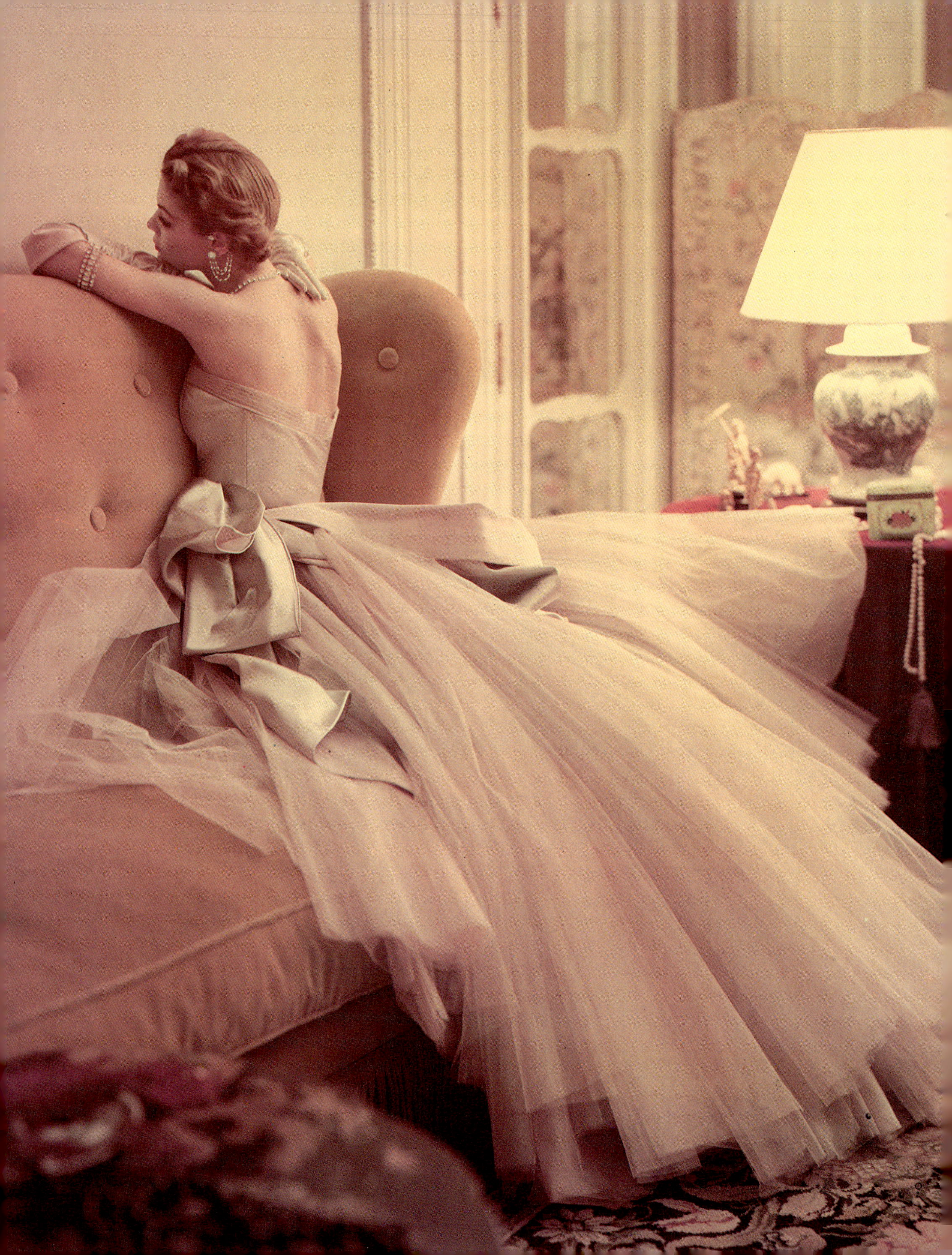

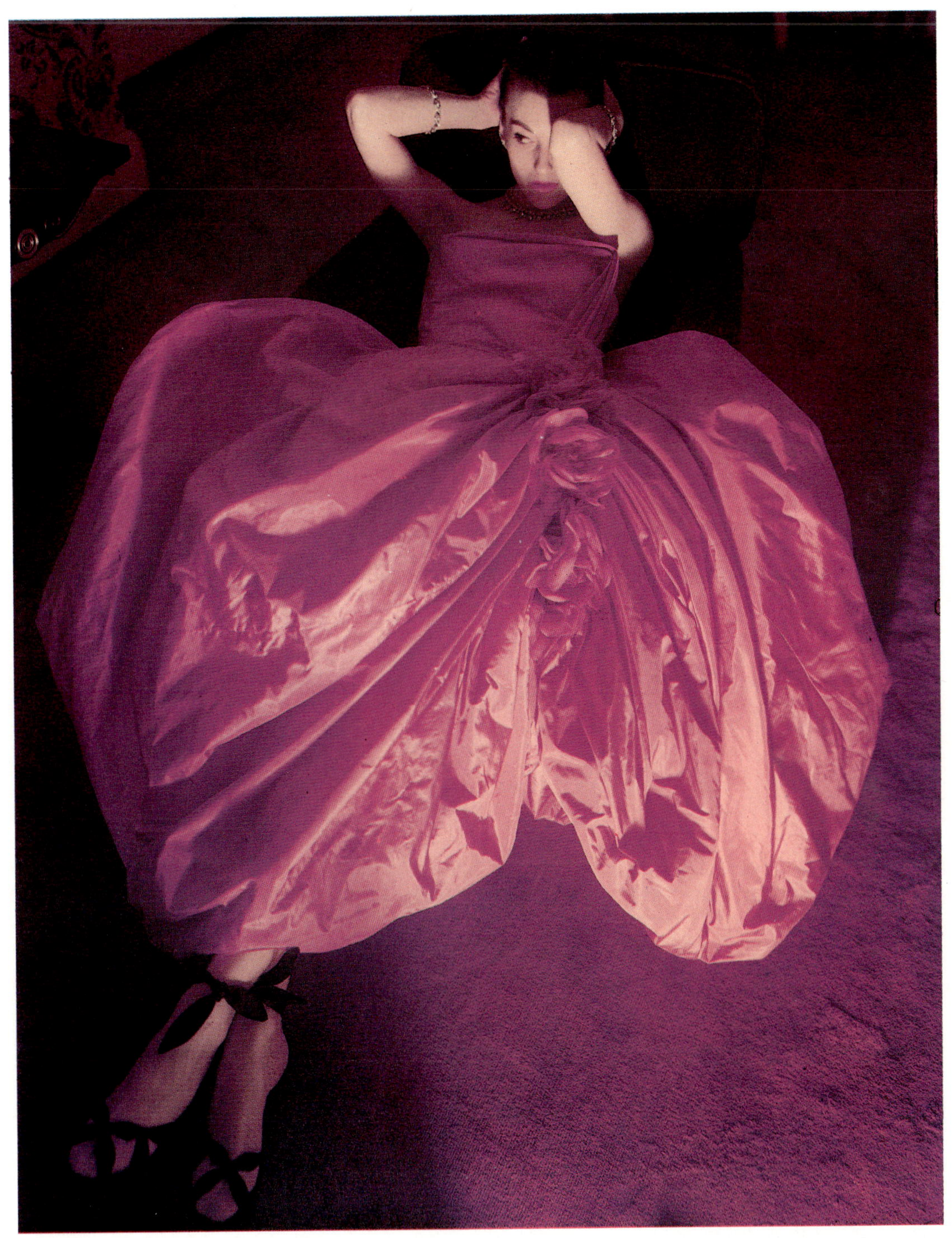

*37* **Balenciaga dress Régine 1950**

*36* **Jean Desses evening dress Paris Jeannie Patchett 1950**

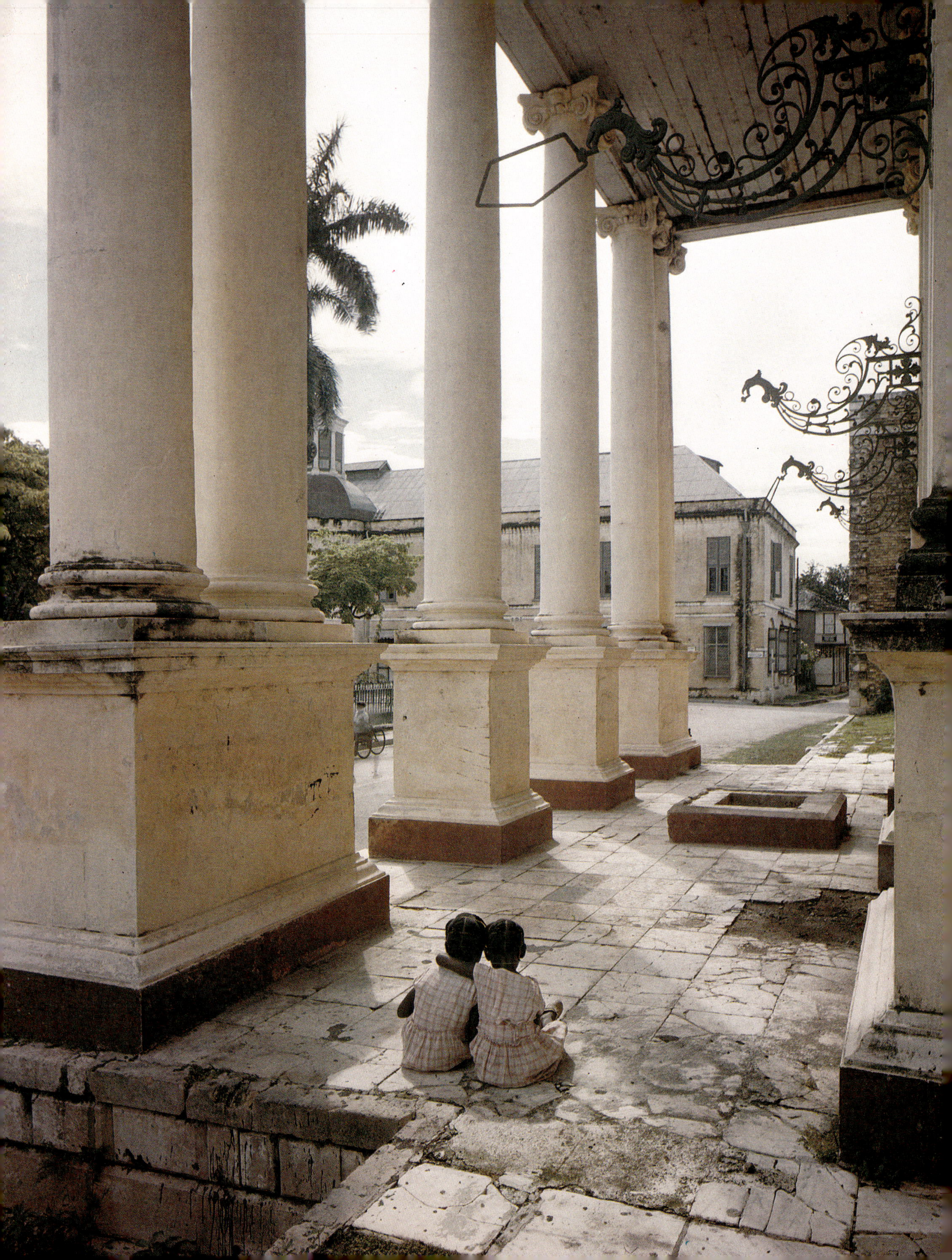

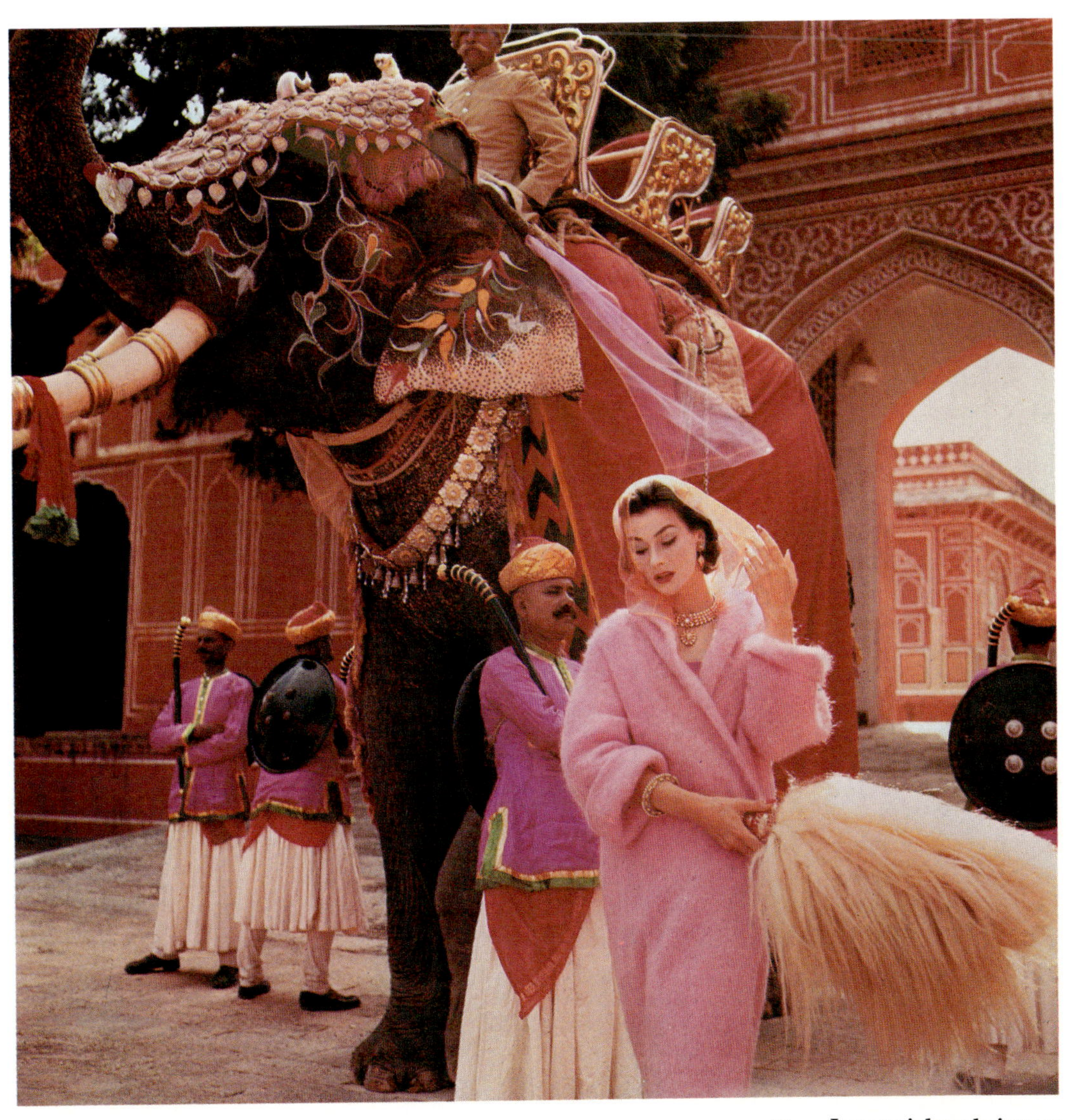

*39* **Jaeger pink mohair coat**
**Jaipur India**
**Anne Gunning 1956**

*38* **Jamaican twins Spanish Town 1950**

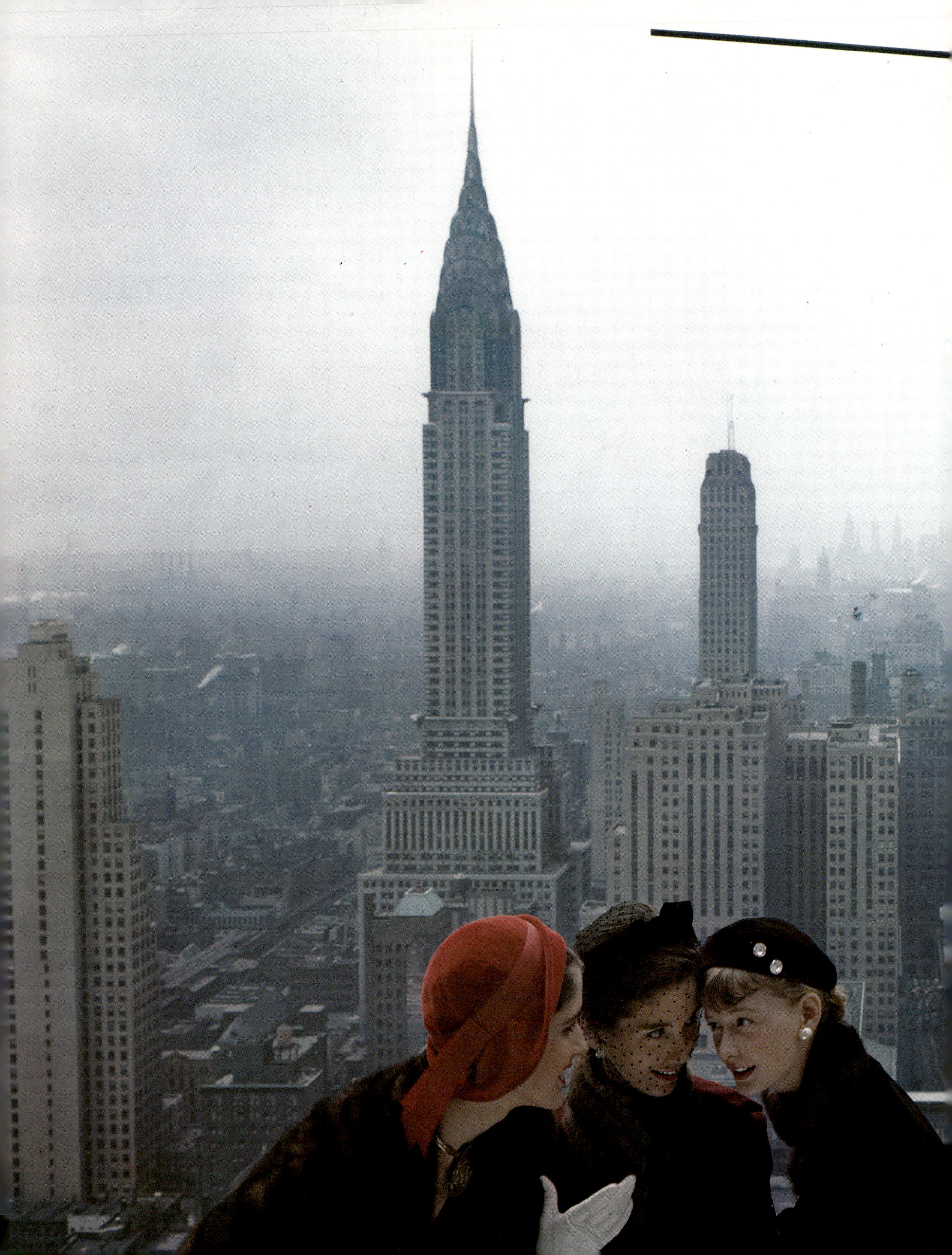

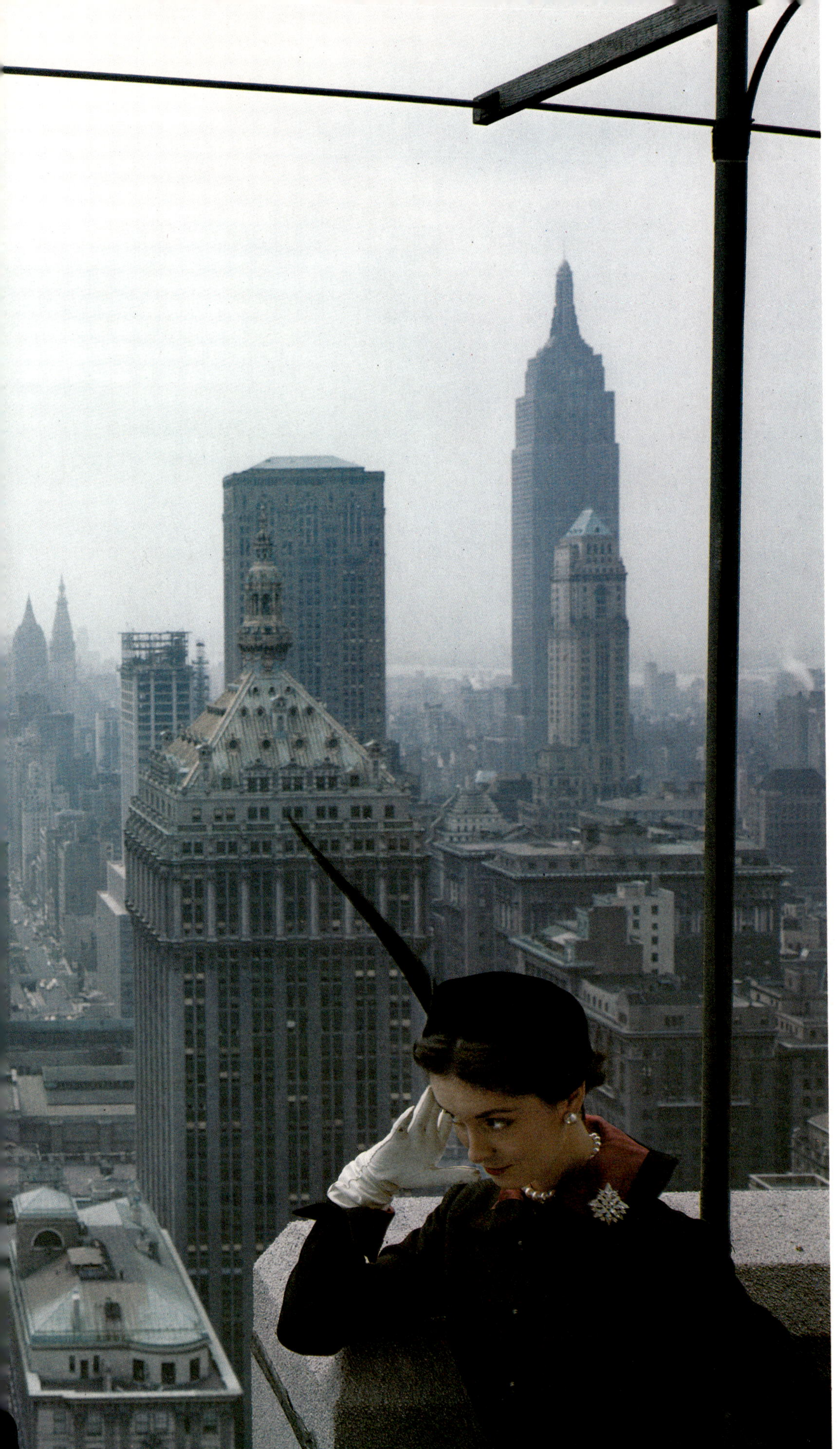

*40* **Hat fashions**
**New York 1949**

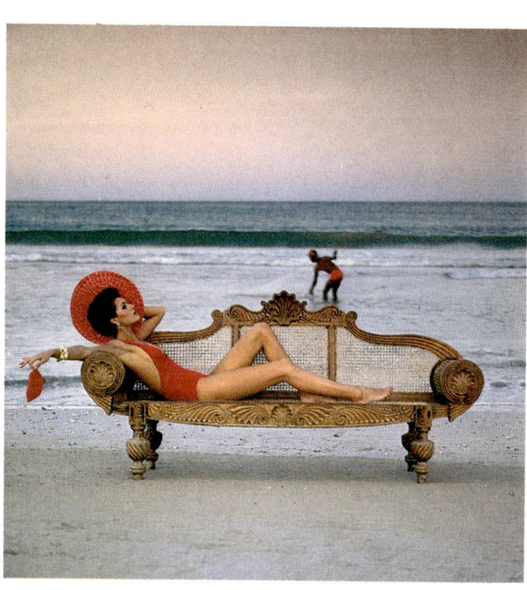

*41* **Trincomalee Sri Lanka Pilar Crespi 1980**

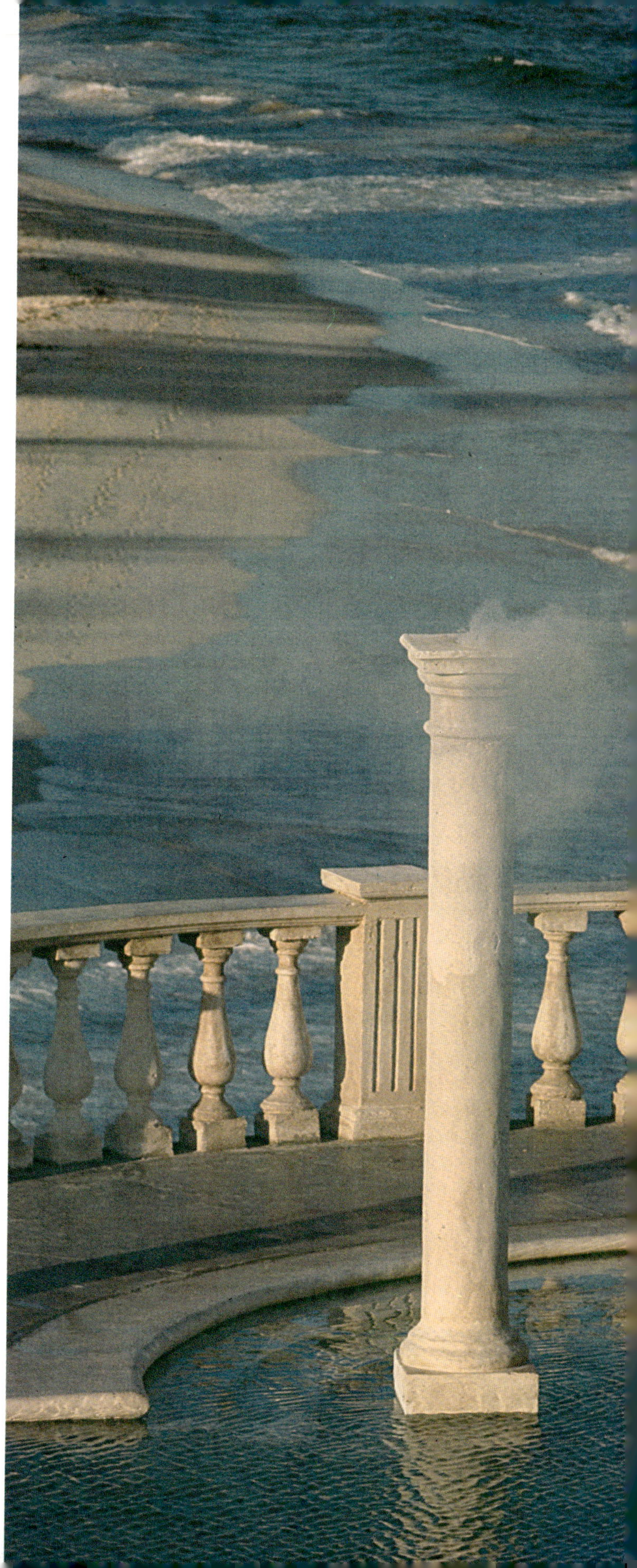

*42* **Crane Beach Hotel Barbados Appollonia Van Ravenstein 1973**

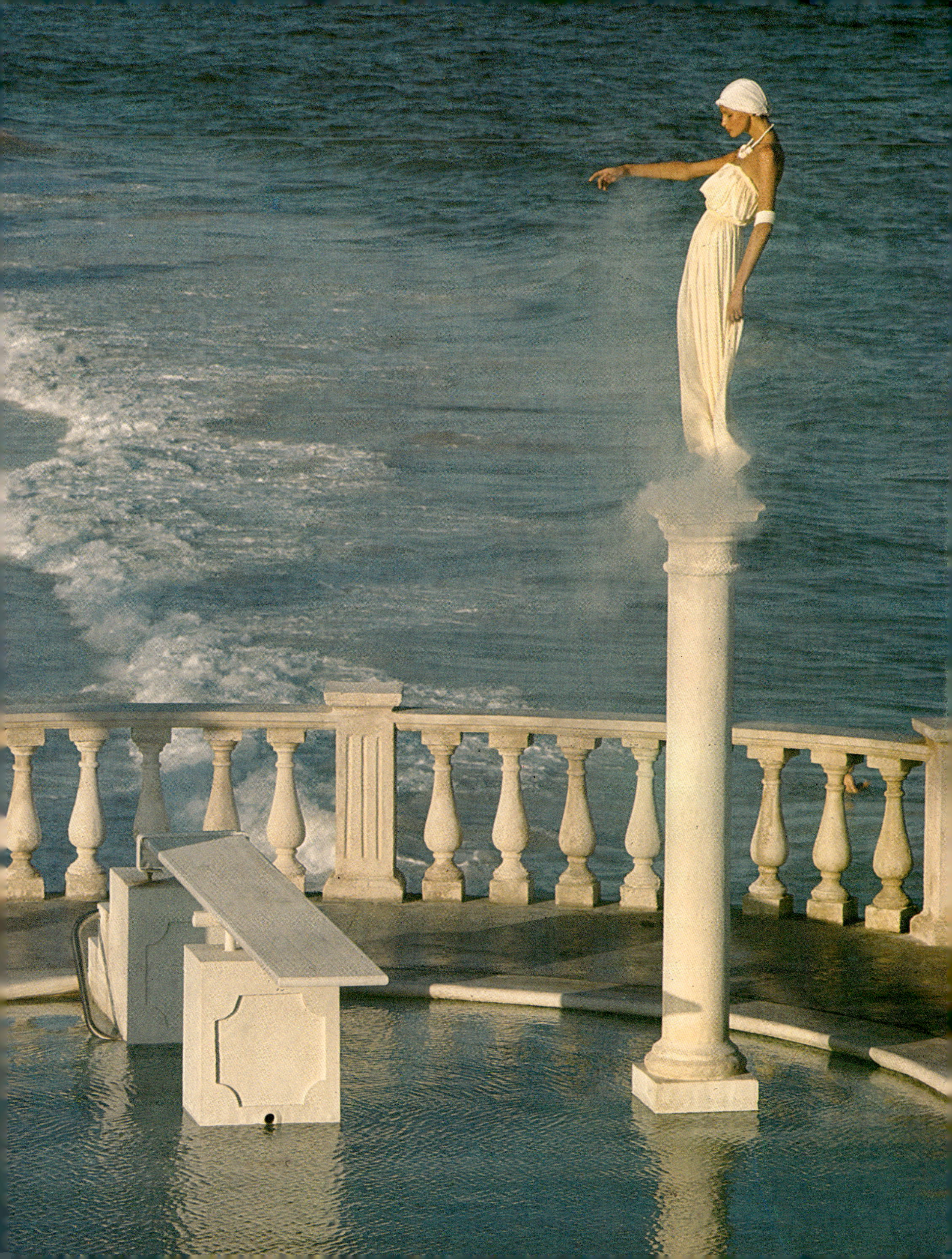

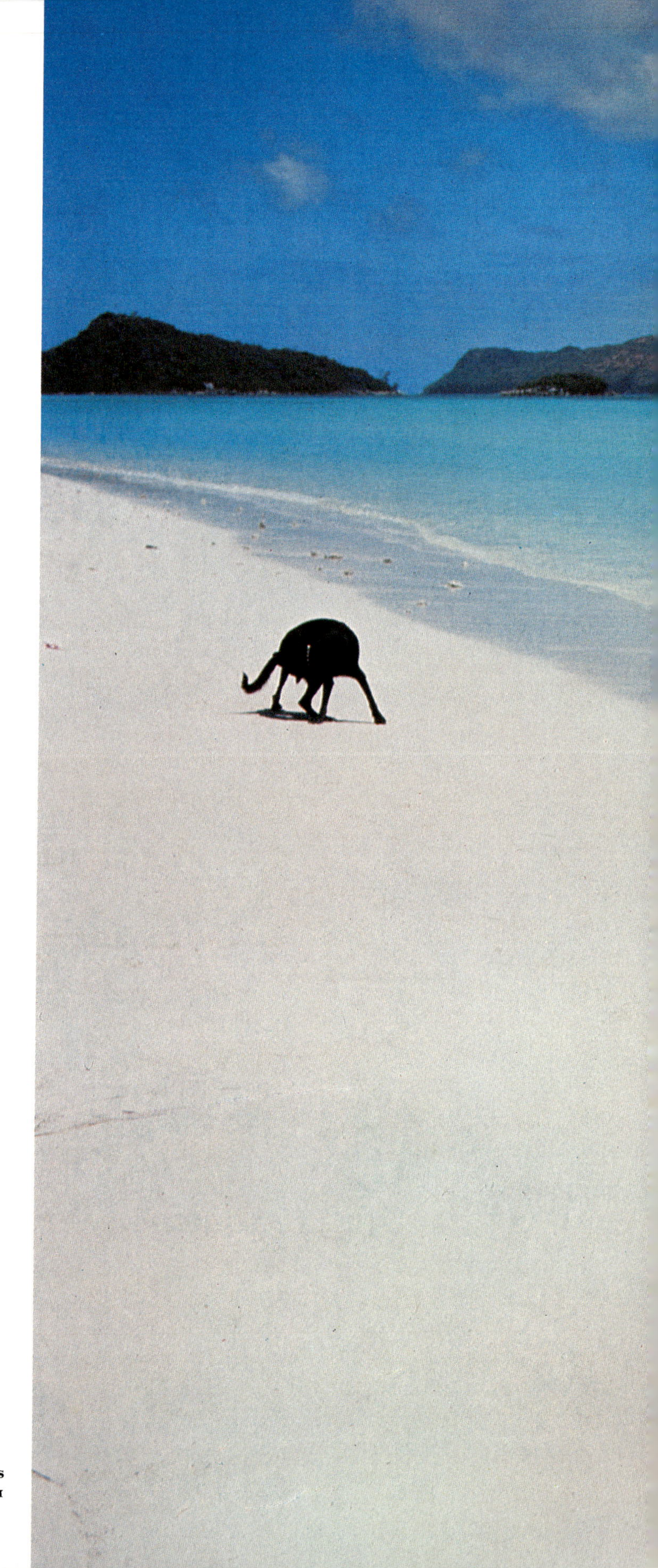

*43* **Dog Friday Praslin Island Seychelles**
**Appollonia Van Ravenstein 1971**

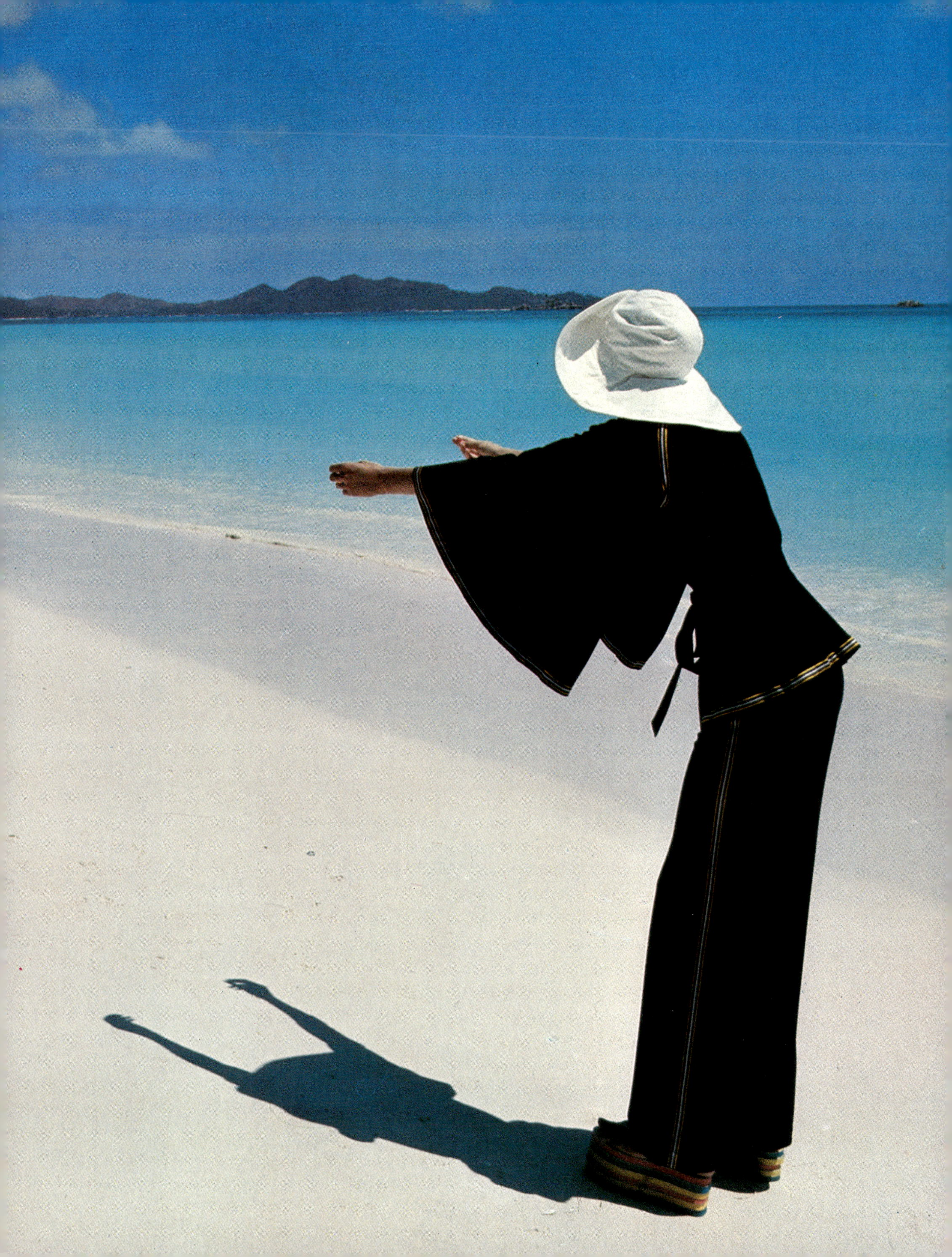

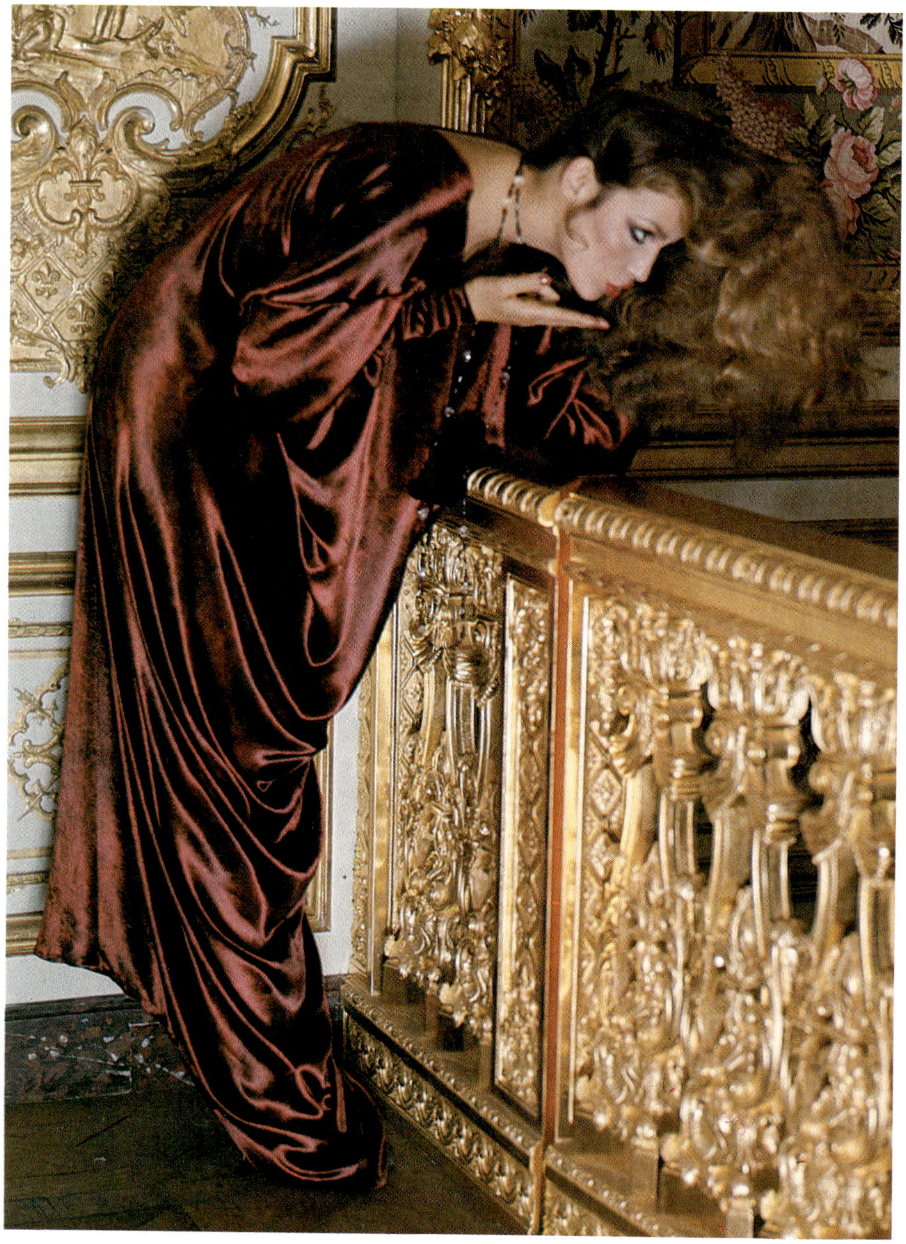

*44* **Yves Saint Laurent's garnet velvet robe**
**Marie Antoinette's bedroom**
**Versailles**
**Jerry Hall 1975**

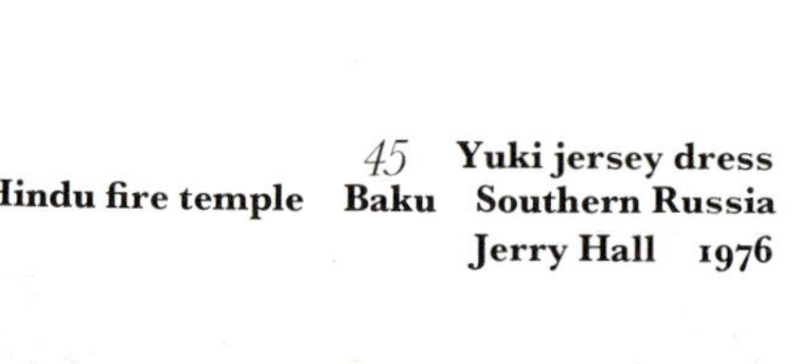

*45* **Yuki jersey dress**
**Hindu fire temple Baku Southern Russia**
**Jerry Hall 1976**

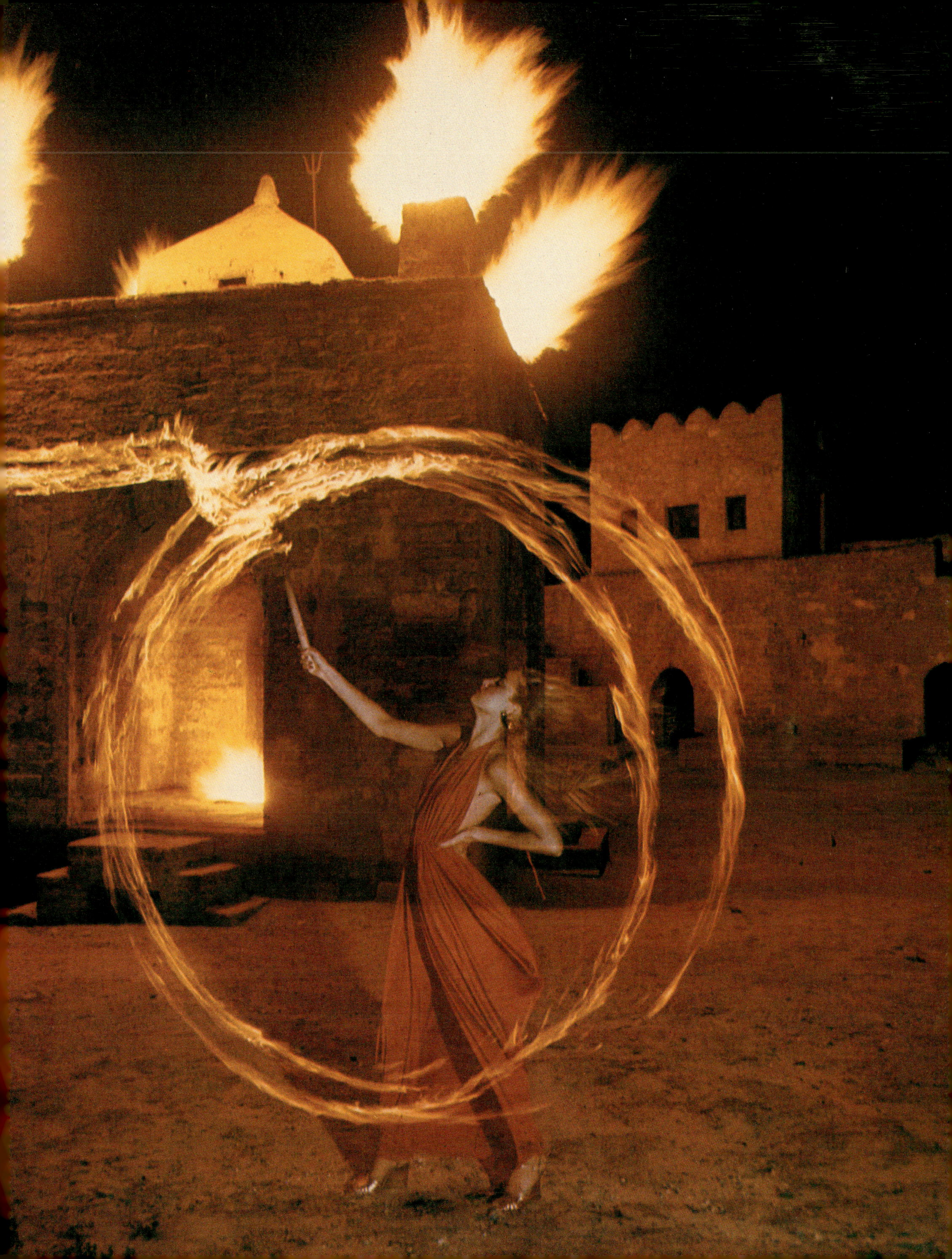

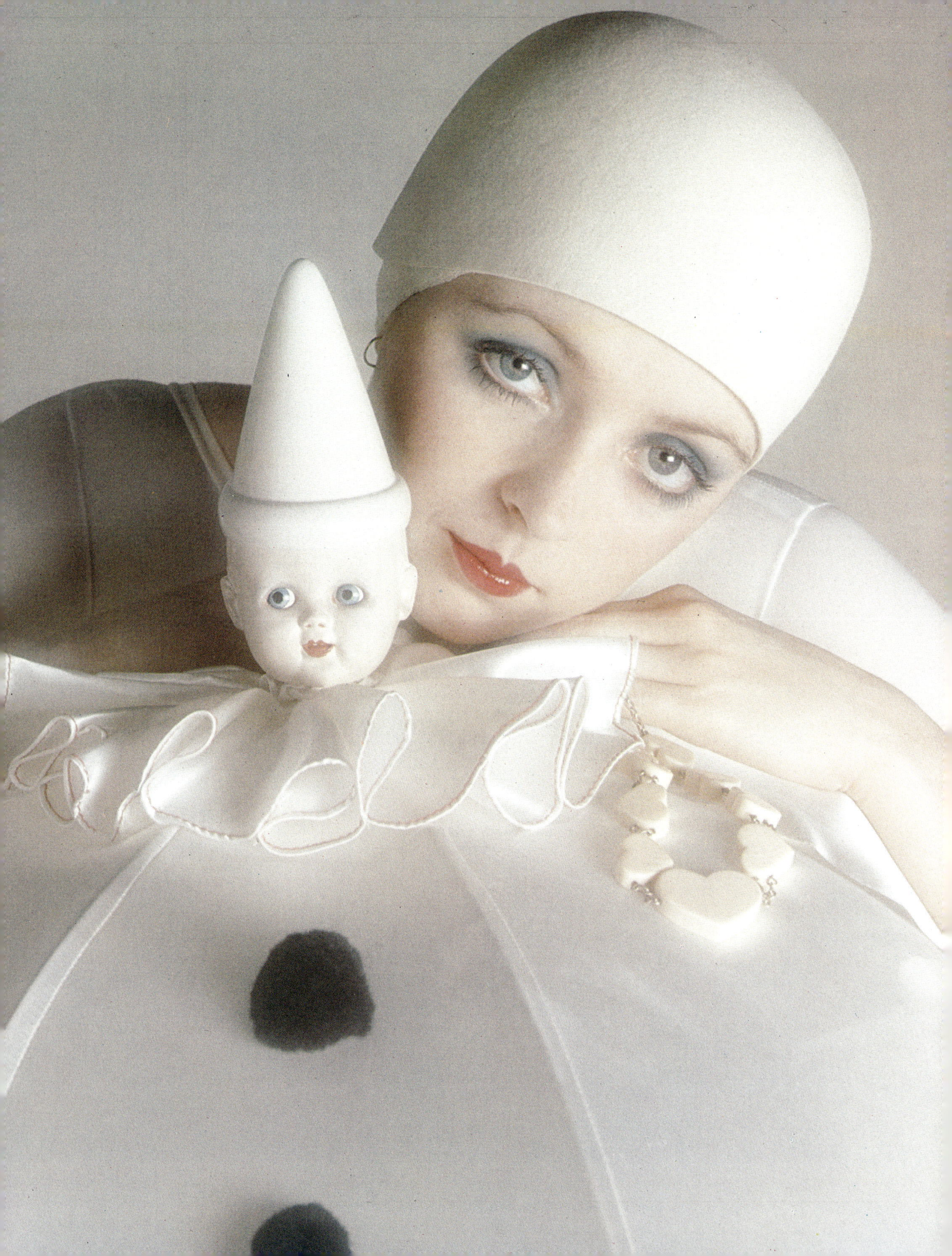

46 **Pierrot**
**Dior make-up**
**Linda Deganais** 1973

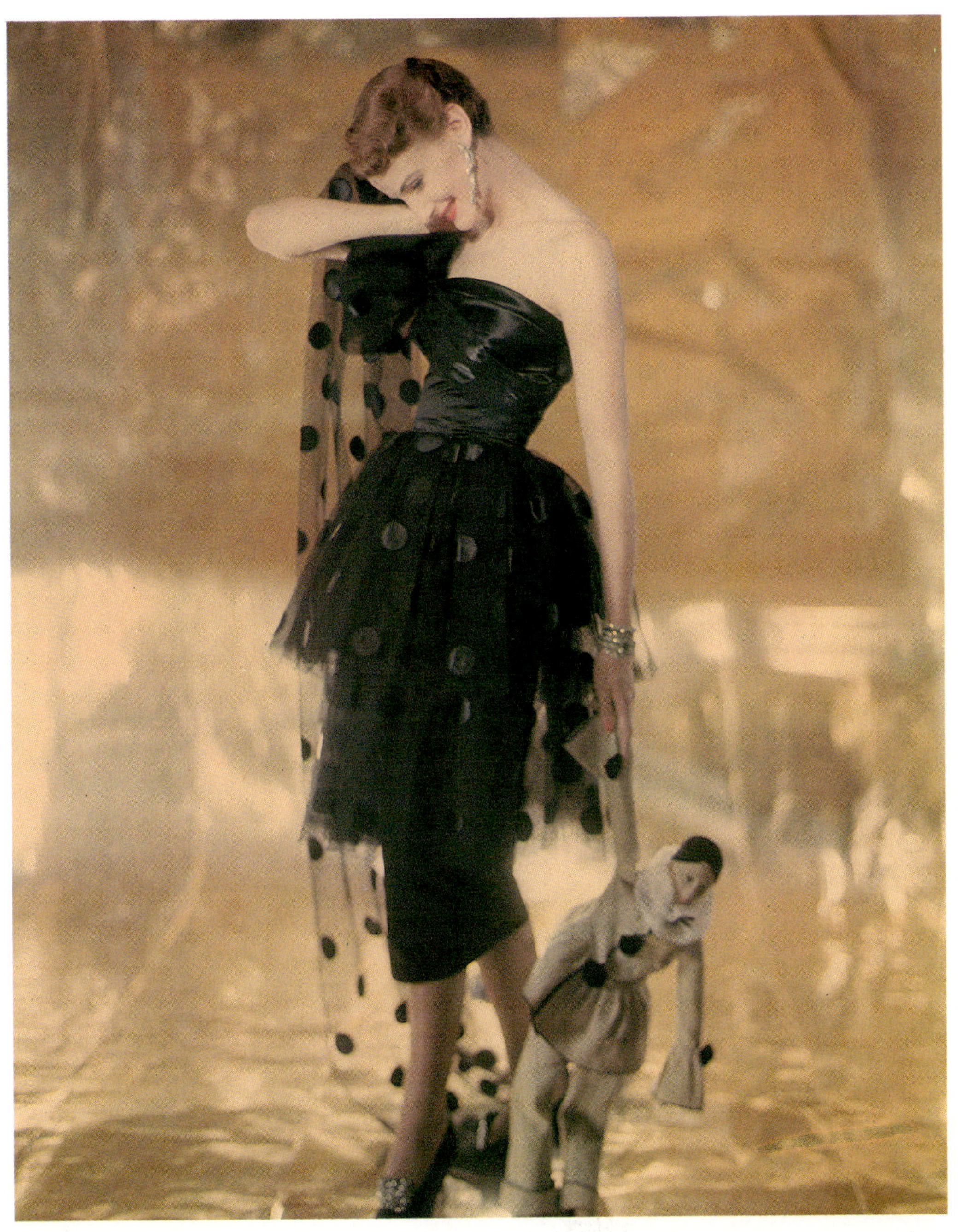

47 **Hardy Amies short evening dress** **Wenda Rogerson** 1950

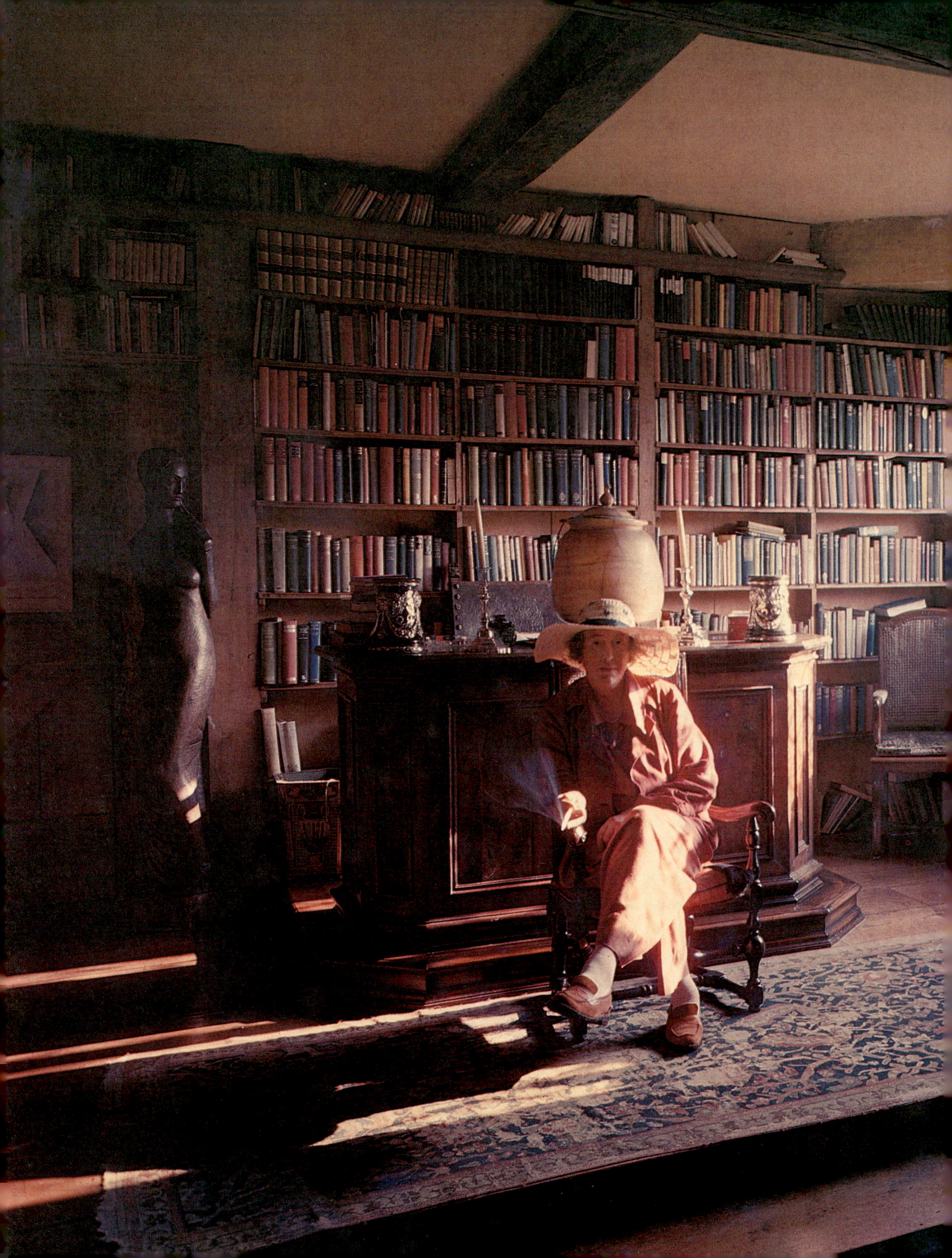

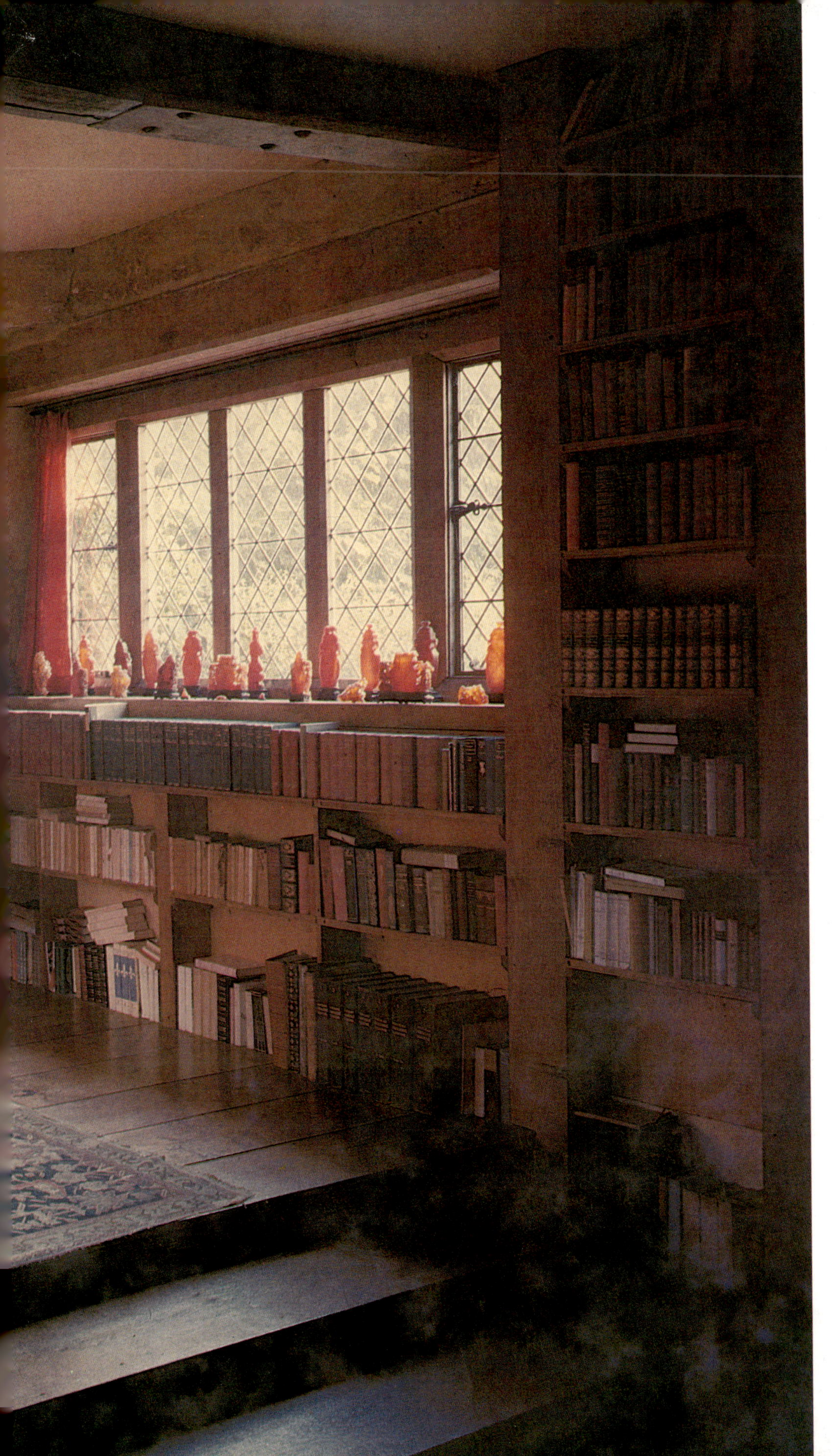

48 **Vita Sackville-West**
**Sissinghurst Castle** **1949**

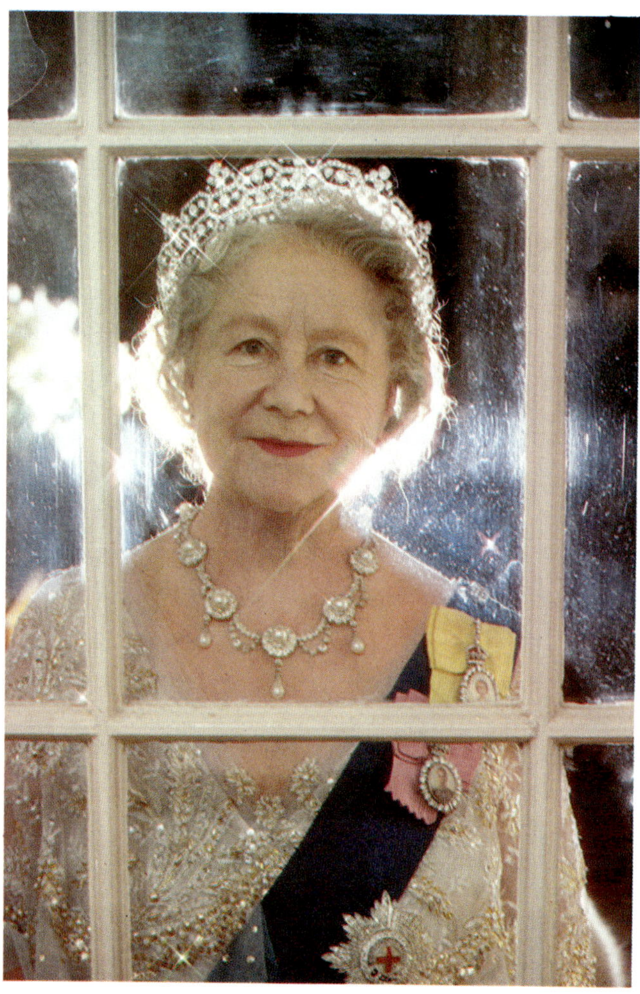

*49* **H.M. Queen Elizabeth The Queen Mother**
**Clarence House 1980**

*50* **H.R.H. Princess Anne and Captain Mark Phillips**
**The Long Gallery**
**Windsor Castle 1973**

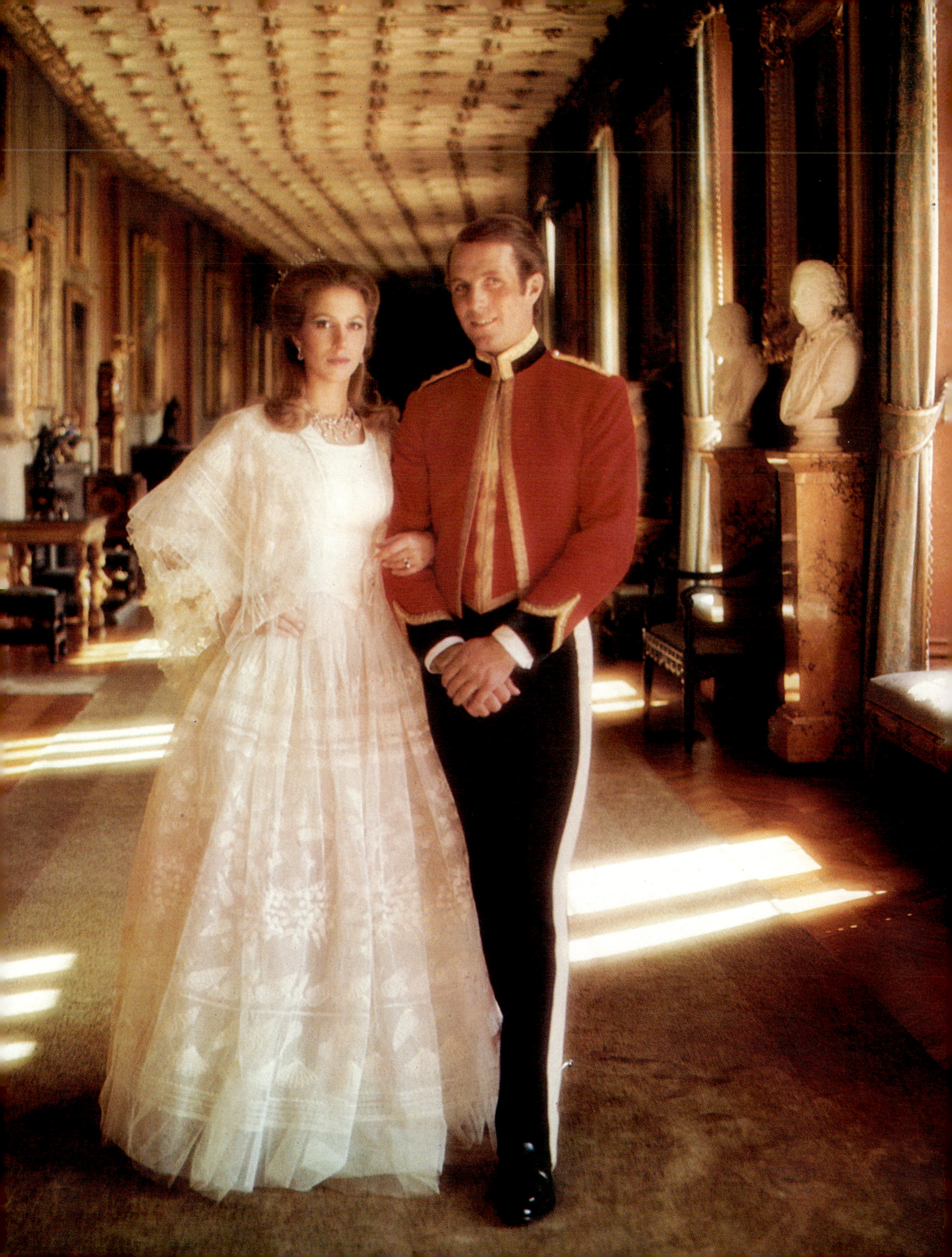

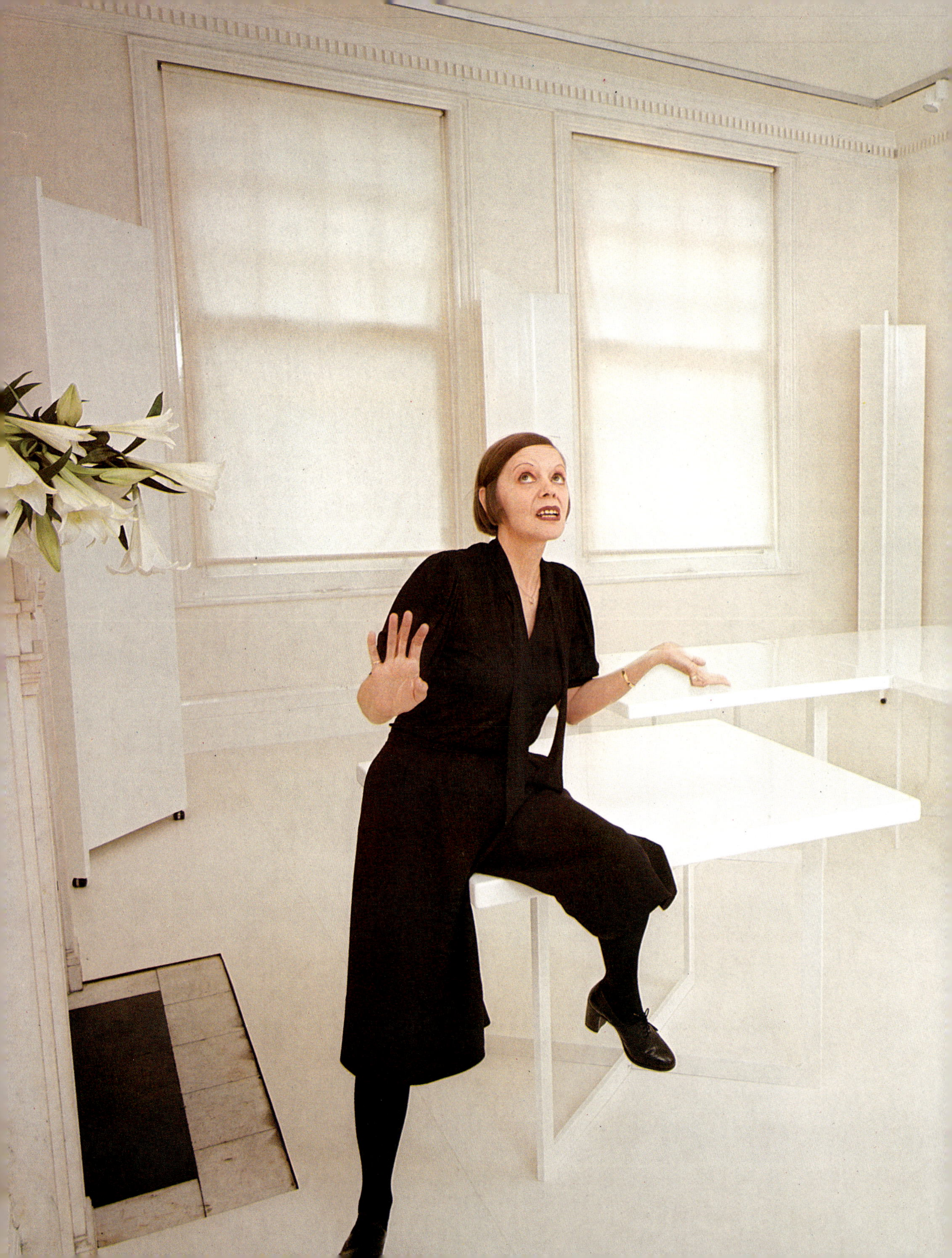

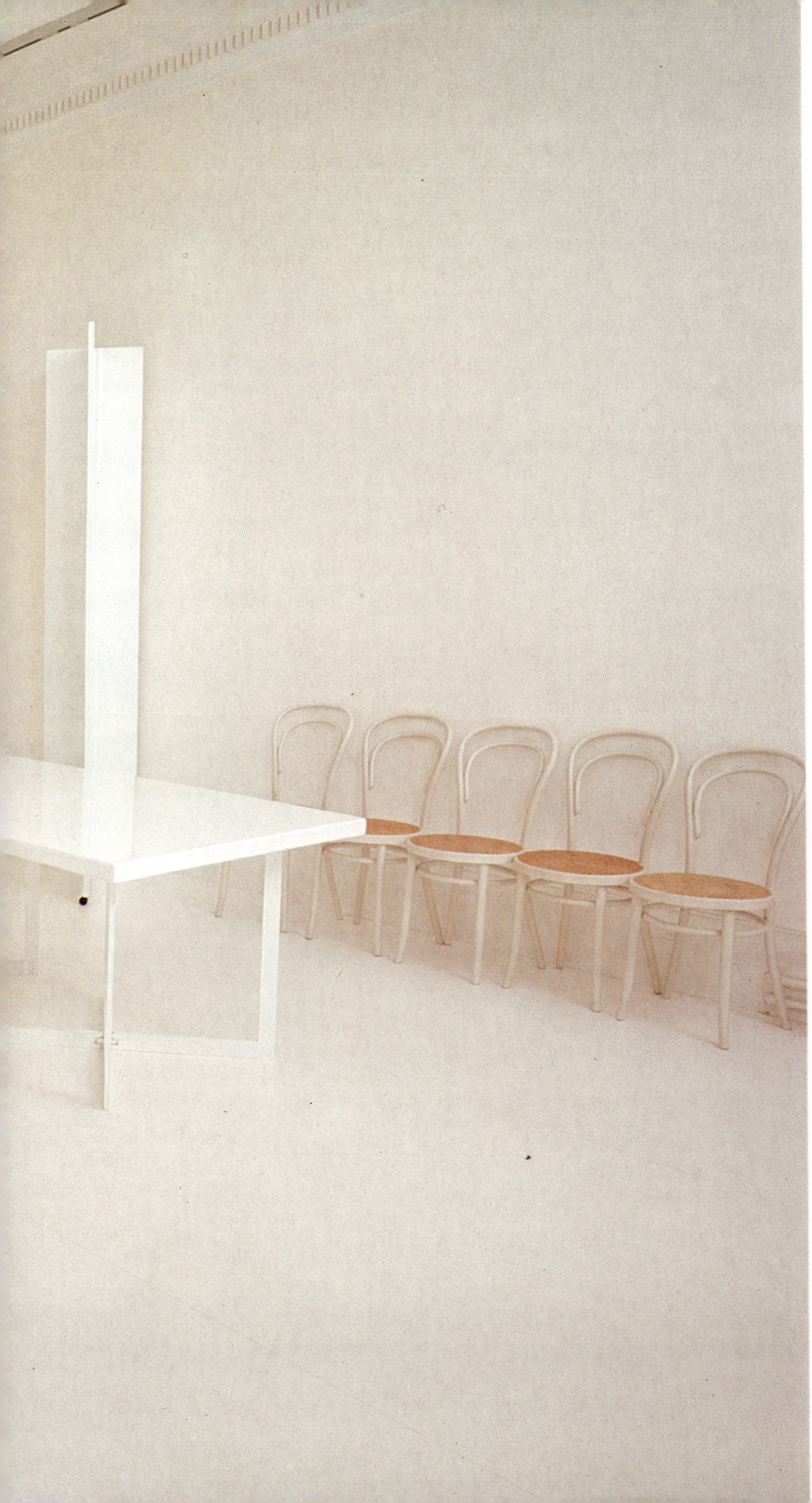

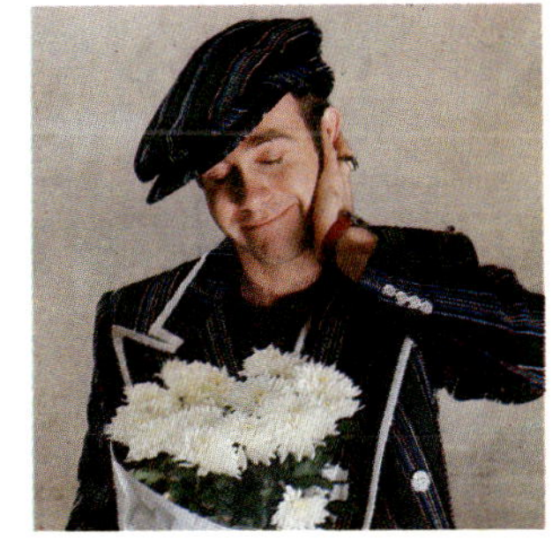

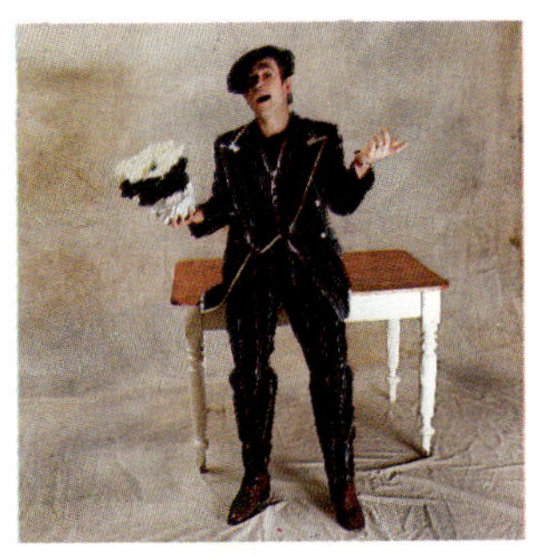

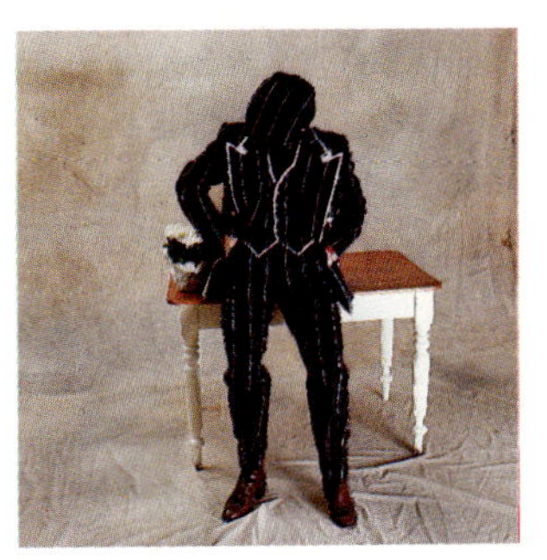

*52* **Elton John 1978**

*51* **Jean Muir 1979**

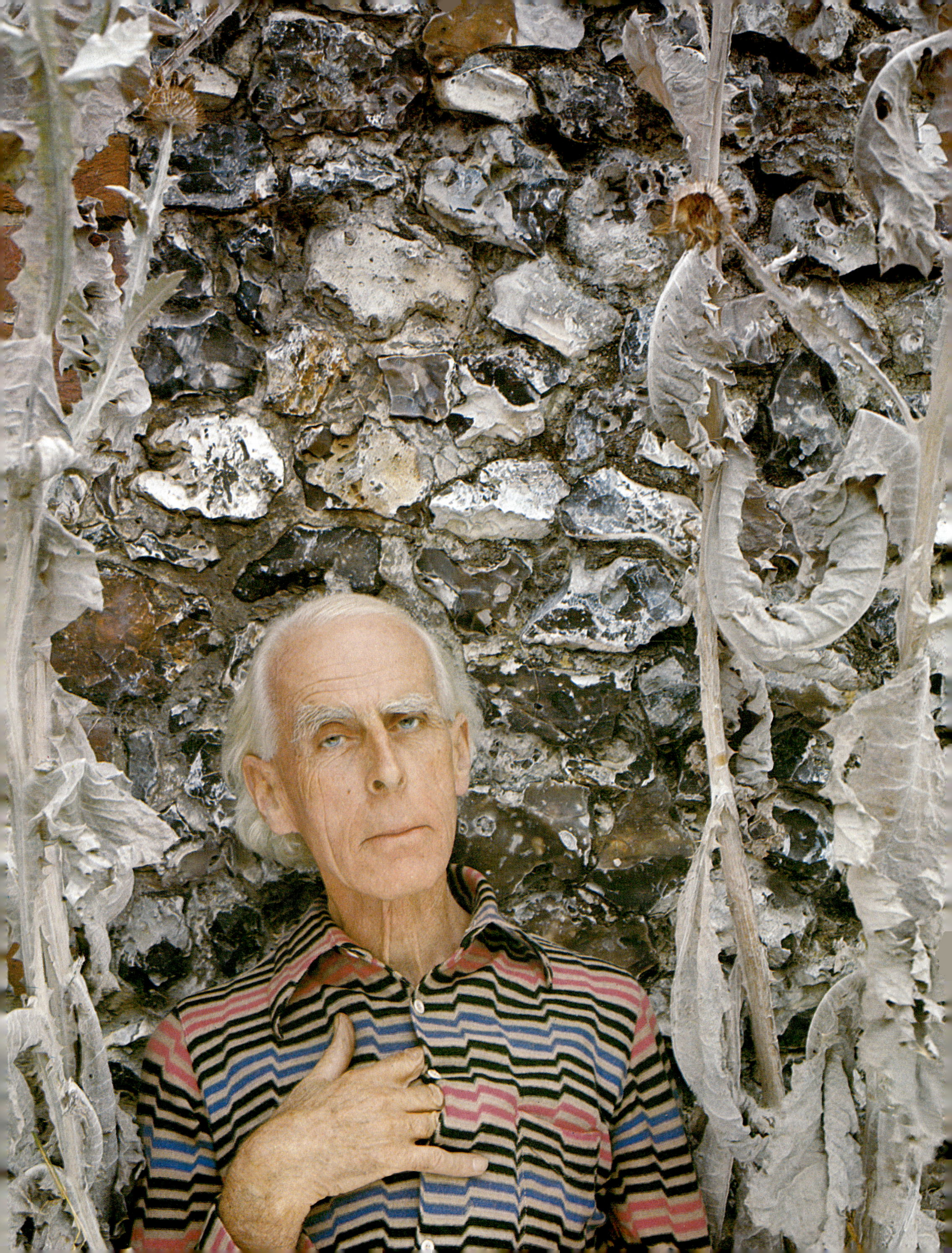

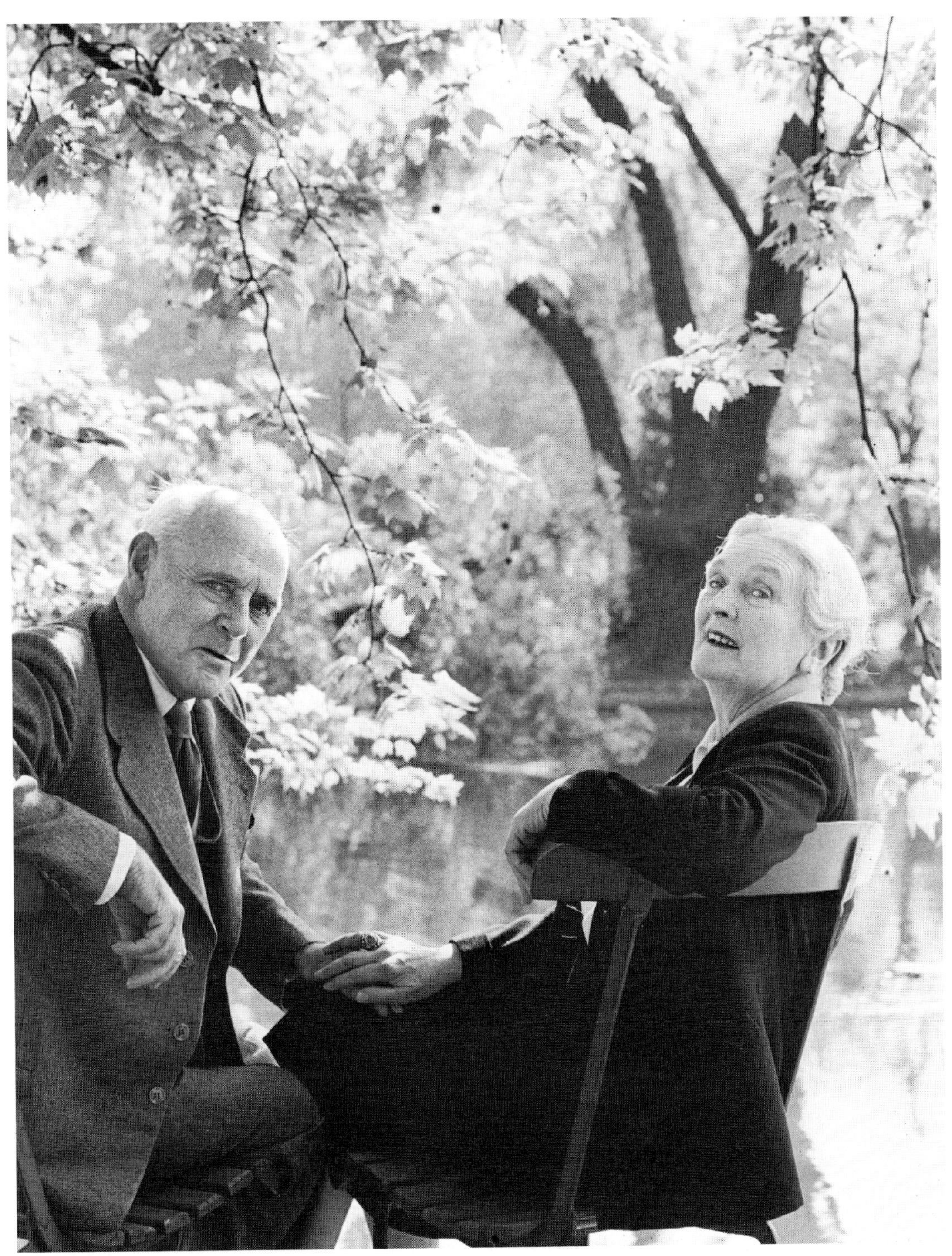

*54* **Lewis Casson and Sybil Thorndike 1956**

*53* **John Piper 1976**

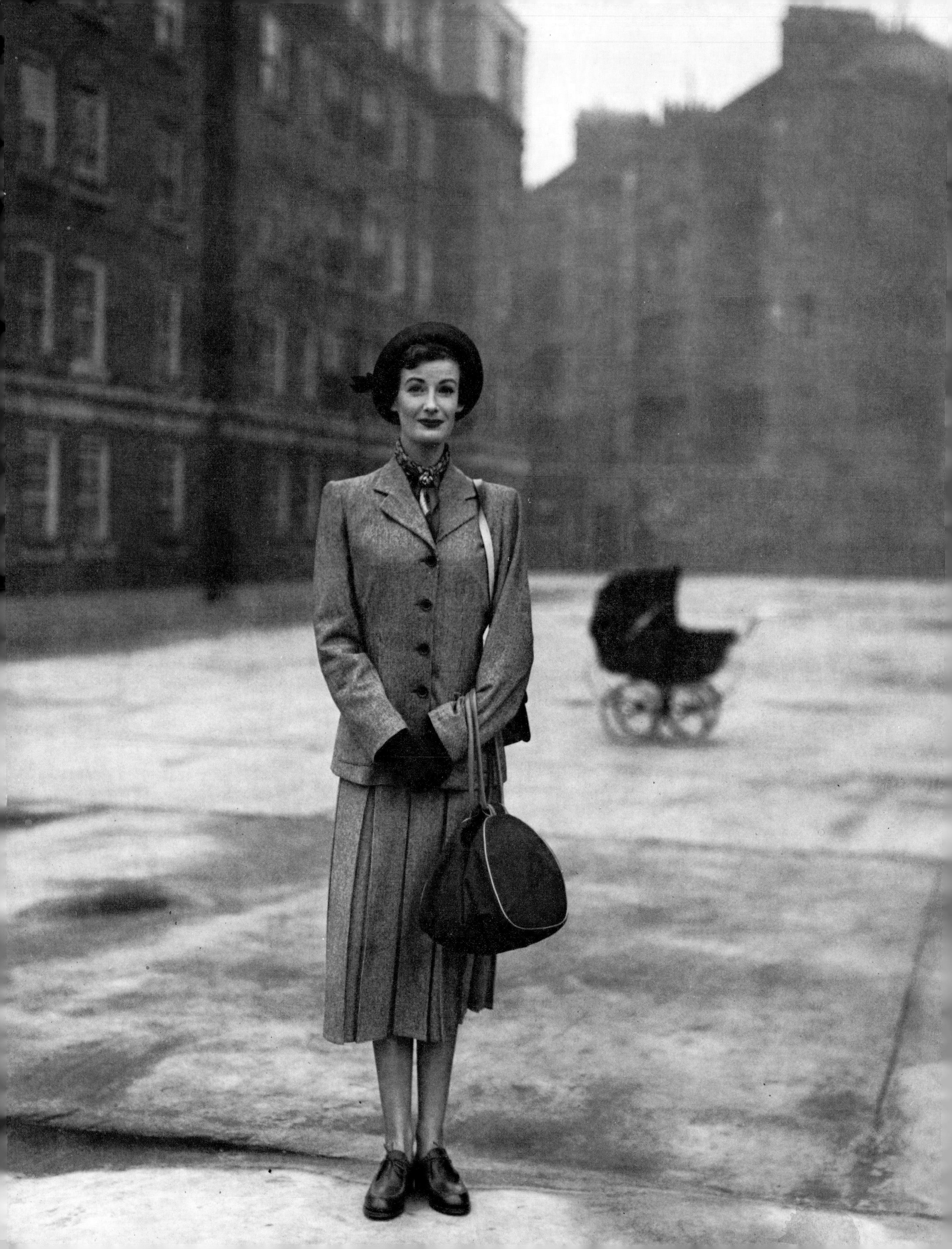

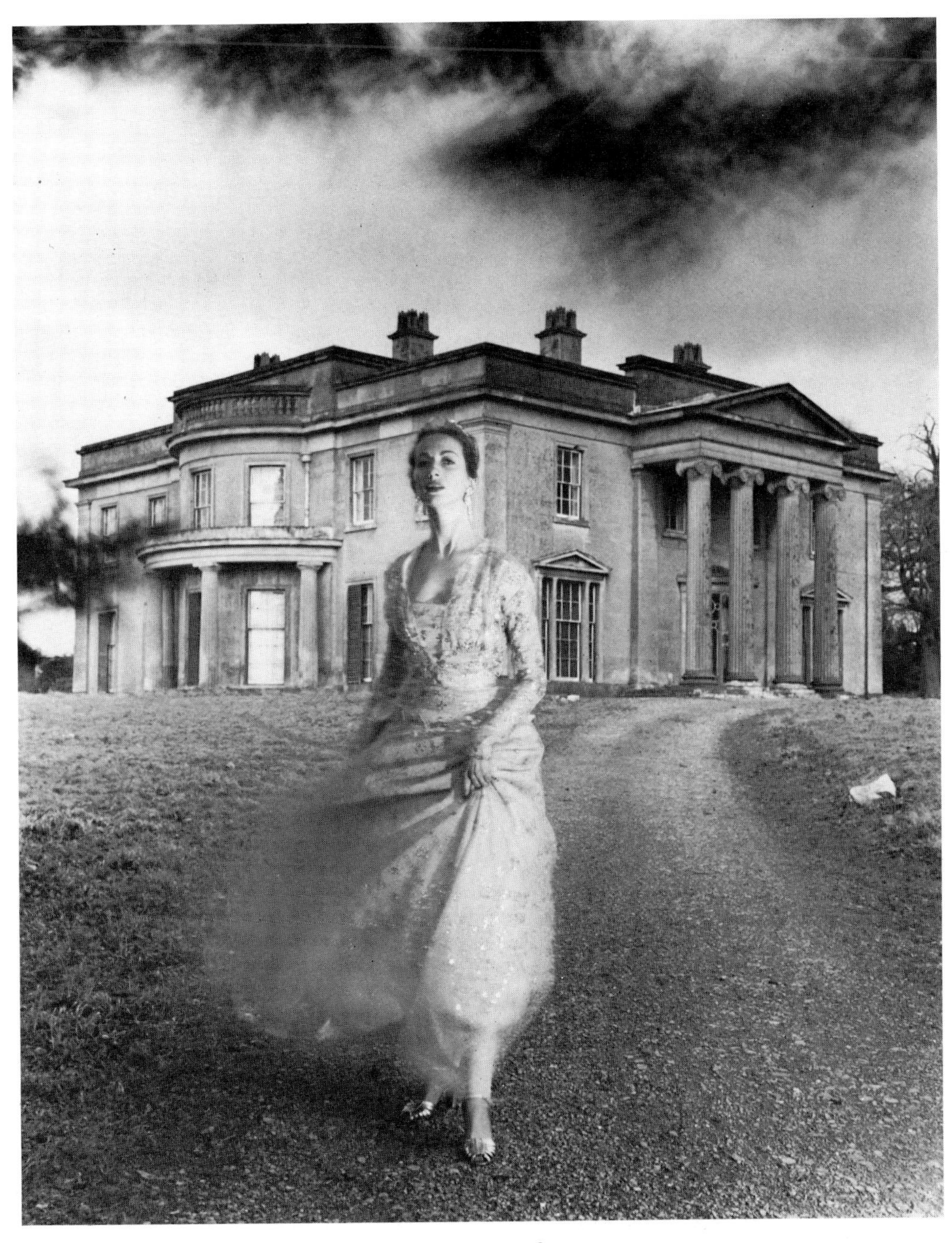

*56* **Hartnell strapless evening dress and jacket**
**Clytha Park Monmouthshire**
**Della Oak 1951**

*55* **Simpsons' suit**
**Peabody Trust Buildings Fulham Road**
**Wenda Rogerson 1950**

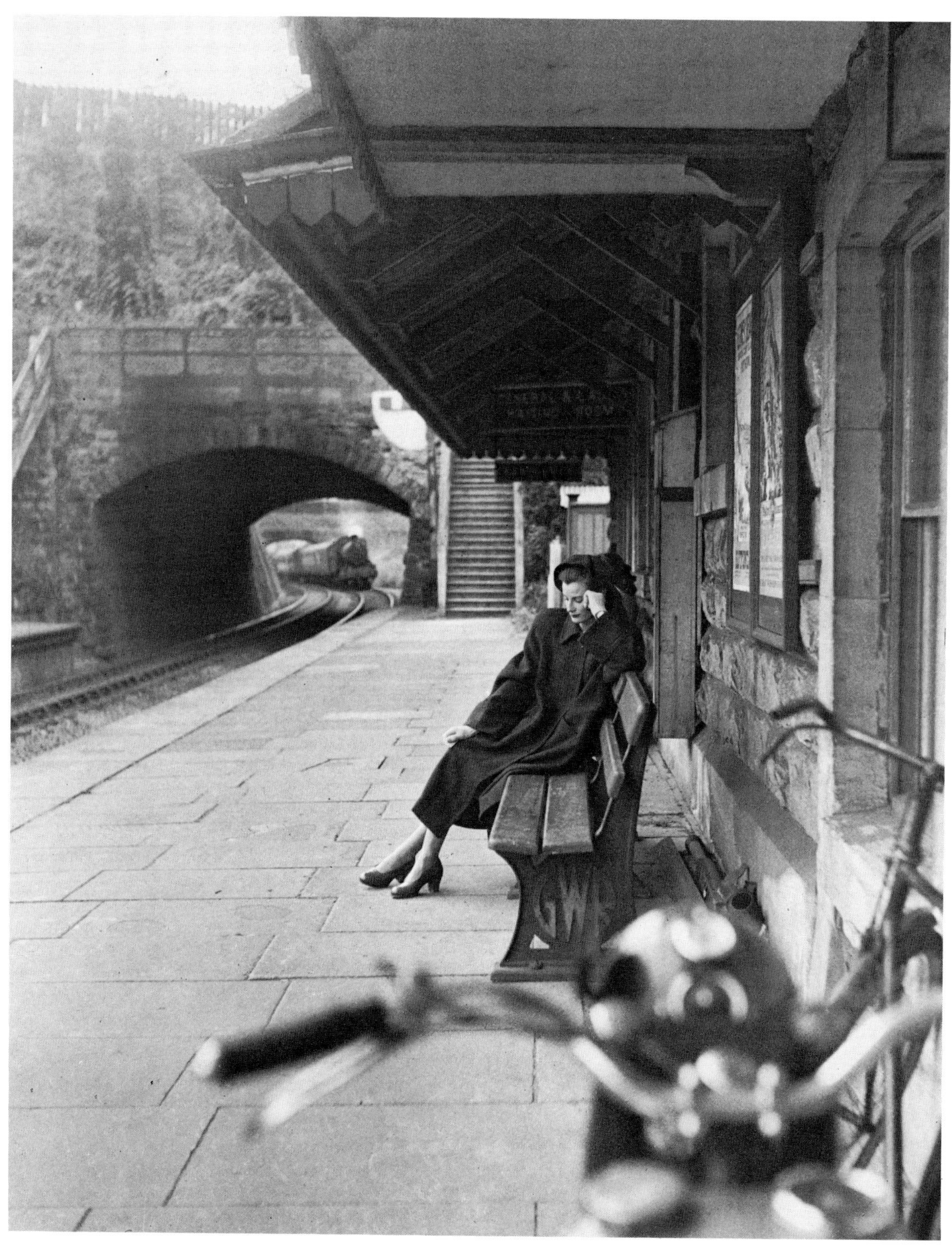

*57* **The Iron Road  Wenda Rogerson  1947**

*58* **Hand-knit cashmere twinse**
**Public bar Hobnails Inn  Little Washbourn**
**Wenda Rogerson  195**

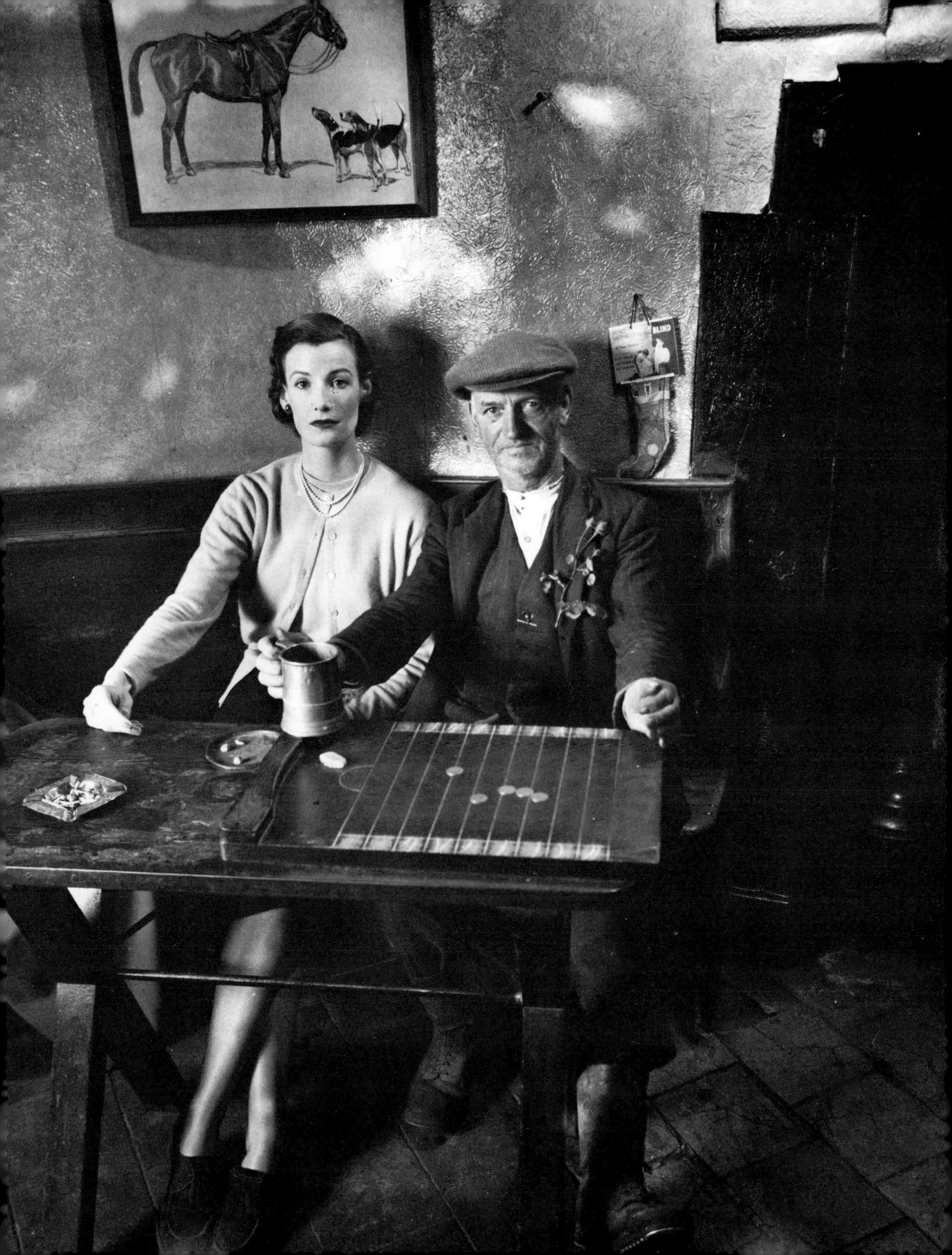
BLIND

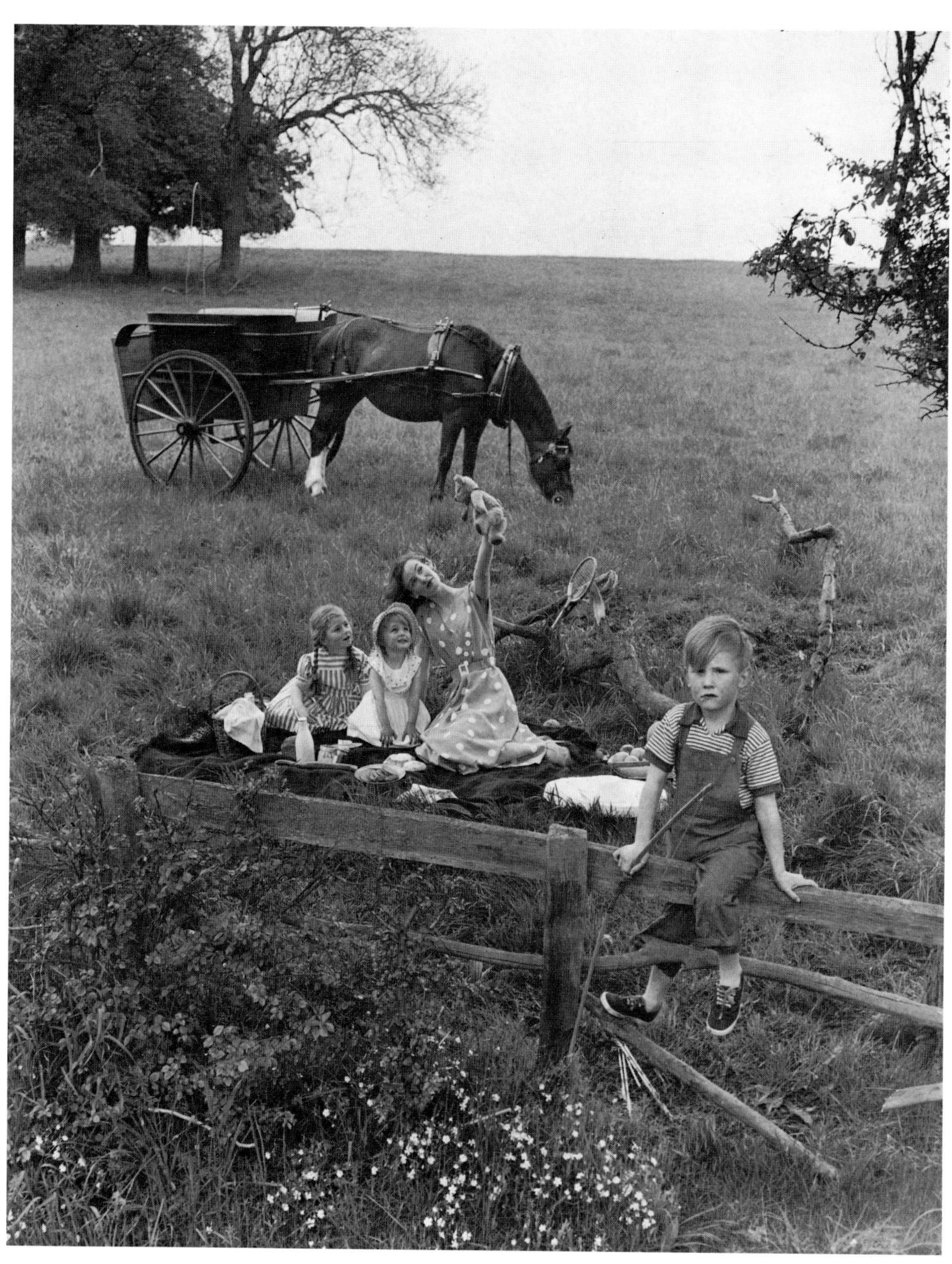

*59* **The Picnic**
**Wenda Rogerson**
**her niece Caroline Owen**
**Mary Robertson and Simon Parkinson** **1951**

*60* **Country Classic tweed suit** **Wenda Rogerson** **195**

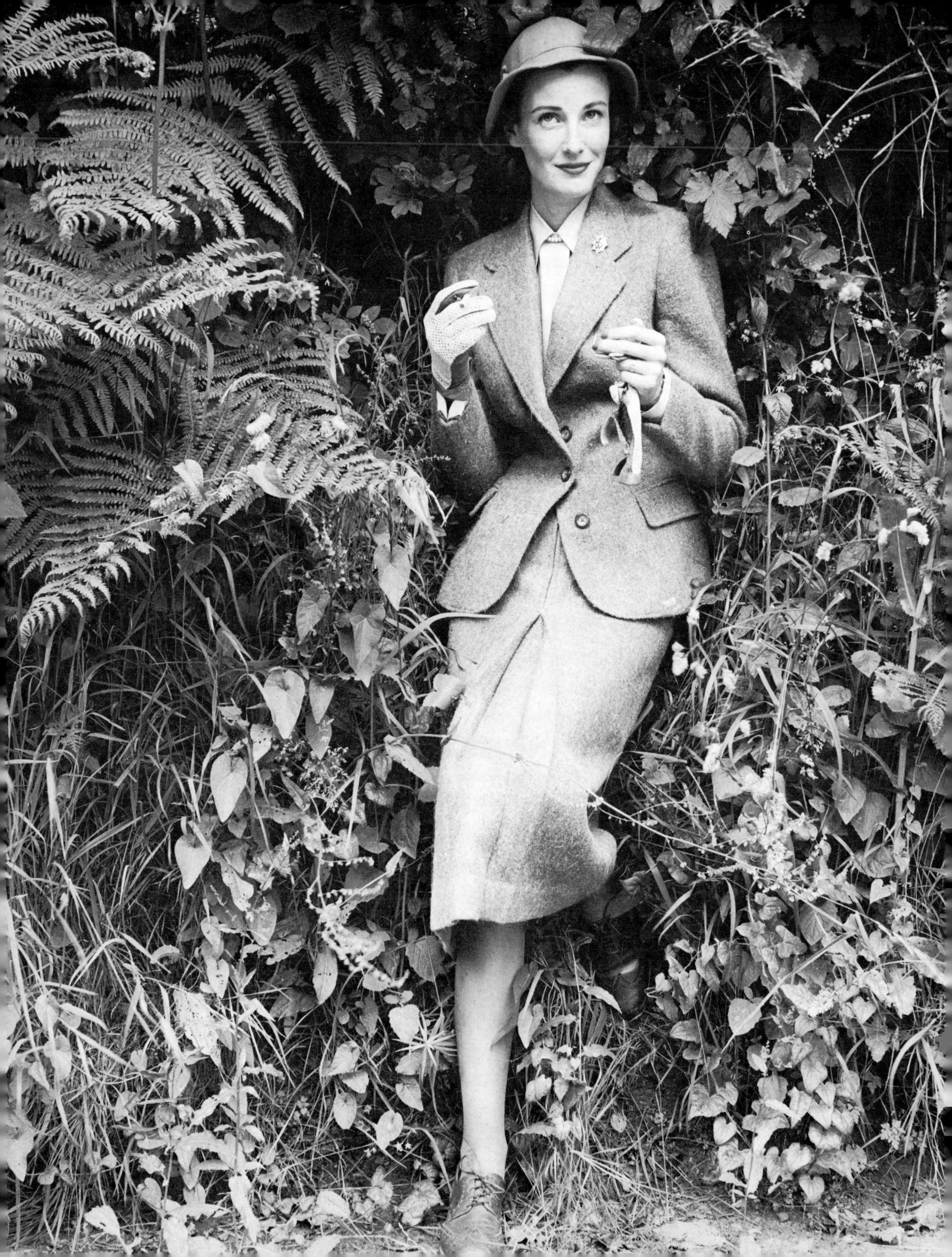

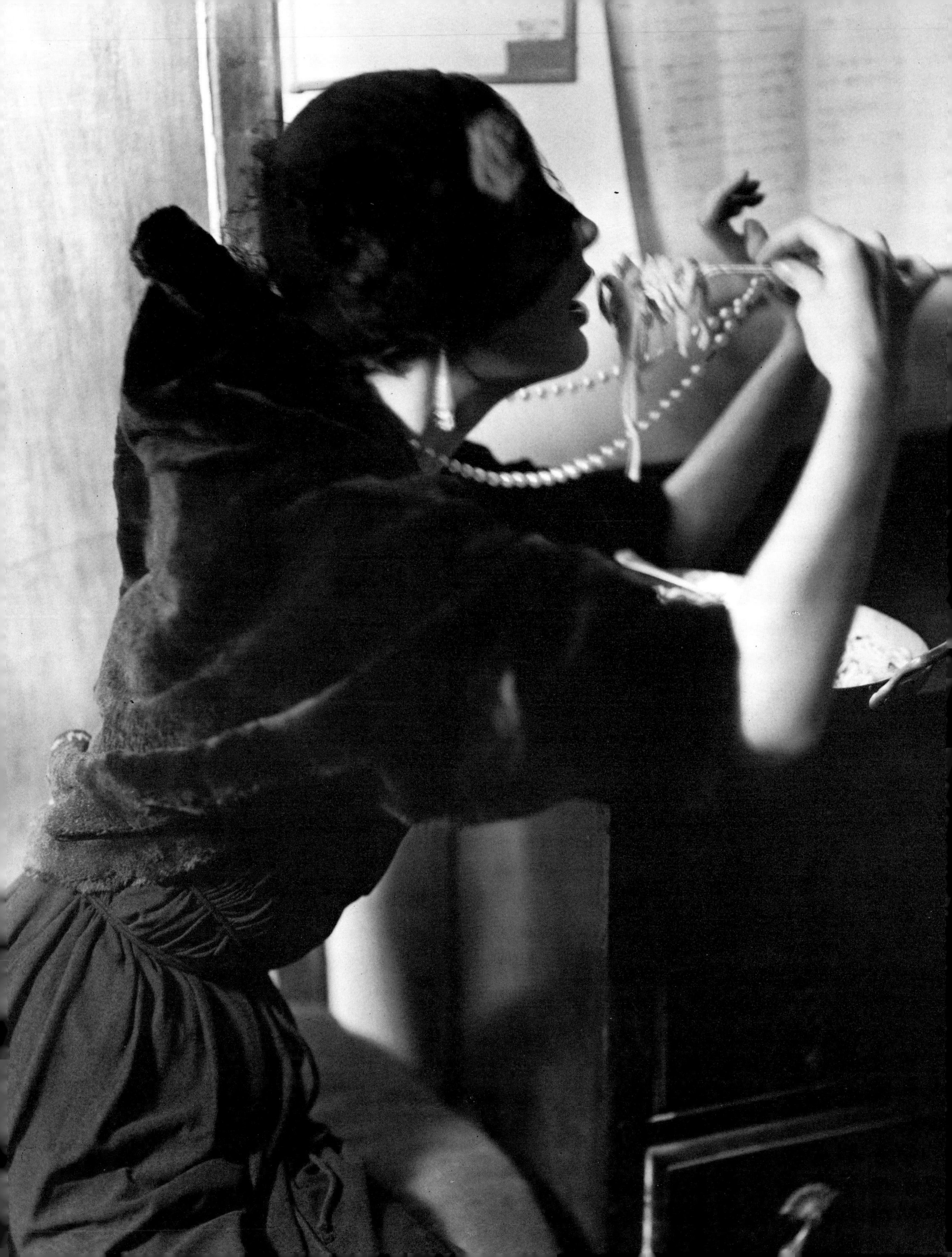

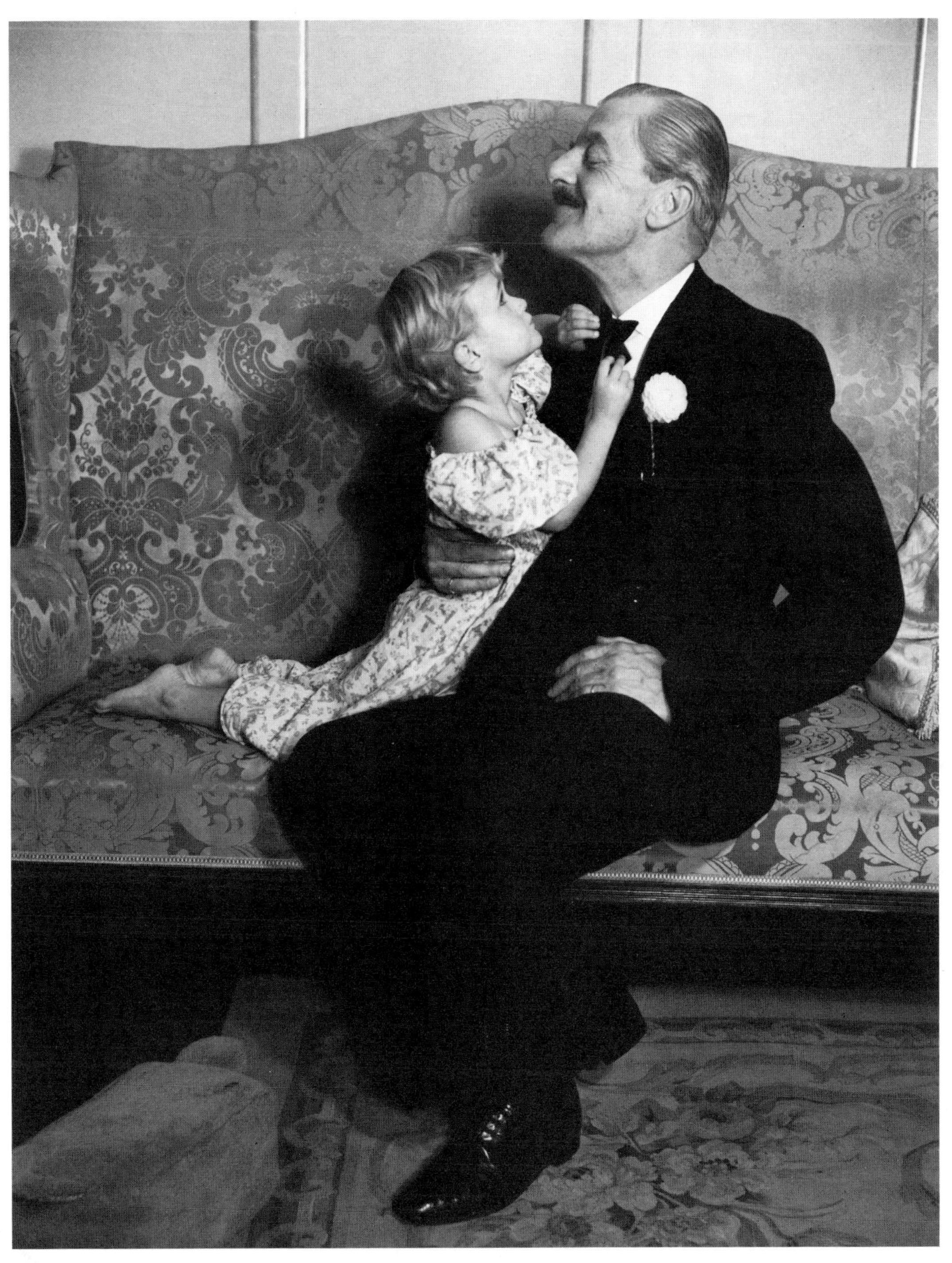

*62* **Dinner-jacket**
**Aquascutum advertisement Archie Campbell and Mary Robertson 1952**

*61* **More dash than cash Taste**
**Wenda Rogerson 1950**

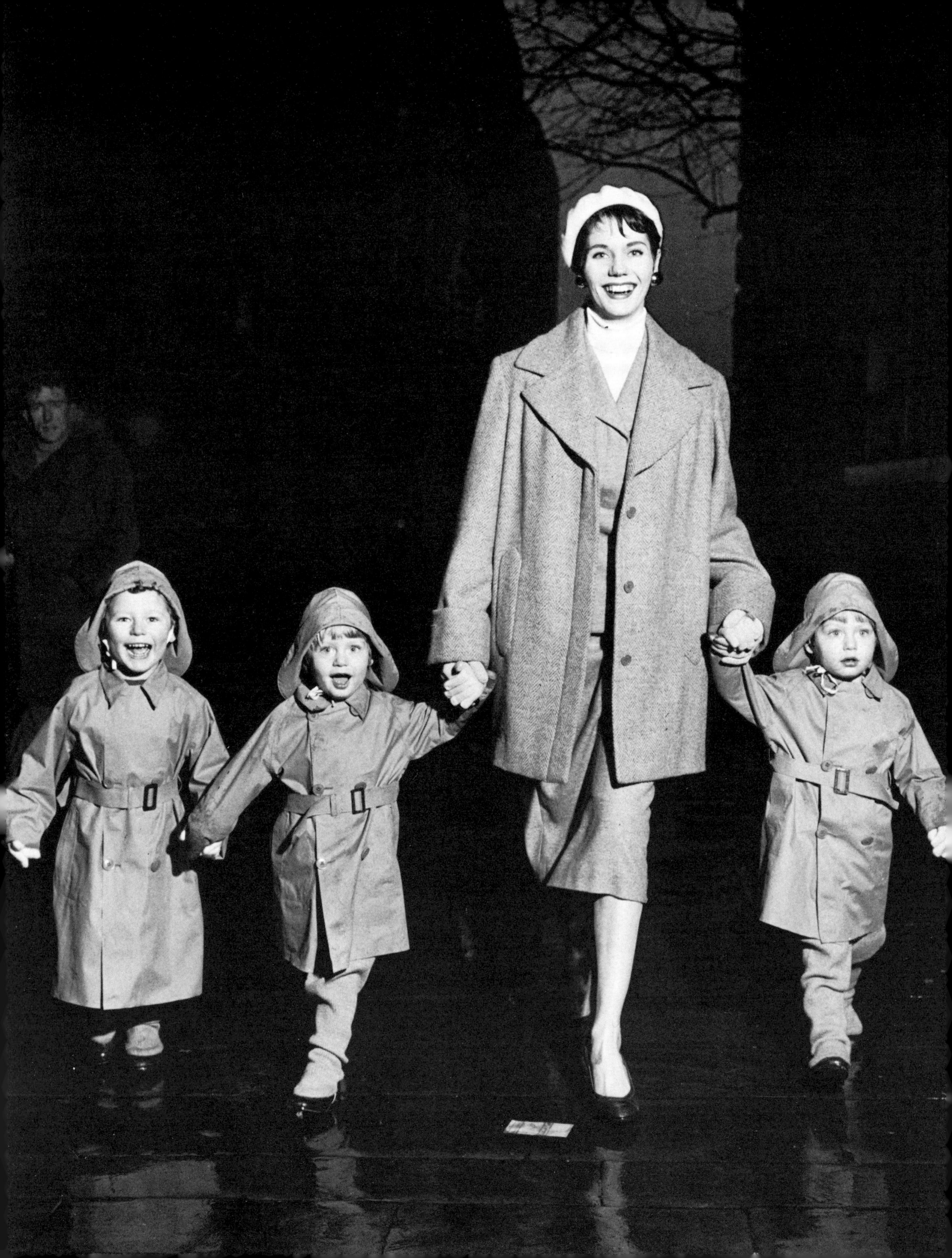

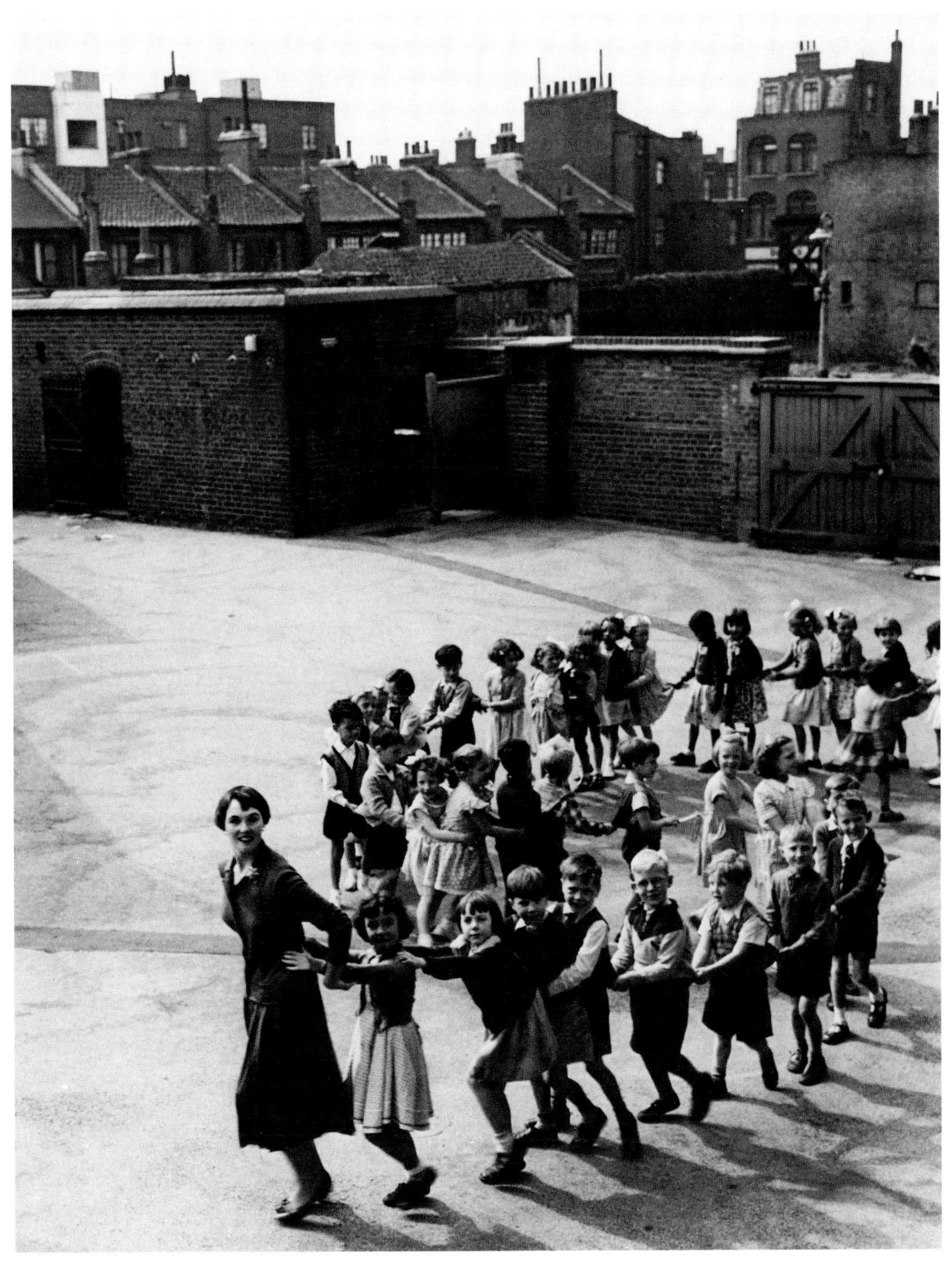

64 **Young Idea Starting a career**
**Infant school teacher**
**Jaeger separates Joan Cox 1955**

63 **A cheerful crowd go out in dirty weather**
**Enid Boulting and her children 1955**

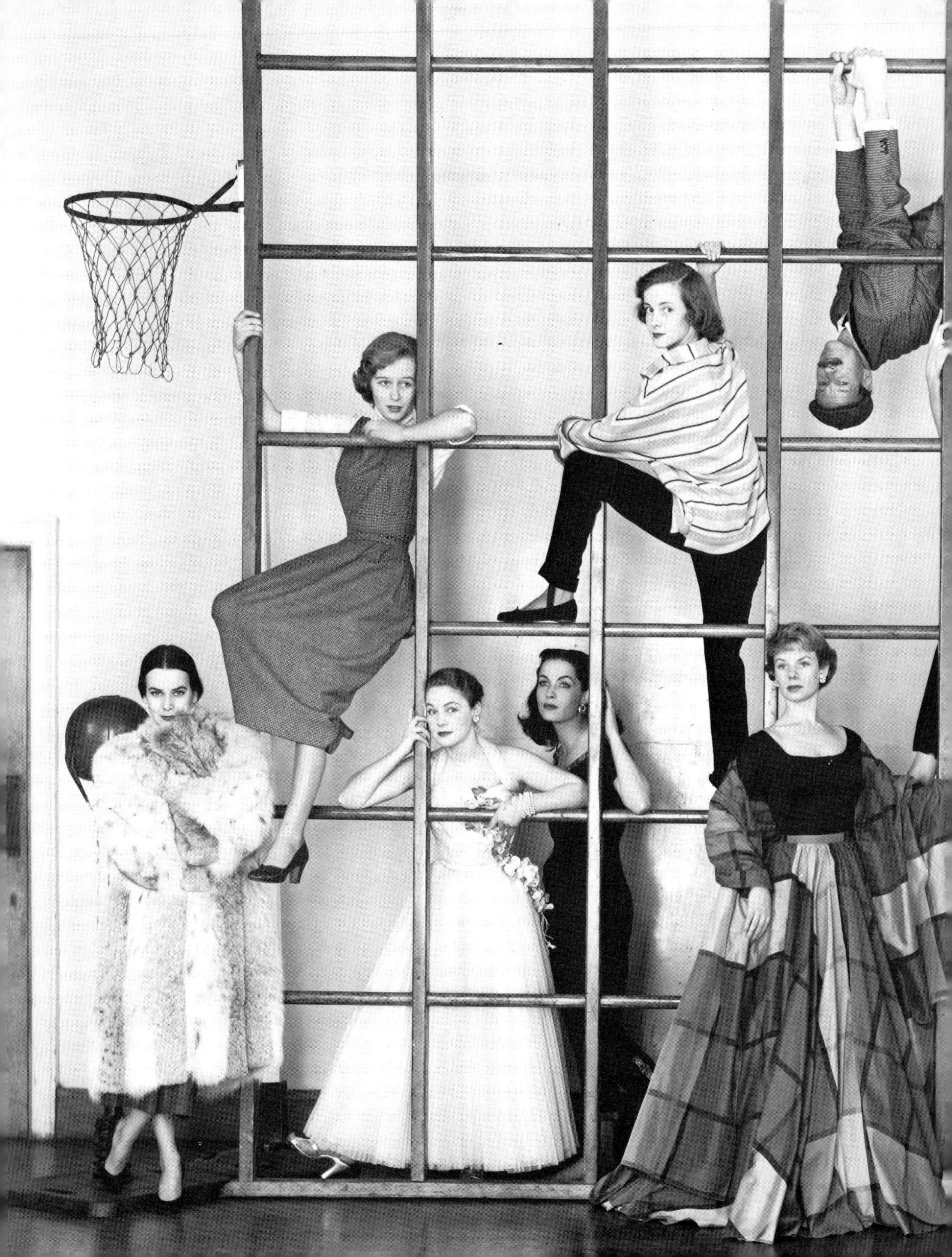

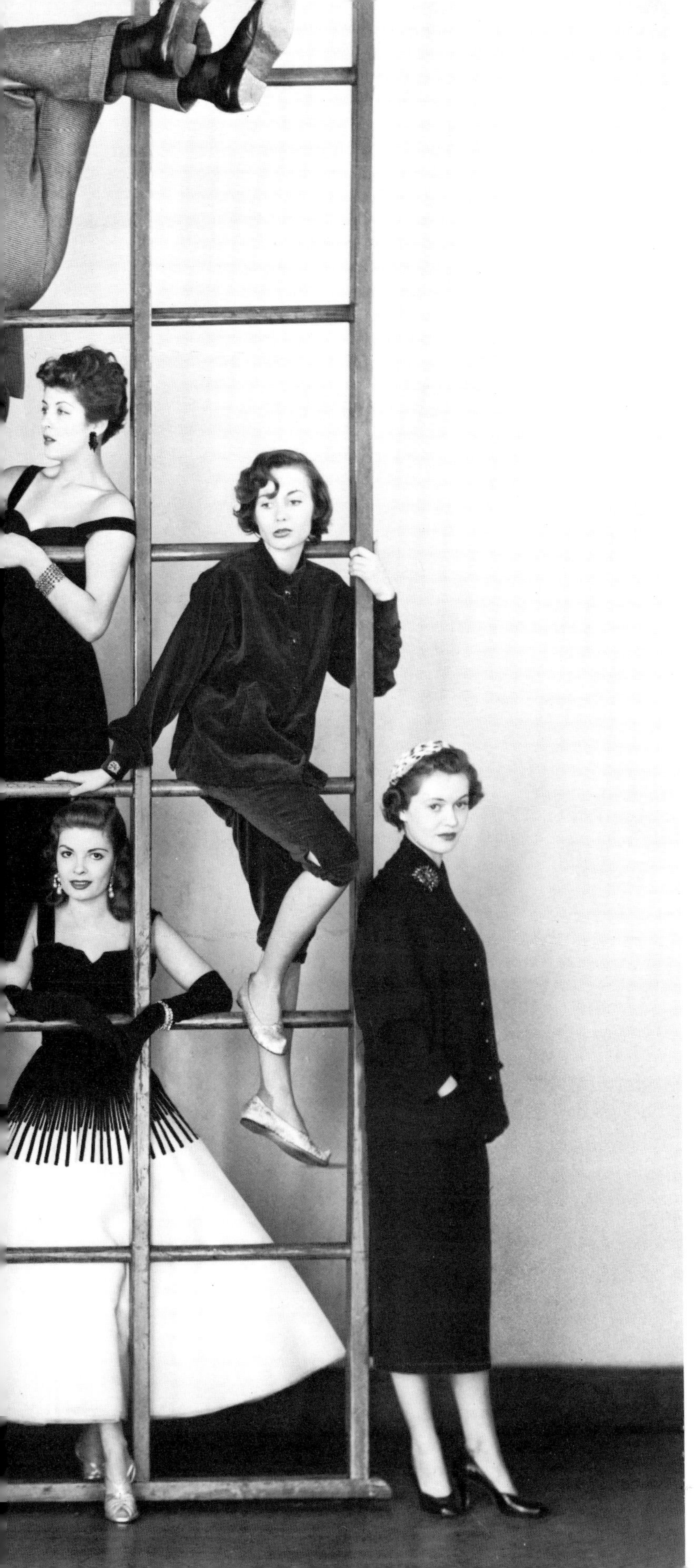

65 **The young look in the theatre**
**Top: Norman Parkinson**
**Middle (l to r): Virginia McKenna Elizabeth Henson Patricia McCarron Josephine Griffin**
**Ground (l to r): Hazel Penwarden Zena Walker Yvonne Furneaux Jill Bennett Patricia Owens Ruth Trouncer 1953**

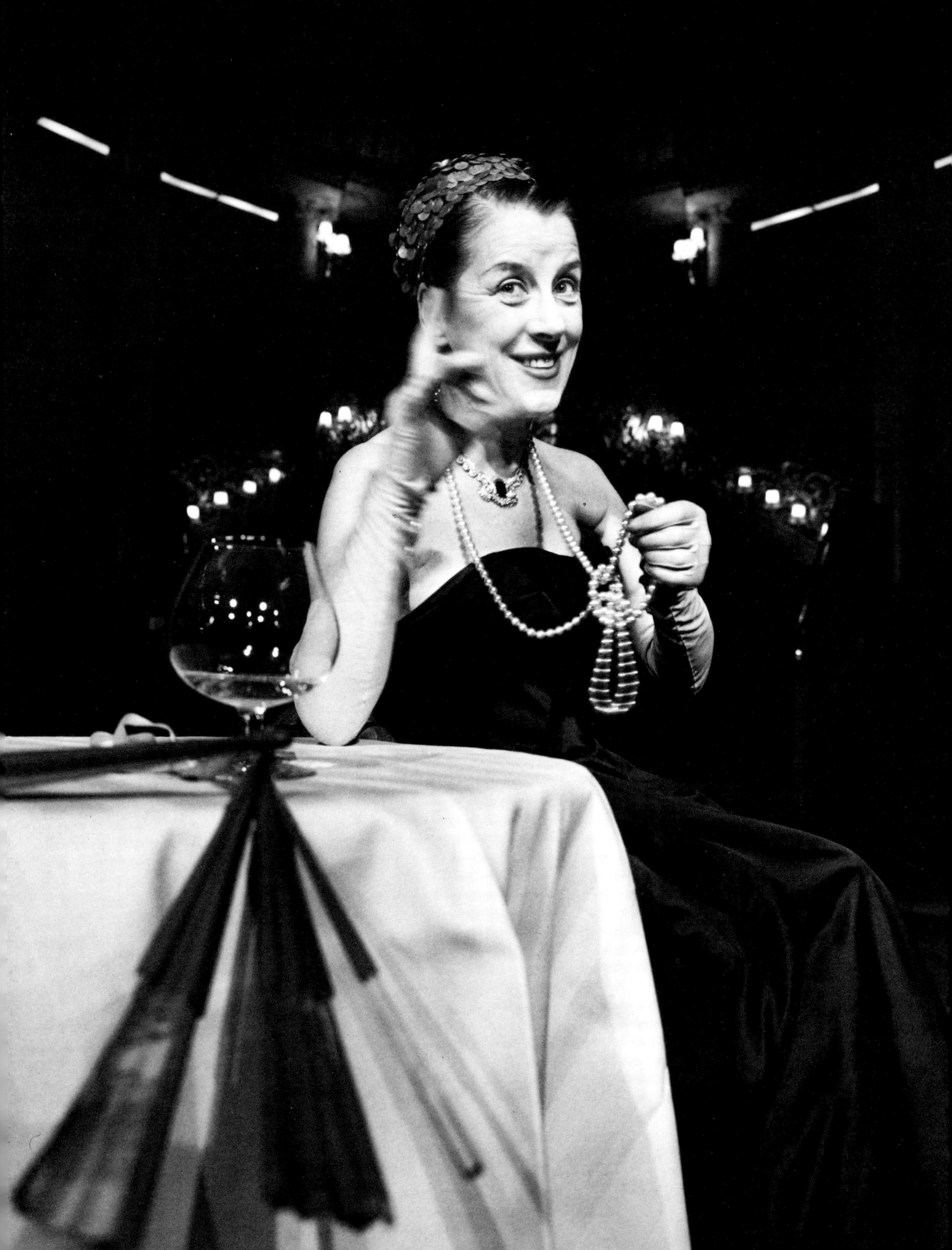

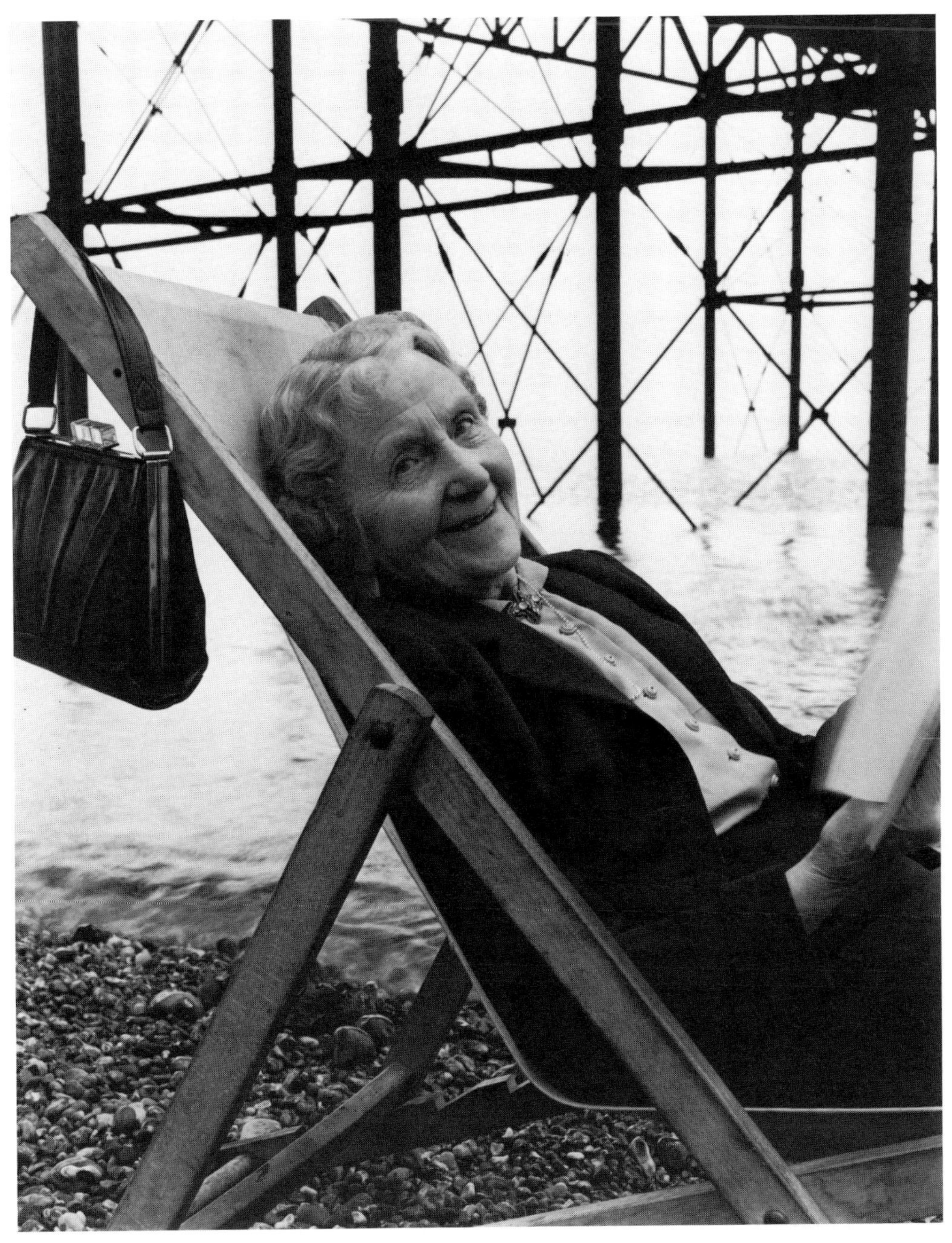

*67* **Mary Jerrold Brighton Pier 1954**

*66* **Beatrice Lillie Café de Paris London 1951**

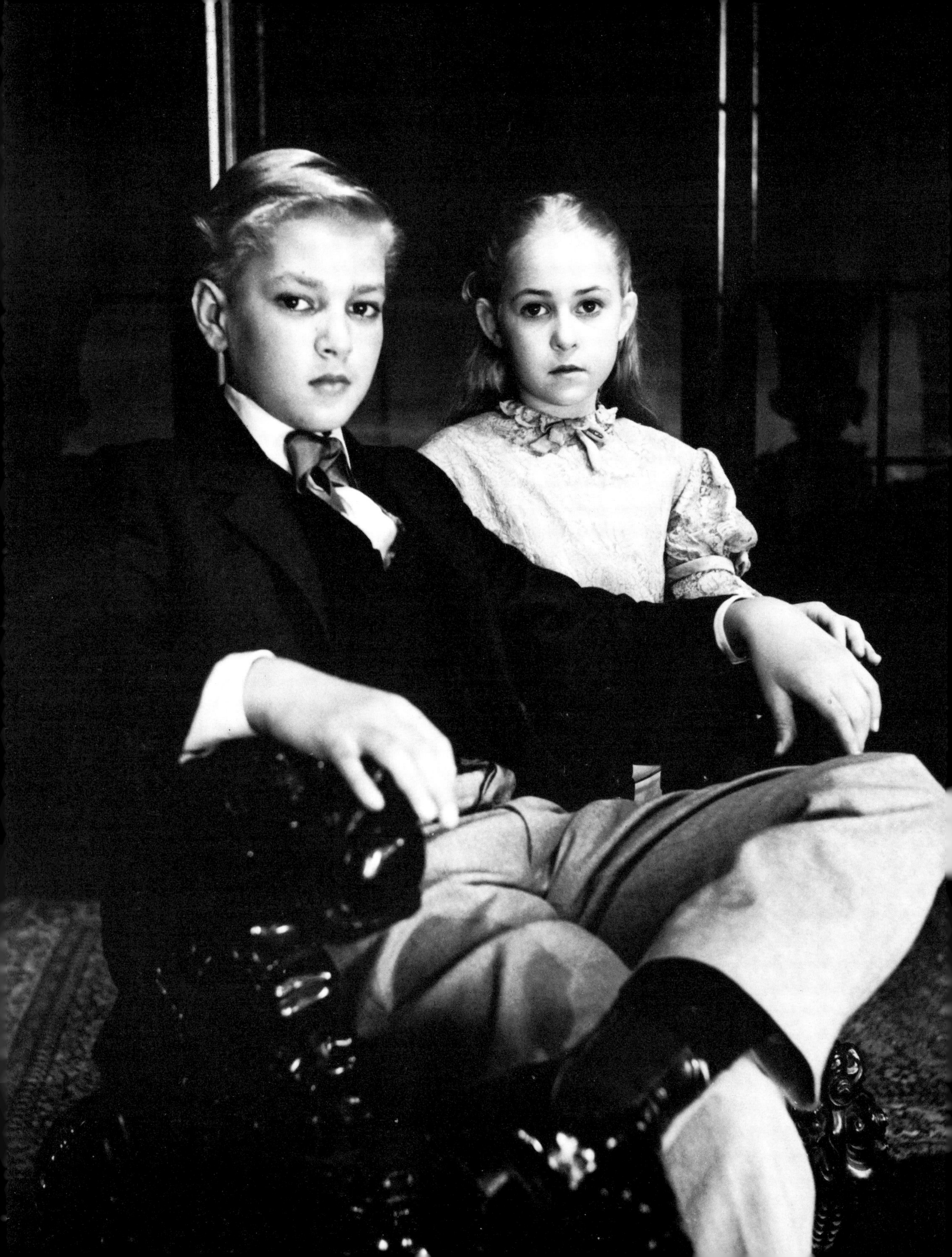

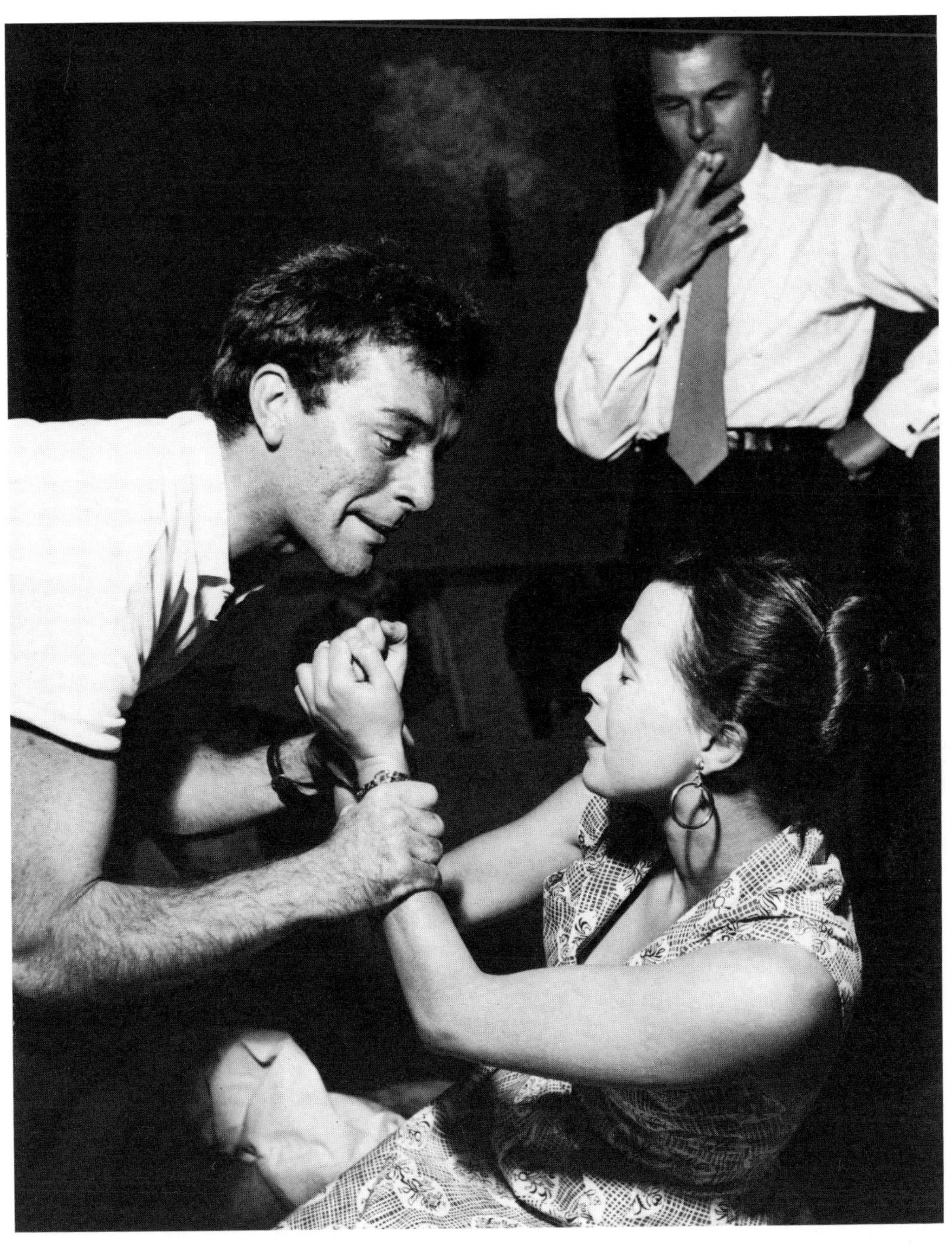

69 *Hamlet* rehearsal at the Old Vic
Richard Burton Claire Bloom Michael Benthall 1953

68 *The Innocents* Jeremy Spencer Carol Wolveridge 1952

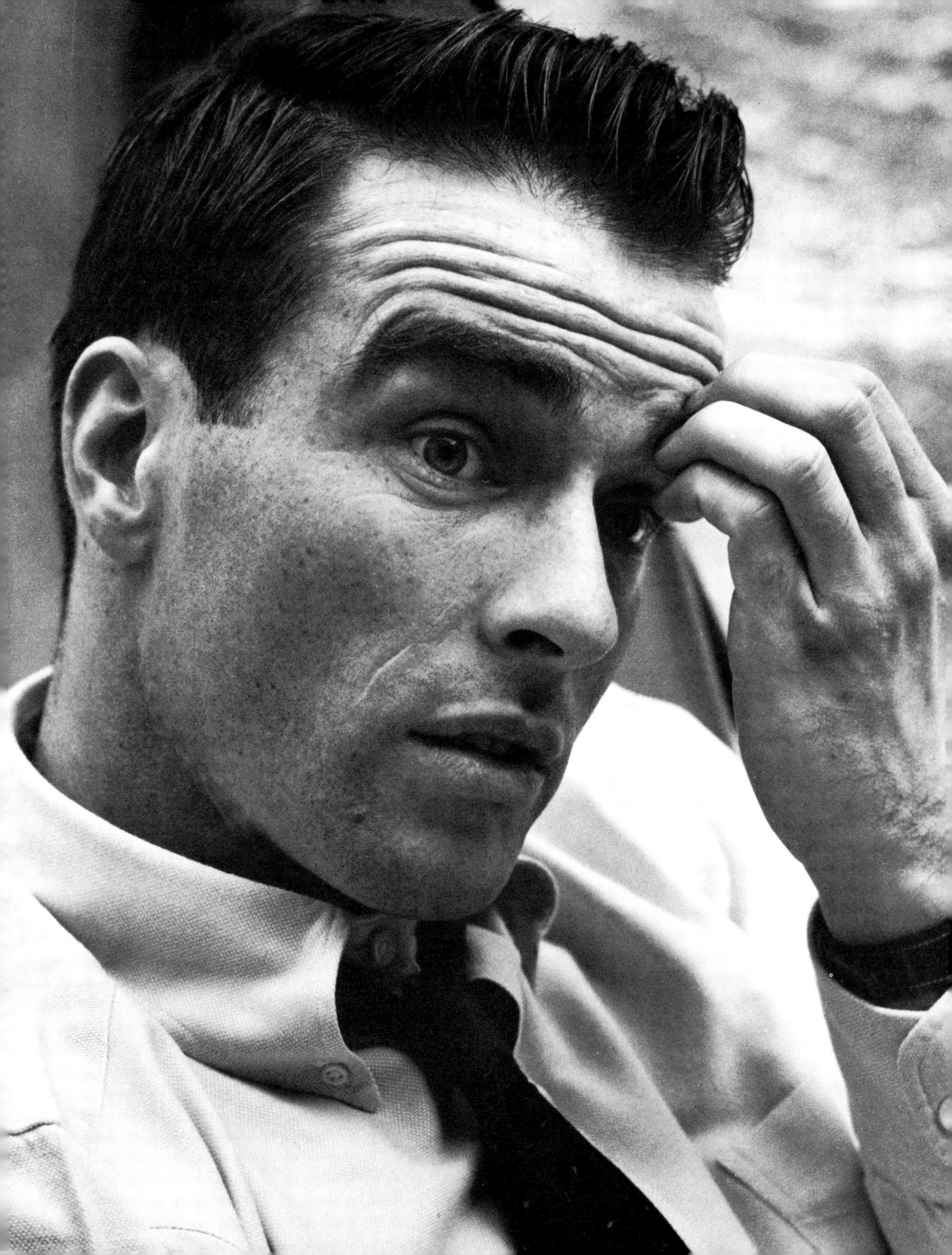

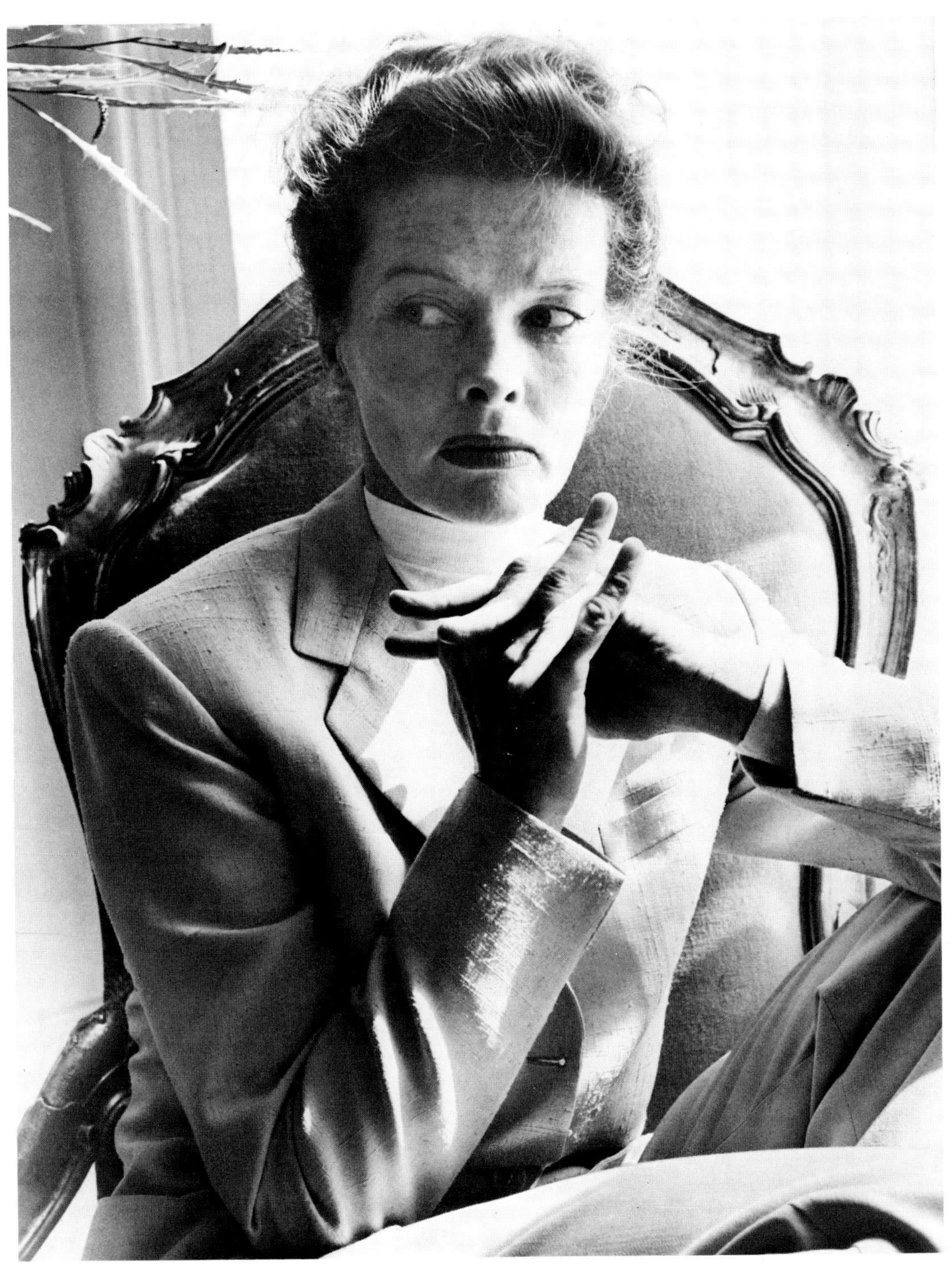

*71* **Katherine Hepburn 1952**

*70* **Montgomery Clift New York 1952**

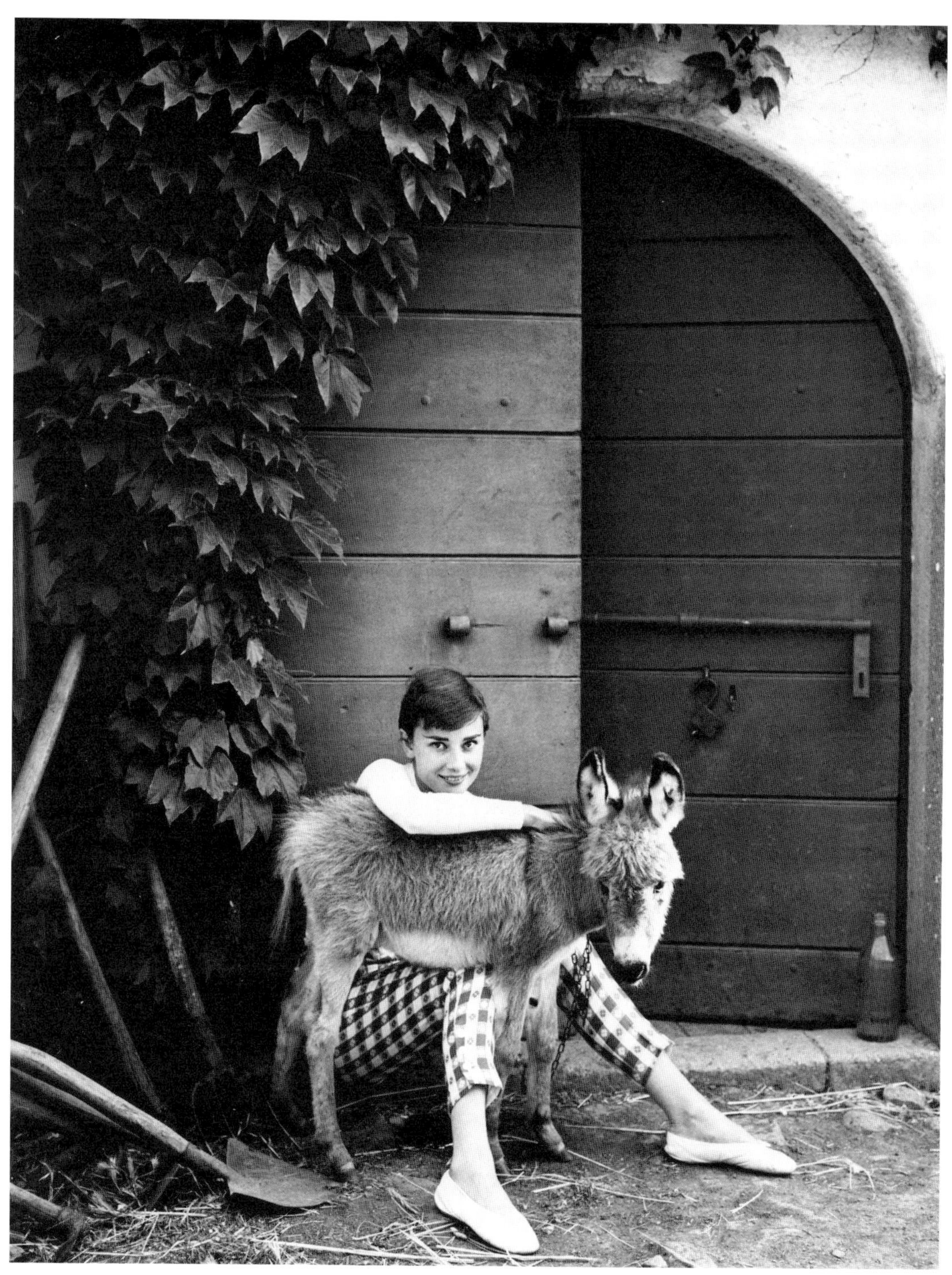

*72* **Audrey Hepburn Rome 1955**

*73* **John Huston between takes of the filming of *Moby Dick* 1955**

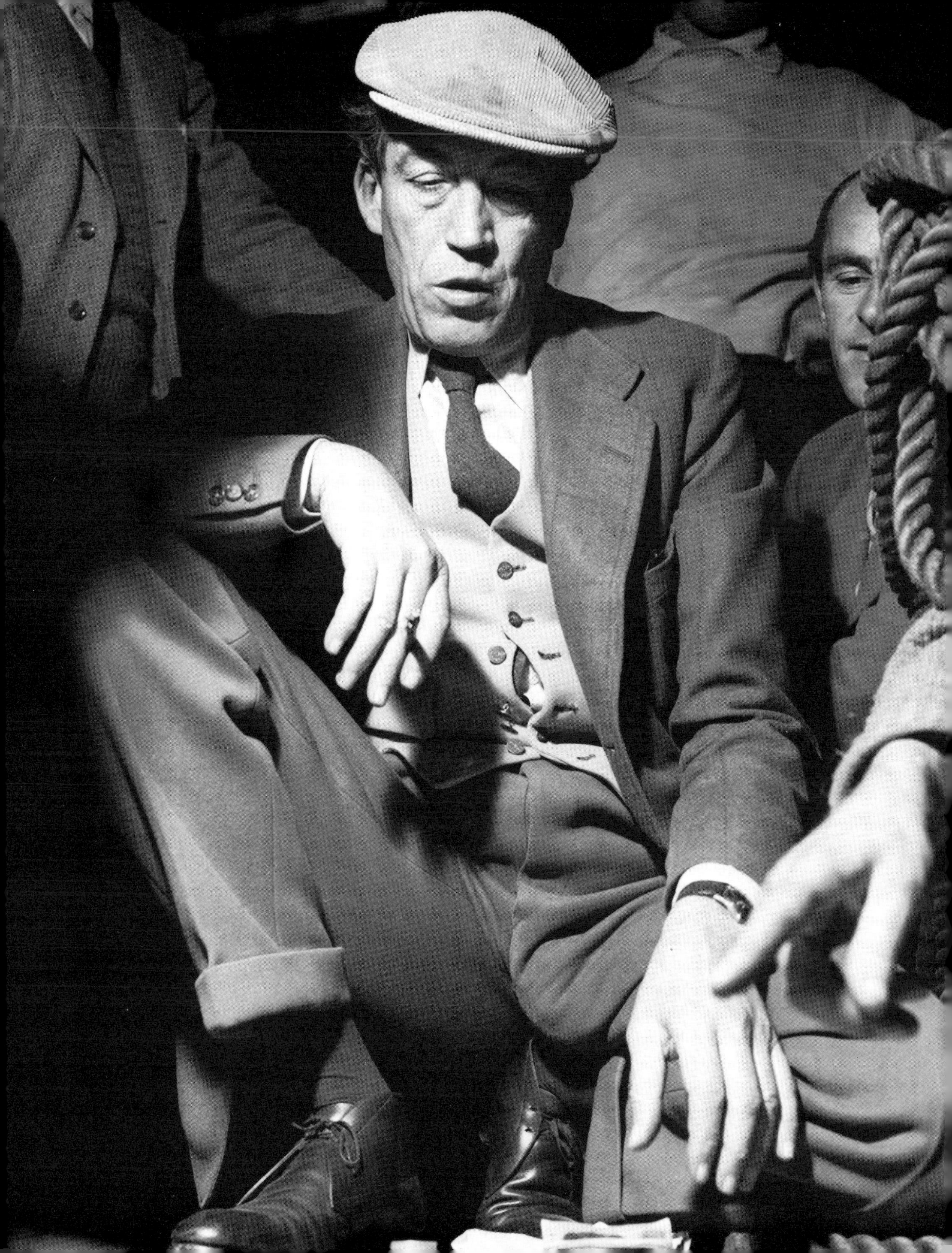

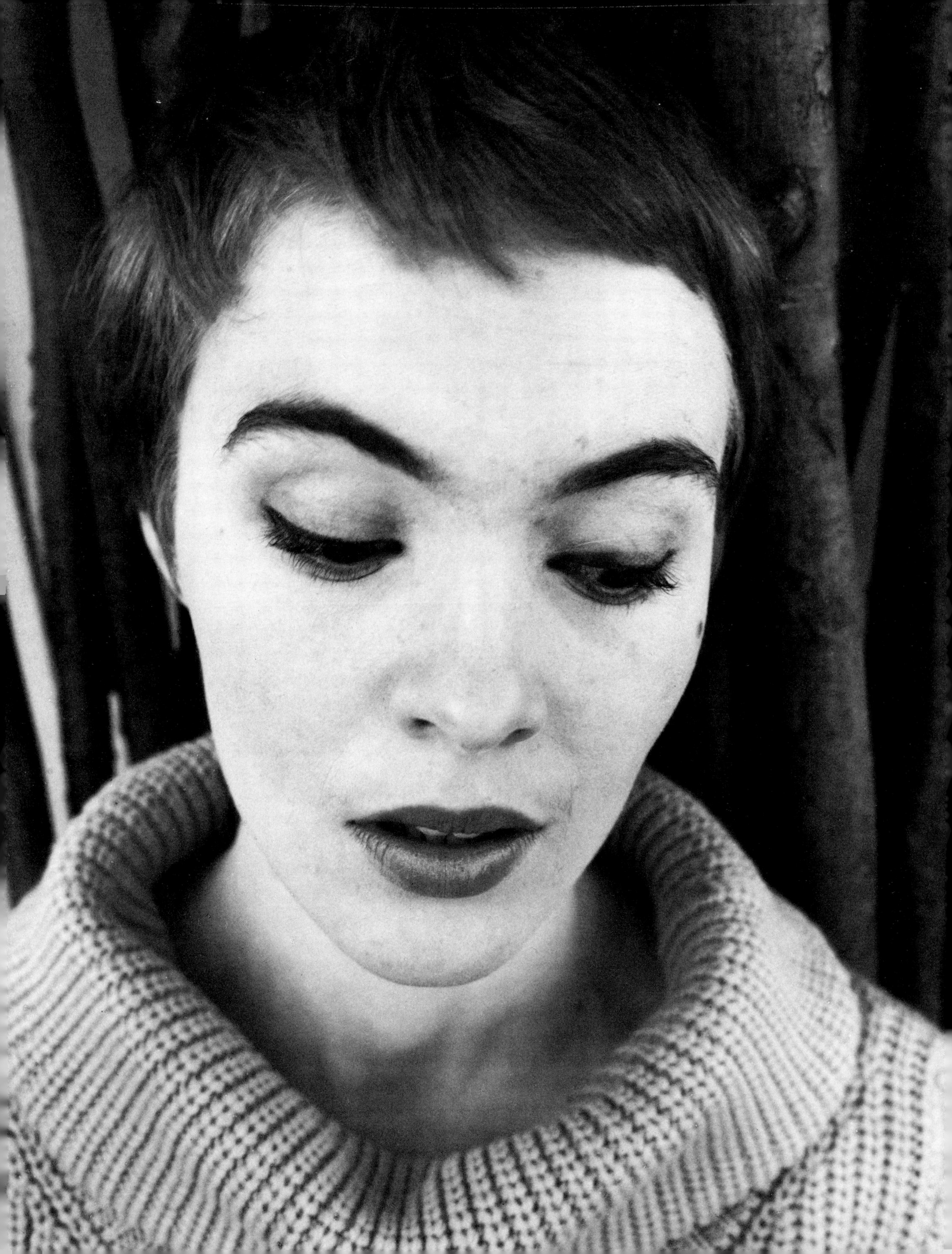

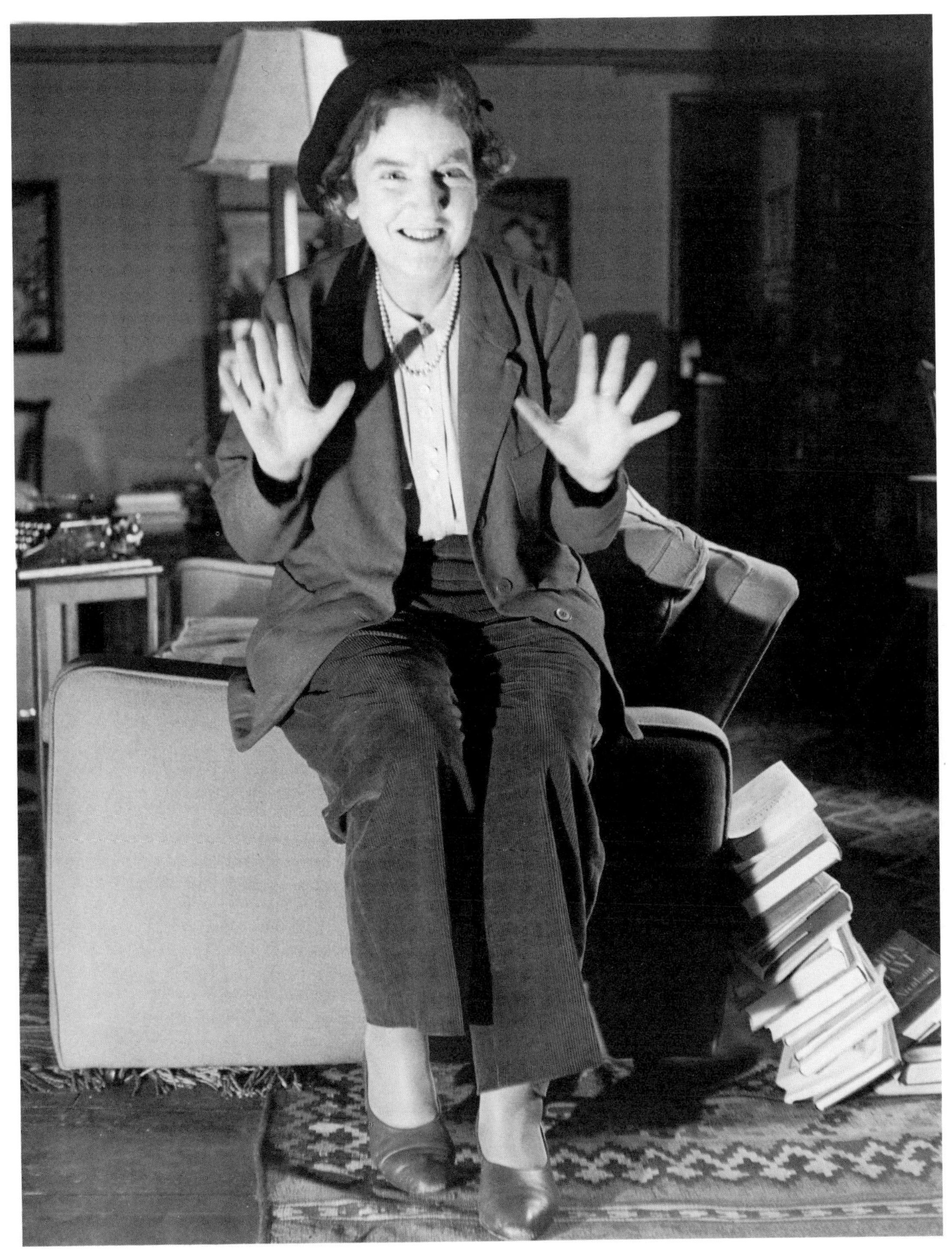

*75* **Enid Starkie Oxford 1951**

*74* **Jean Seberg 1957**

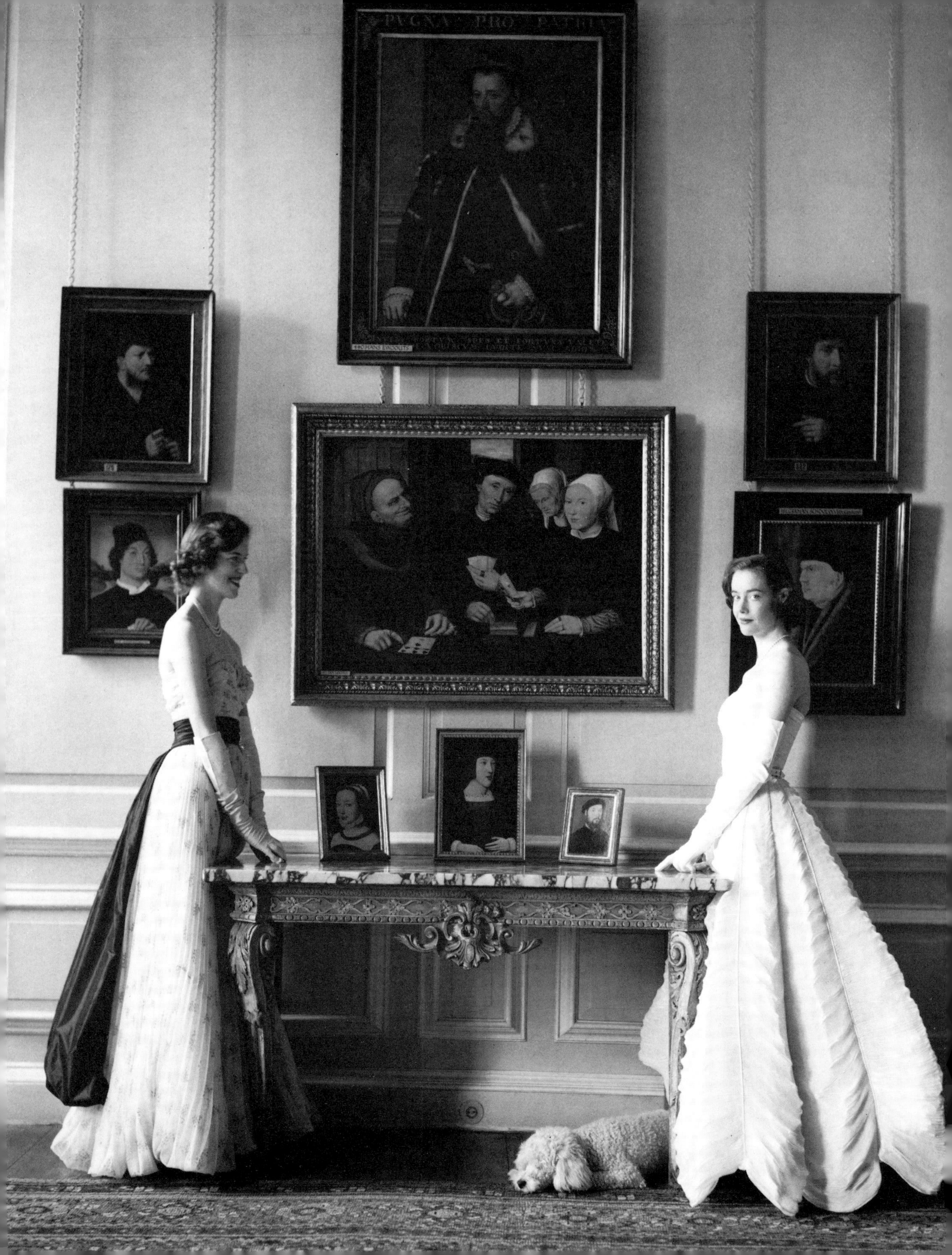
PVGNA PRO PATRIA

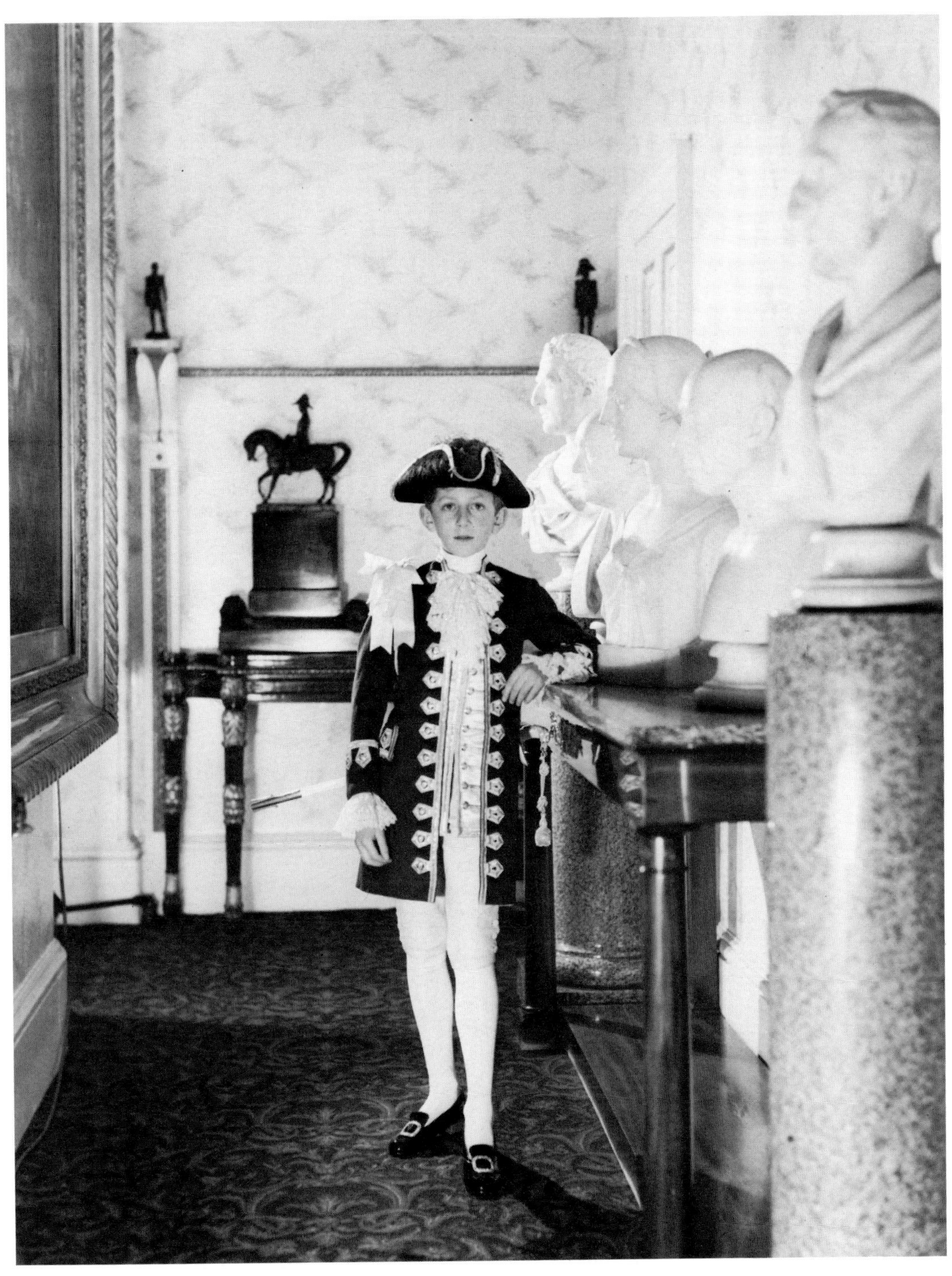

*77* **Jeremy Clyde**
**page-boy to the Duke of Wellington**
**Apsley House 1953**

*76* **Lady Melissa and Lady Caroline Wyndham-Quin**
**posing in Sybil Connolly dresses**
**The Little Dining Room Petworth 1954**

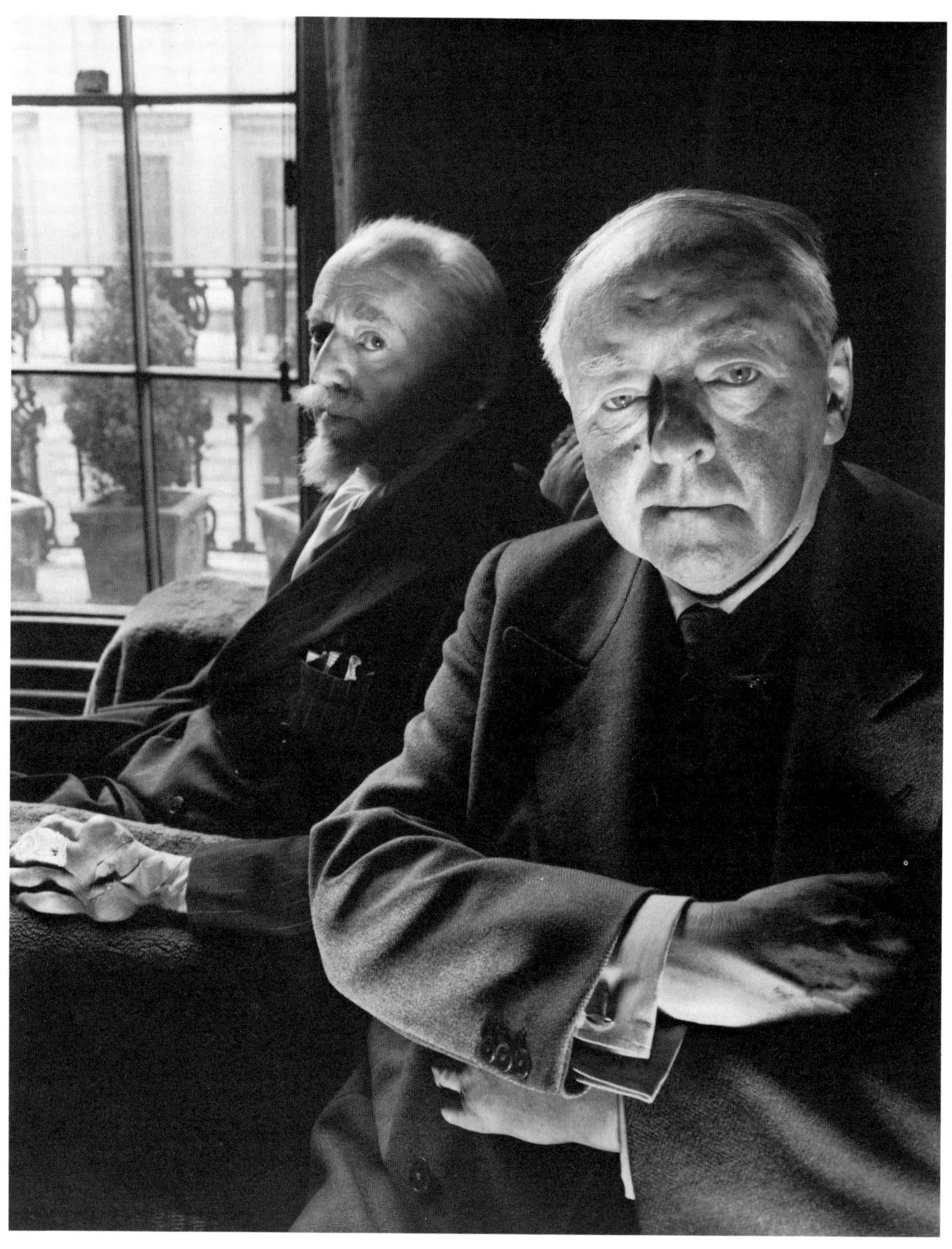

*78* **Clifford and Arnold Bax** **1953**

*79* **Arthur Bliss** **Hampstead** **1956**

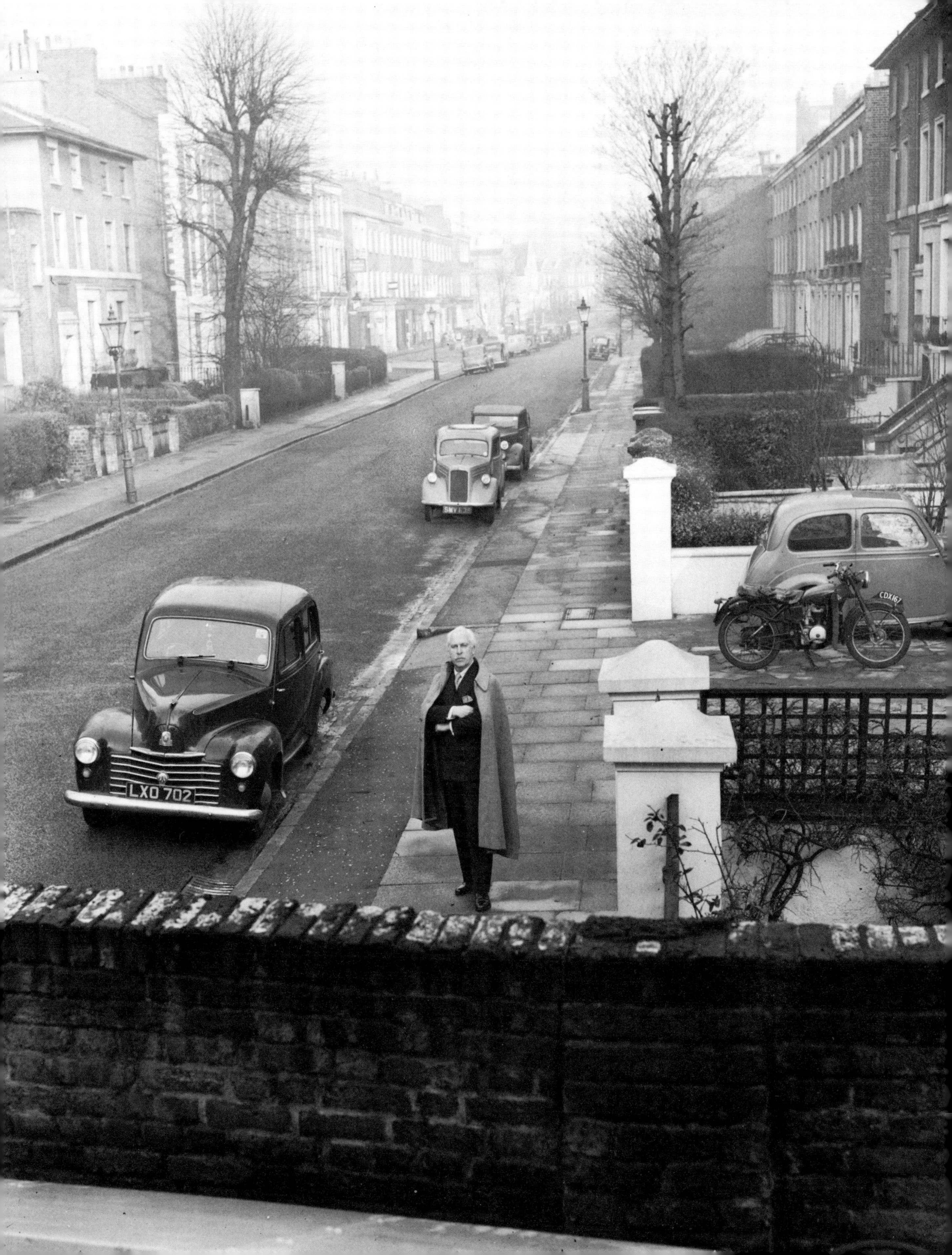
LXO 702
CDX167

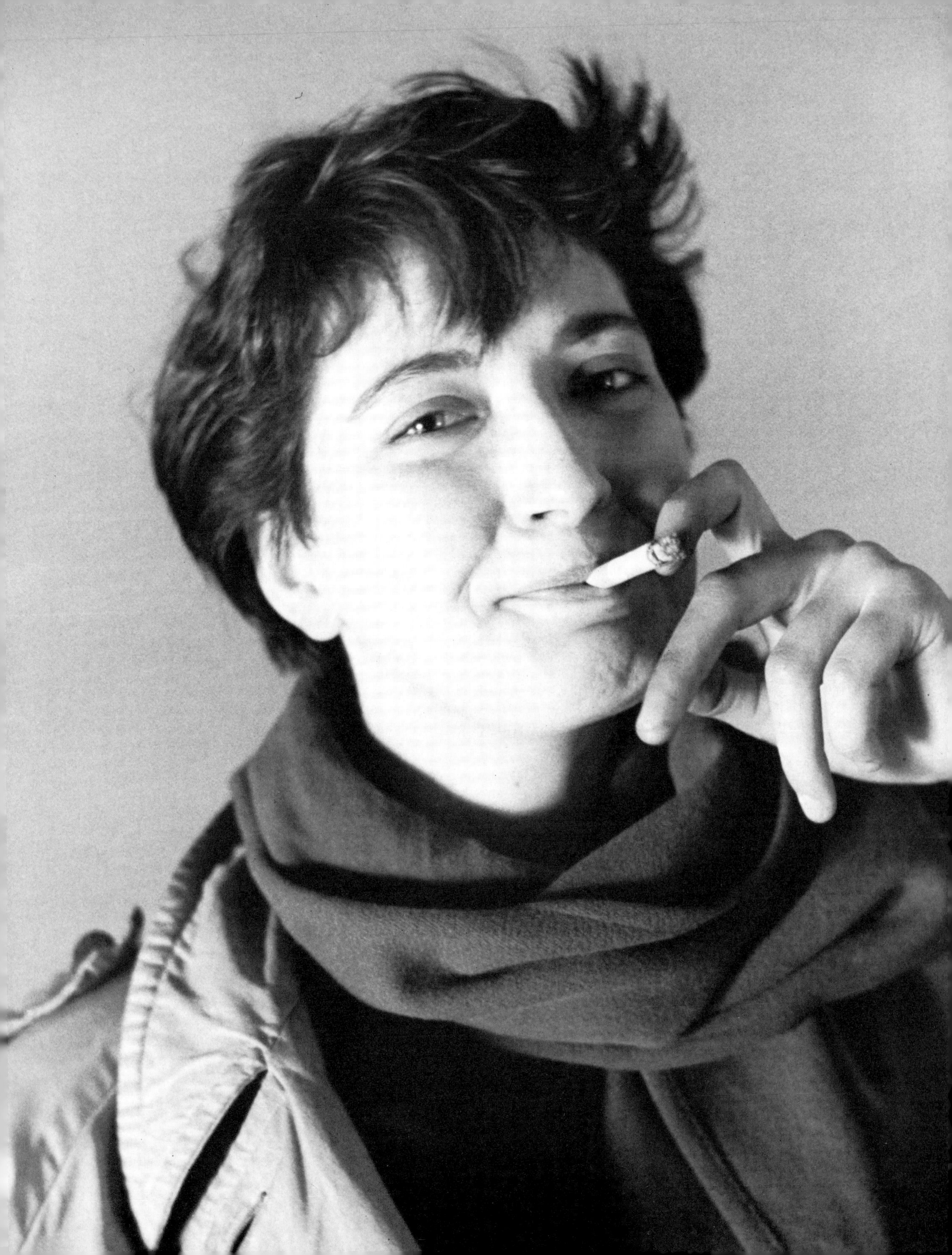

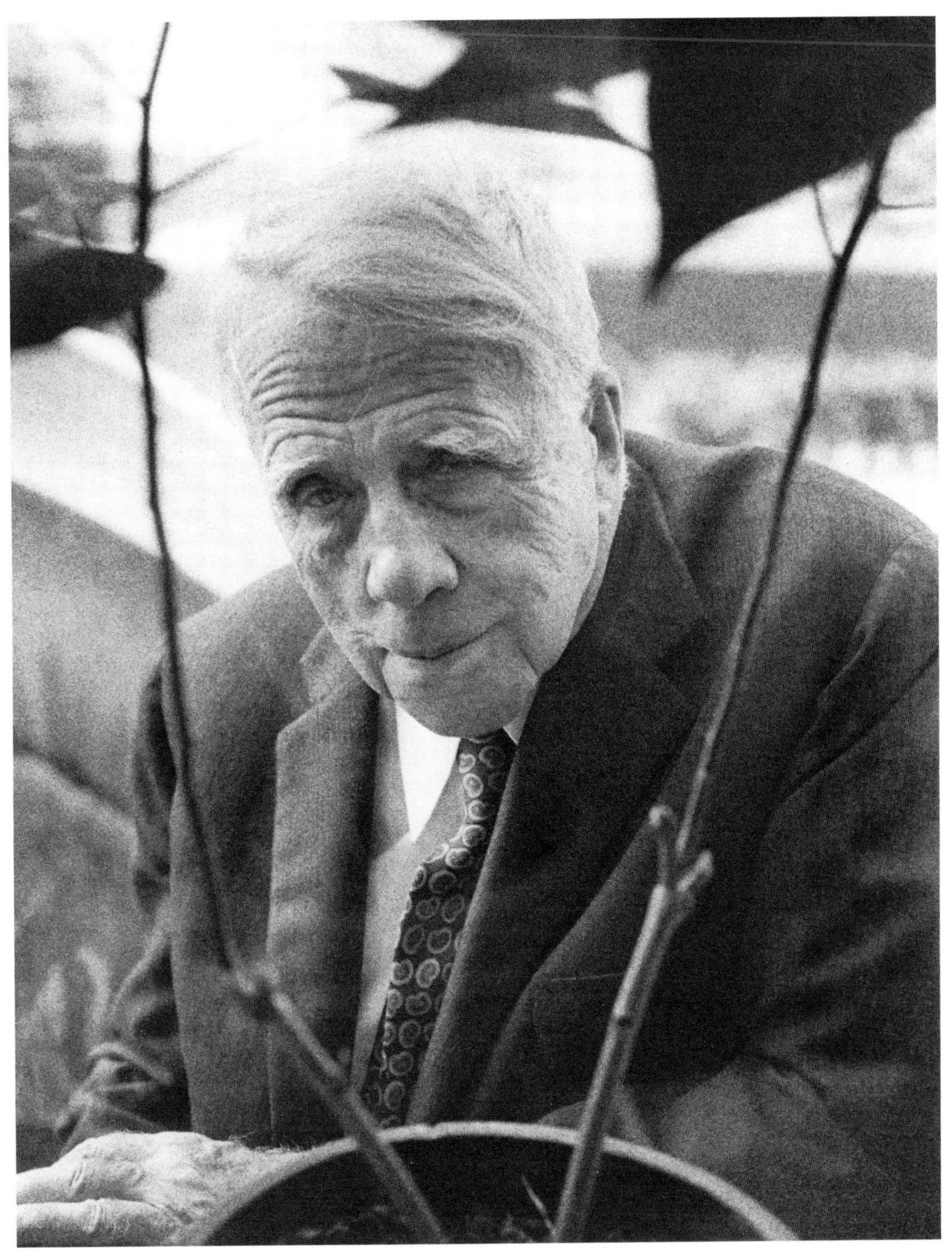

*81* **Robert Frost American Embassy Grosvenor Square 1958**

*80* **Shelagh Delaney 1959**

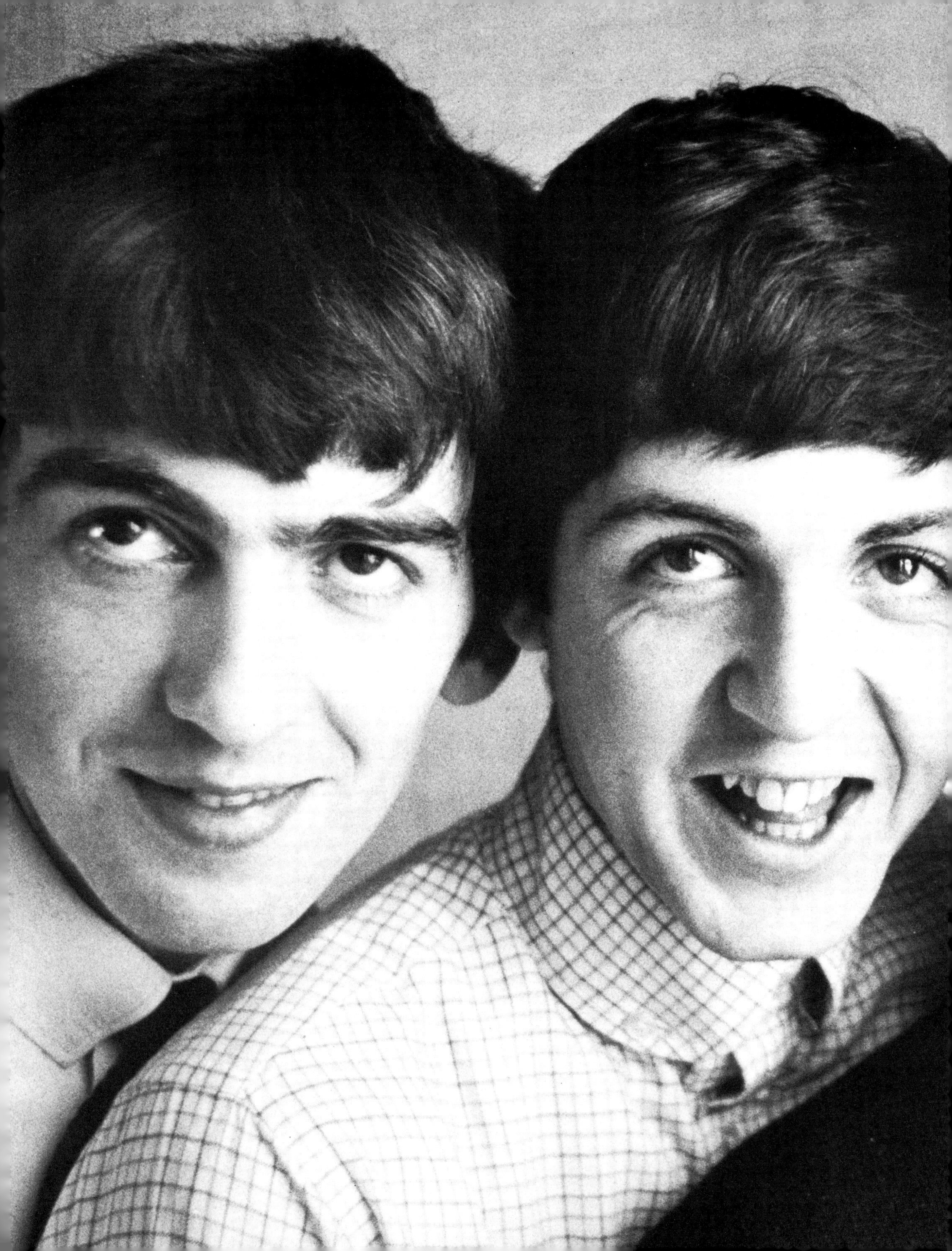

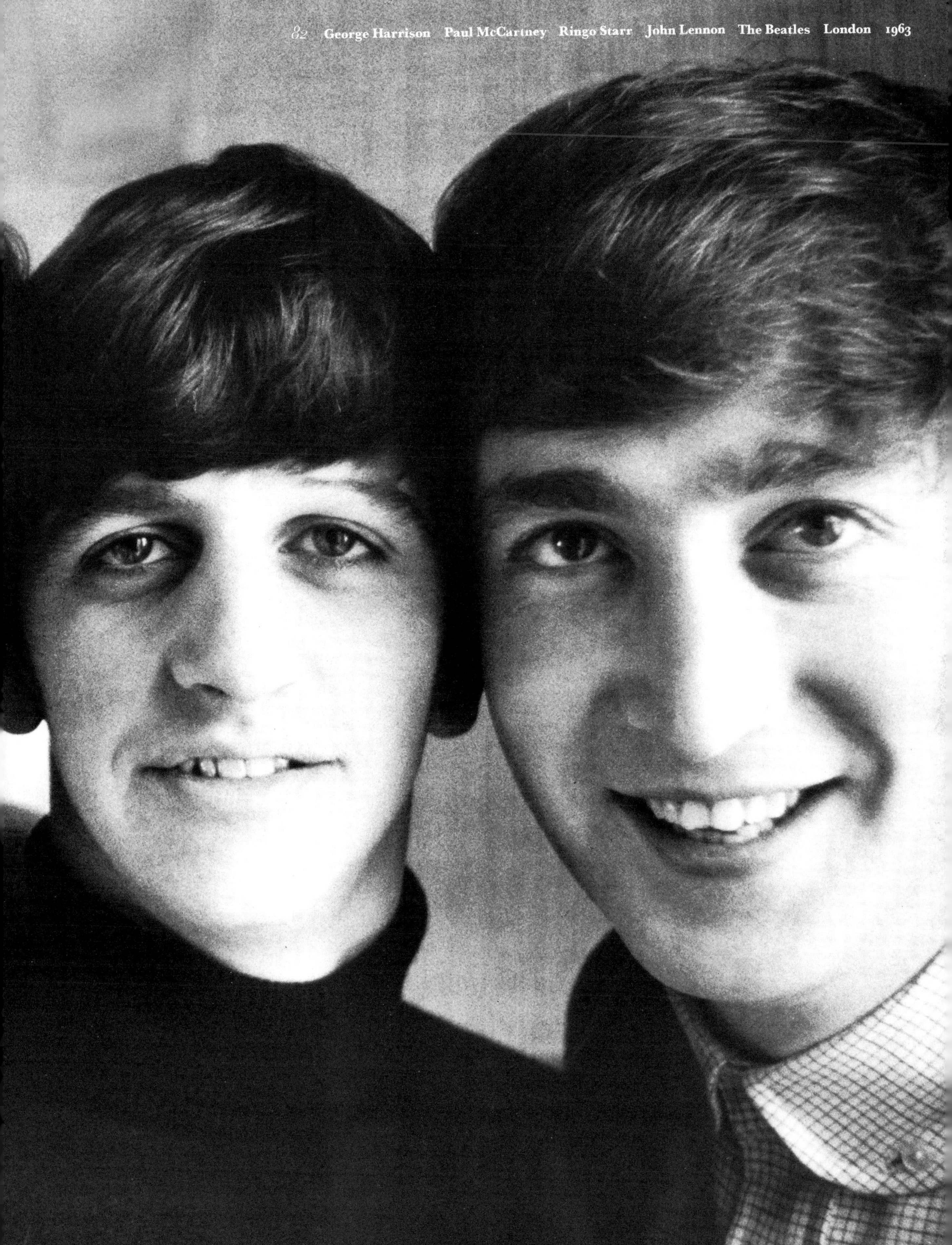

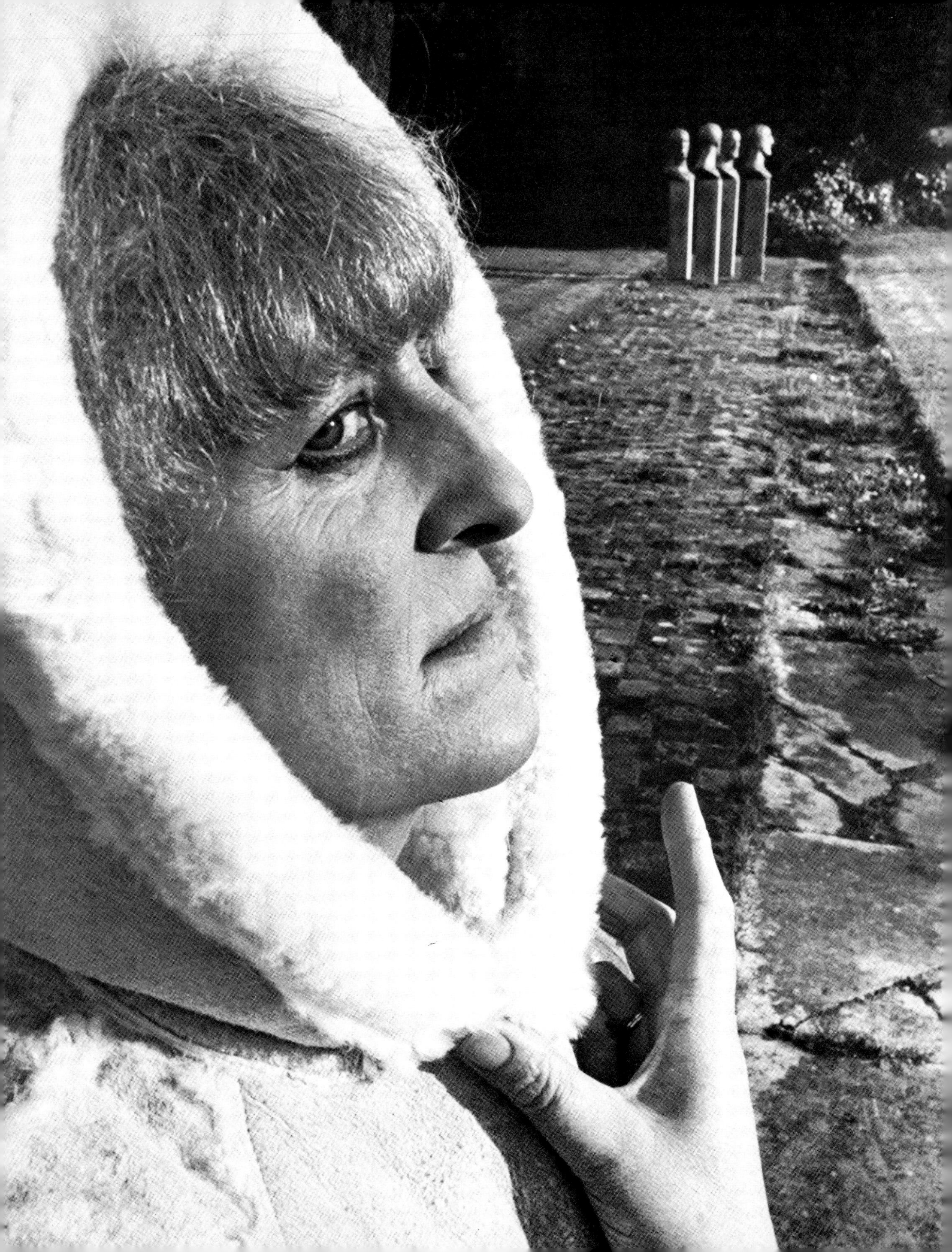

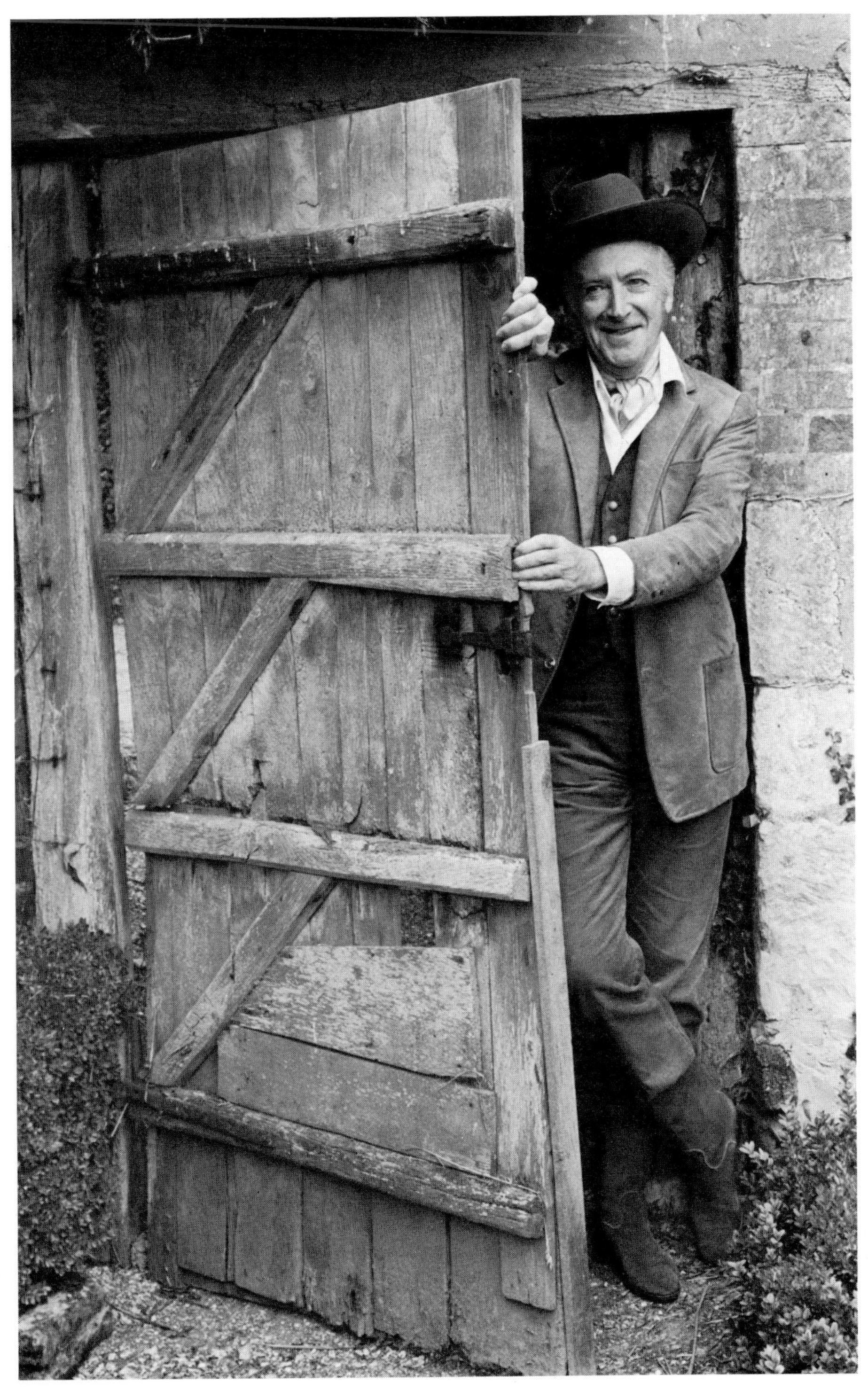

*84* **Cecil Beaton 1969**

*83* **Elisabeth Frink 1977**

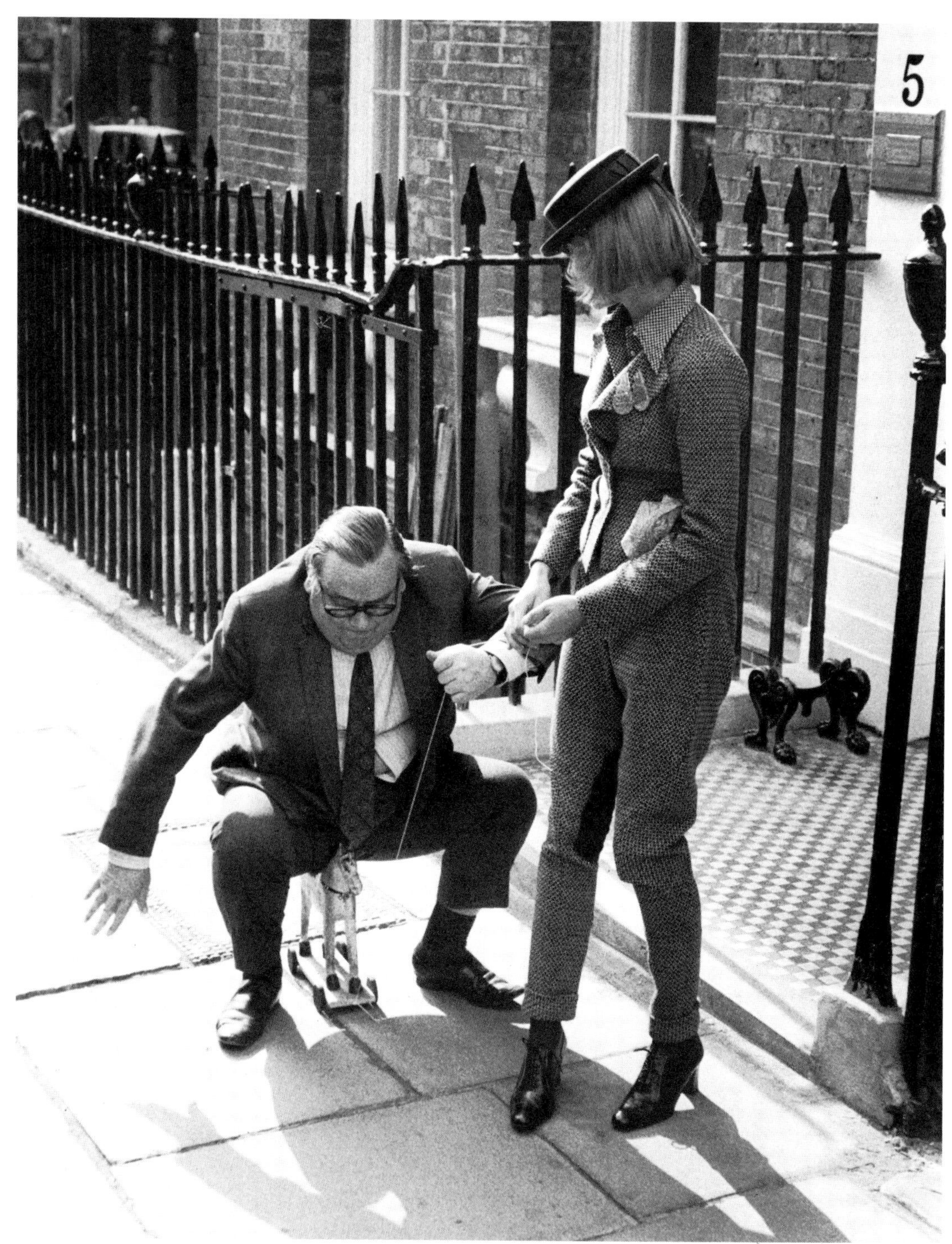


*85* **Equestrian fashion Clifford Street 1972**

*86* **Lancashire coal miners 1960**

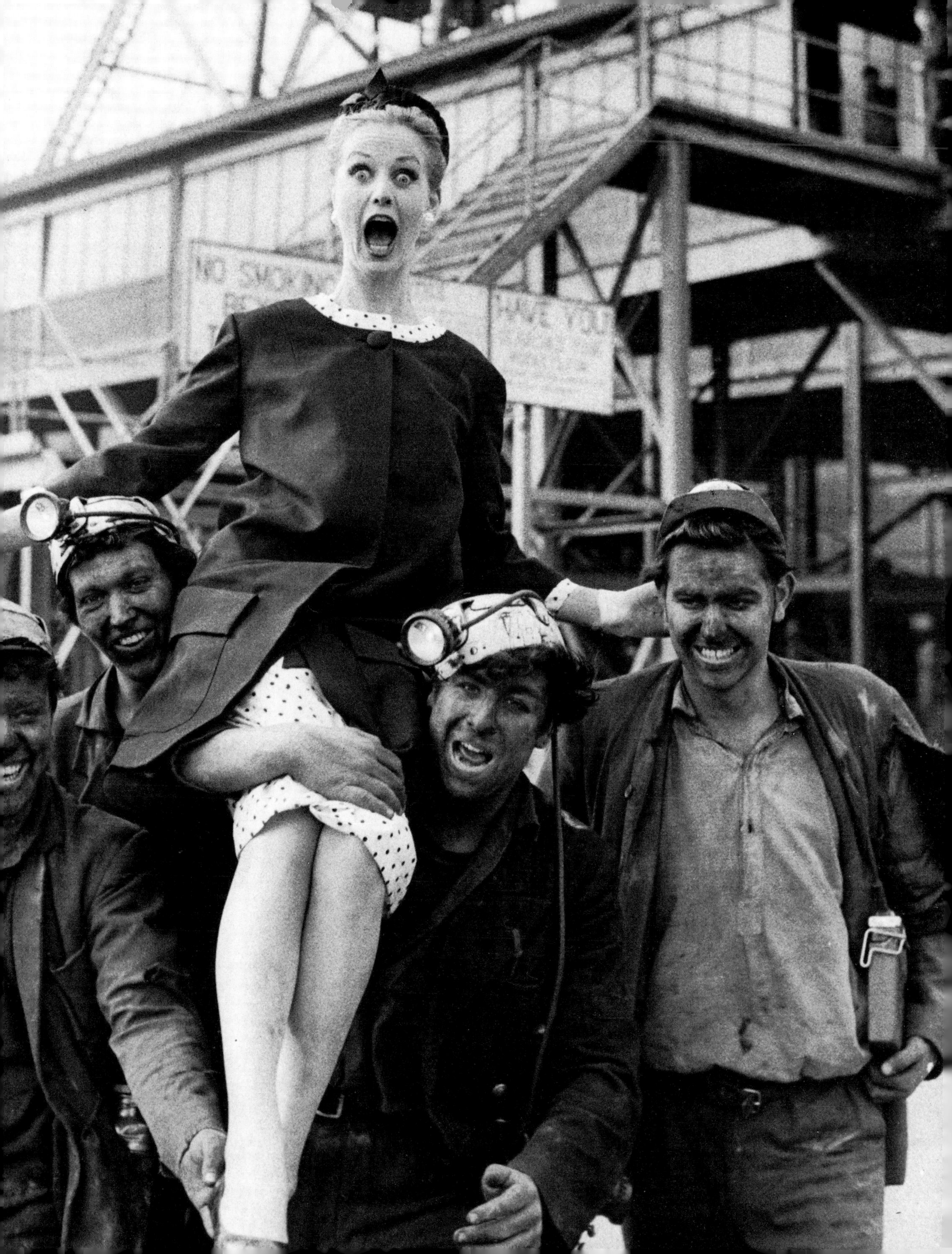
NO SMOKIN
HAVE YOU

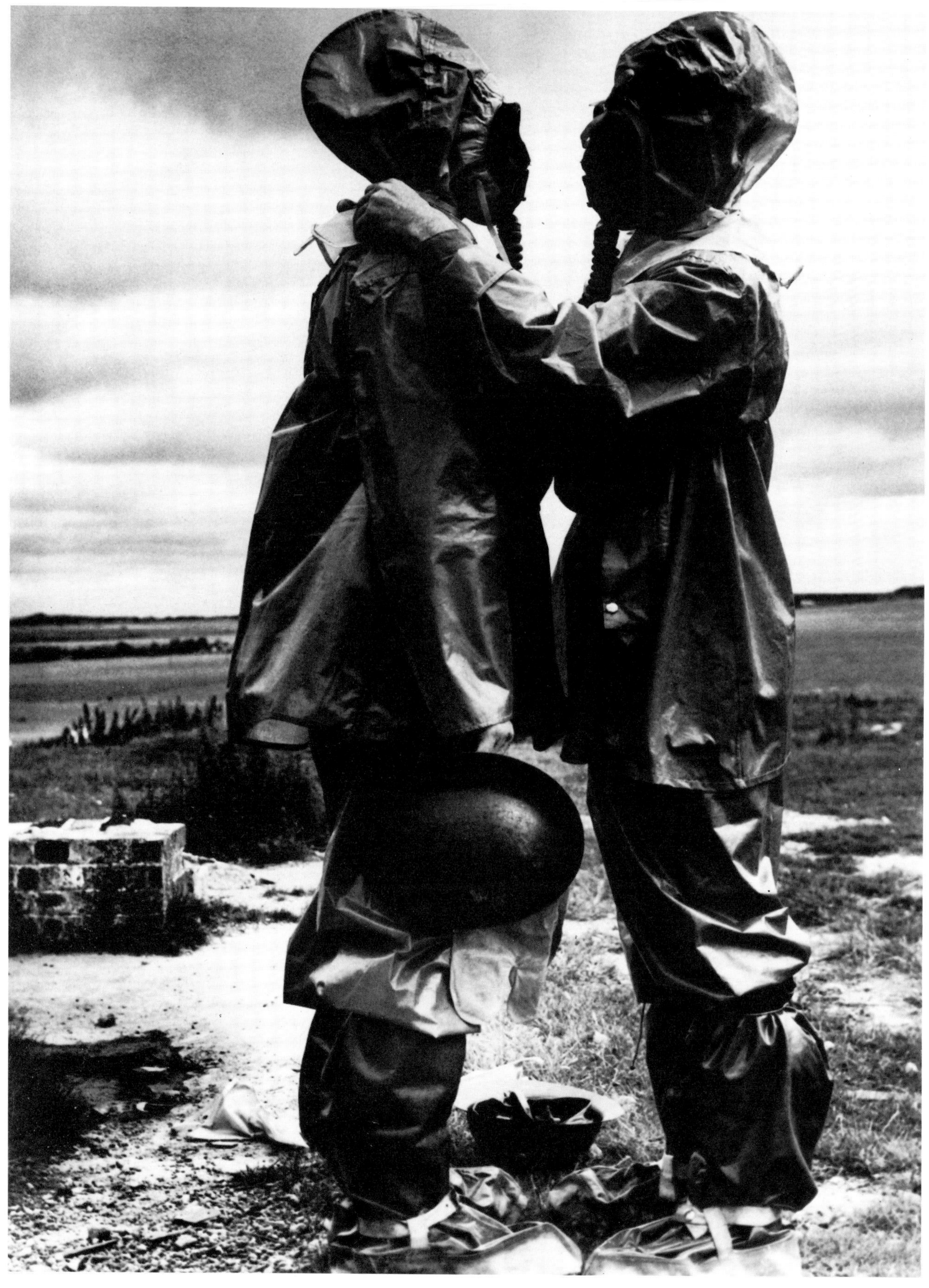

*87* **Protective clothing anti gas-masks 1938**

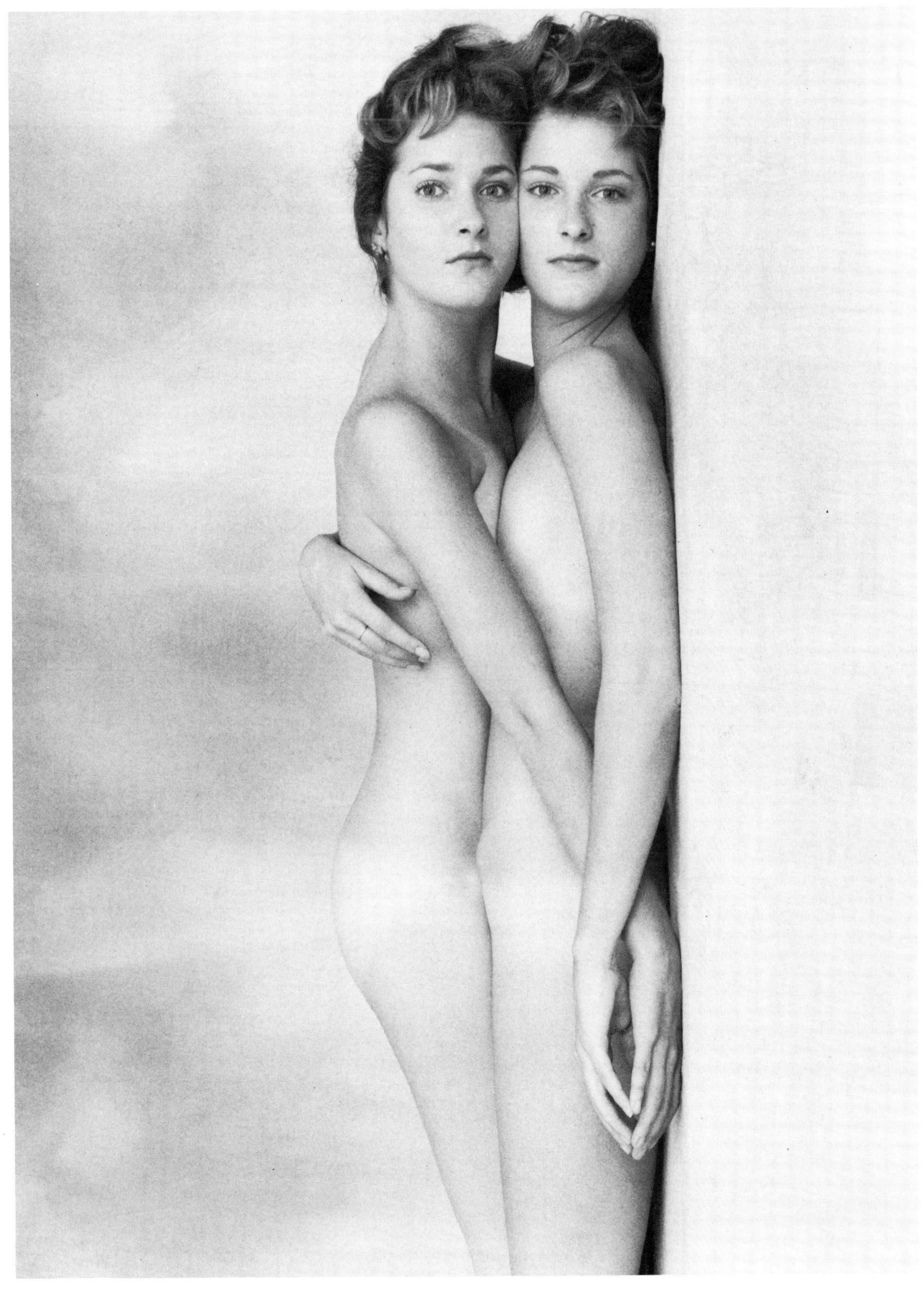

 Amy and Ann McCandless **1978**

## Select bibliography

*(In chronological order)*


The portrait as a piece of furniture. **Photography**, April 1935

What type of background shall I use? New ideas from the London studios. **Photography**, August 1935

Joanna Gordon Forbes, Parkinson of *Harper's*, Rawlings of *Vogue*. **Art and Industry**, March 1940

Norman Parkinson, Back to the land. **Vogue**, July 1944

H. W. Yoxall, Fashion photography. **Penrose Annual**, Vol. 43, 1949

Alexander Liberman (editor), **Art and techniques of color photography**. Simon & Schuster, New York, 1951

John Parsons, Fashion in fashion photography. **Penrose Annual**, Vol. 49, 1955

Mary Gowing, Norman Parkinson, fashion photographer. **Art and Industry**, May 1956

Siriol Hugh-Jones, Introduction to catalogue of exhibition of Norman Parkinson's photographs at Jaeger's, 1960

The sensible magic of Norman Parkinson. **Kodak View**, No. 2, 1961

Alan Vines, Norman Parkinson interviewed. **British Journal of Photography**, 12 October 1962

Norman Parkinson, *Formula for success*. **New Photograms**, 1962

Siriol Hugh-Jones, You can hold the light meter. **The Listener**, 31 October 1963

Alan Vines, Norman Parkinson. **Photography**, March 1964

Norman Parkinson, Celia Hammond: cameo in camera. **Women's Mirror**, 24 August 1964

Norman Parkinson, Parkinson's lore. **The Sunday Times**, 27 June 1965

Norman Parkinson, Fashion and the talented mechanic. **The Sunday Times Magazine**, 18 September 1966

Suzanne Patterson, Norman Parkinson: great photographers of the world series. **Realities**, July 1971

**Image**, Vol. 1, No. 6, 1972

Maureen Cleave, The gentle giant with an eye for women. **Woman**, 9 December 1972

Polly Devlin, Norman Parkinson talking to Polly Devlin: 'I'm the world's most famous unknown photographer'. **Vogue**, November 1973

Cecil Beaton and Gail Buckland, **The Magic Image**. Weidenfeld & Nicolson, 1975

Georgina Howell, **In Vogue: six decades of fashion**. Allen Lane, 1975

Linda Blandford, Focus on Parks. **Cosmopolitan**, December 1976

Marina Warner, Norman Parkinson at work. **The Daily Telegraph Sunday Magazine**, 22 October 1978

Janet Watts, Snapping up the sisters. **The Observer**, 19 November 1978

Nancy Hall Duncan, **History of fashion photography**. IMP/Alpine Books, 1979

Roger Clark, Norman Parkinson: an interview. **British Journal of Photography Annual**, 1982 (forthcoming)

George Walsh (editor), **Contemporary Photographers**. St James Press (forthcoming)

## Index of sitters

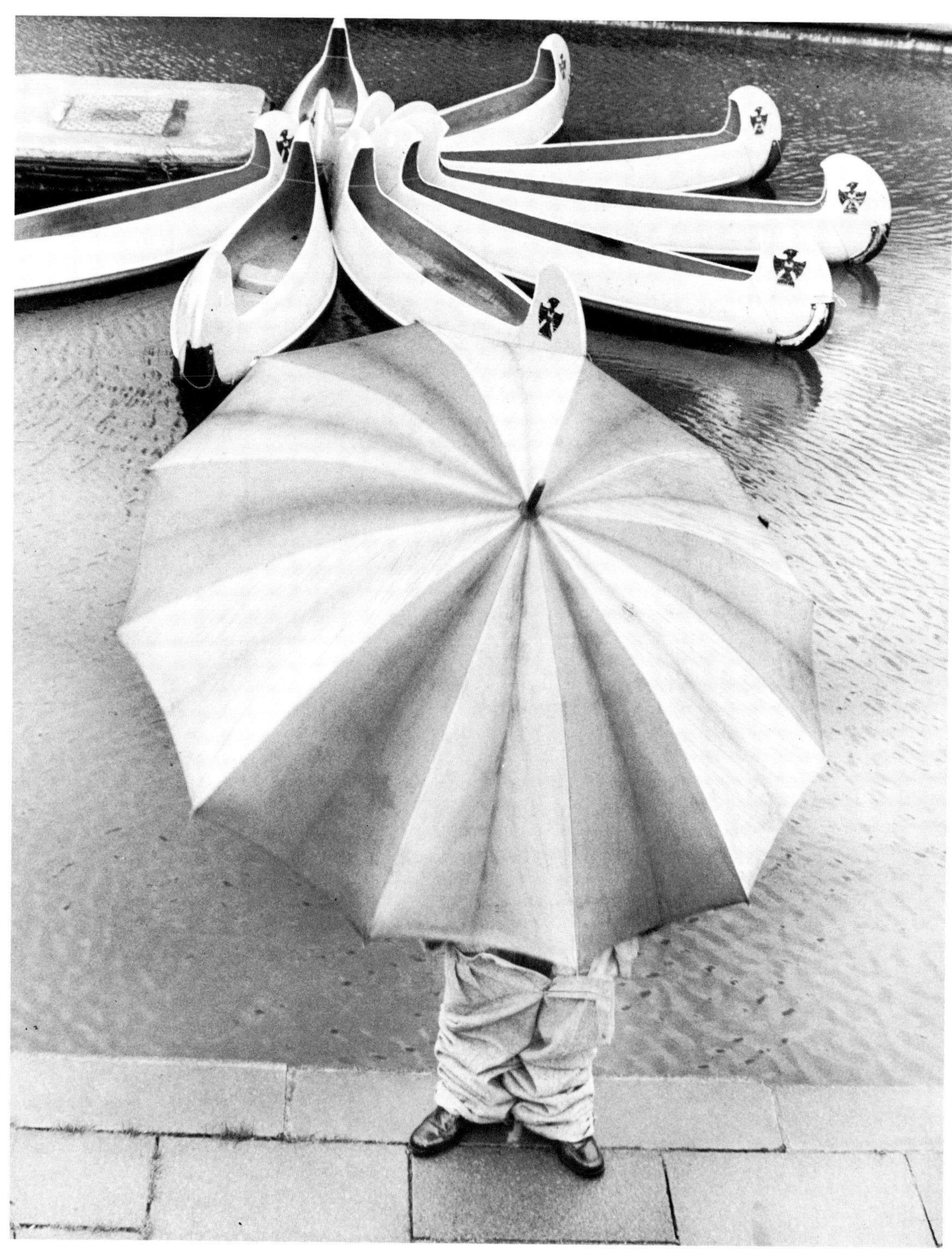

*89* **Tinka Paterson Brighton 1974**